Principles of Constitutional L

This book is written for anyone anywhere sitting down to write a constitution. The book is designed to be educative even for those not engaged directly in constitutional design but who would like to come to a better understanding of the nature and problems of constitutionalism and its fundamental building blocks – especially popular sovereignty and the separation of powers. Rather than being a "how-to" book that explains what to do in the sense of where one should end up, it instead explains where to begin – how to go about thinking about constitutions and constitutional design before sitting down to write anything. Still, it is possible, using the detailed indexes found in the book, to determine the level of popular sovereignty one has designed into a proposed constitution and how to balance it with an approximate, appropriate level of separation of powers to enhance long-term stability.

Donald S. Lutz is a professor of political philosophy in the department of political science at the University of Houston, where he has been teaching since 1968. He received his Ph.D. from Indiana University. He is the author of eleven books, including *Colonial Origins of the American Constitution: A Documentary History* (1998), *A Preface to American Political Theory* (1992), and *The Origins of American Constitutionalism* (1988), as well as numerous articles published in the *American Political Science Review*, *American Journal of Political Science*, *Journal of Politics*, *Publius: The Journal of Politics*, *Social Science Quarterly*, *Annals of Political Science and History*, and *Western Political Quarterly*, among others.

Principles of Constitutional Design

DONALD S. LUTZ
University of Houston

CAMBRIDGE
UNIVERSITY PRESS

CAMBRIDGE UNIVERSITY PRESS
Cambridge, New York, Melbourne, Madrid, Cape Town, Singapore, São Paulo

Cambridge University Press
32 Avenue of the Americas, New York, NY 10013-2473, USA

www.cambridge.org
Information on this title: www.cambridge.org/9780521861683

First published 2006
This digitally printed version 2008

A catalog record for this publication is available from the British Library.

Library of Congress Cataloging in Publication Data

Lutz, Donald S.
Principles of constitutional design / Donald S. Lutz.
p. cm.
Includes bibliographical references and index.
ISBN 0-521-86168-3 (hardback)
1. Constitutions. 2. Comparative government. 3. Separation of powers.
4. Sovereignty. I. Title.
JF128.L88 2006
342.02 – dc22 2005037370

ISBN 978-0-521-86168-3 hardback
ISBN 978-0-521-06376-0 paperback

In memory of Daniel J. Elazar

In memory of Charles S. Hyneman

With thanks for the continuing presence of Vincent Ostrom

Contents

Preface

What follows will disappoint those looking for a "how-to" manual on constitutional design. Certainly there is much here that can be used by those writing or rewriting a constitution, but the major intent of this book is to help us understand constitutional design rather than lay out guidelines for constitutional construction – to help us think about the constitutional project rather than direct us toward specific institutional or constitutional outcomes. Even if one wanted to provide a set of instructions for those framing a constitution, it would be unwise for an outsider to do so. A fundamental fact about constitutional design is that there is no optimal model, no clear set of rules for matching a people and their situation with a set of institutions, and no inherently stable or superior constitutional system. We do know a great deal more about institutional design than Aristotle did, and even a good deal more than we did half a century ago. The empirical knowledge we now possess, however, tends to be piecemeal, theoretically unfocused, and sometimes contradictory. As important as the contributions of empirical and analytic approaches have been over the past half century, there is no substitute for just backing off and asking, How do we go about thinking about constitutionalism and the design of constitutions as an integrated project? That is the deep focus of this book, and that is why it is best to think of it as an exercise in political theory.

The book is aimed at political theorists, especially students of constitutionalism and institutional design, as well as those in the field of comparative politics. Portions may interest those working in international relations, particularly Chapter 2 on the concept of sovereignty. Chapters 3, 4, 5, and 8 present empirical analyses of a cross-national data base using several newly developed indexes. Among other things, the parliamentary-presidential dichotomy is completely recast. It is hoped that anyone wrestling with the nature of constitutionalism, the definition of democracy, the design of democratic institutions, or democratization will find something of value. Still, this book is an extended exercise in political theory, which is reflected in the analyses drawn from Plato, Aristotle, Jean Bodin, Thomas Hobbes, John Locke, Baron de Montesquieu, James Madison, and a number of other political thinkers that inform the arguments of every chapter. Overall, constitutional design is approached as a project that recapitulates the structure of political philosophy as laid out in Chapter 7. As befits political theory properly pursued, the project of constitutional design brings together the various methodological strands of modern political science – normative, analytic, and empirical – that have tended to become isolated from each other. In the integrated project we term constitutional design, precise definitions matter, actors may or may not be "rational," human values guide empirical analysis, statistical analyses support propositions from great political theorists who continue to inform our thinking in fruitful ways, power and justice interact with culture, and many voices from a variety of political science subfields chant together – sometimes in harmony, sometimes not.

One basic premise of this book is the contention that constitutionalism, properly conceived, inevitably implies at least de facto popular sovereignty, which in turn implies at least some minimal separation of powers, properly conceived. These connections result in large part from the invention of a written constitution. Although constitutionalism is now heavily predicated on the existence of such a document, there are constitutional systems without a written constitution – witness Great Britain and Israel. Also, even though almost every nation now has a written constitution, most of these nations are not constitutional, and thus their respective peoples are not sovereign in terms of what we will call "the second face" of sovereignty. Therefore, it will be argued here that de facto popular sovereignty is coterminous with constitutional democracy – with or without a written constitution.

Because popular sovereignty will be linked with constitutionalism, and because almost every nation now has a written constitution, independent nations that are sovereign in the constitutional sense will be distinguished from nations that are not. In particular, we will be interested in distinguishing the nature of those limits which make the ultimate power a sovereign so we can determine the extent to which a nation is using the strongest form of sovereignty – popular sovereignty – and which version of popular sovereignty it is using. The ability to make such determinations is one of several reasons why the theoretical portions of the book should be of interest to those working in comparative politics, primarily those working with what are now termed "democracies" but which I prefer to call constitutional republics.

Although inevitably the analysis will involve comparative constitutionalism, its ultimate aim remains to contribute to our theoretical understanding of constitutionalism, principles of constitutional design, and what is termed democratic theory. The book ends by arguing that designers of what initially appear to be highly varied constitutional democracies tend to reach broad solutions that display theoretically explicable regularities, even though the designers themselves do not consciously use these theories. That is, under conditions of liberty, people across cultures seem to arrive at constitutional solutions that display a shared underlying logic despite an astonishingly wide array of institutional arrangements. Institutional diversity reflects a logic of accommodation to the history, culture, circumstances, and hopes of the various peoples living in constitutional democracies. The underlying logic running through constitutional design, on the other hand, reveals the operation of a human nature that is collectively rational in terms of maximizing popular sovereignty, properly understood; or perhaps it is better to speak of minimizing the distance from an ideal of popular sovereignty. The multileveled logic of constitutional design tends to support rational-actor theory in general but illustrates how rationality must be carefully contextualized. That is, in constitutional and institutional design rational-actor analysis must be based on the maximization of goals and values established by historical peoples and not assumed ad hoc by the person doing the analysis.

Framers of constitutions seem to do surprisingly well on their own without assistance from design "experts." Enhancing our understanding of constitutional design may well tend to reassure us that the design process is best left to the people who will live under the constitution being framed. The principles examined in this book all point toward such a conclusion, and the author hopes that as we learn to think more deeply about constitutional design, we will be led to conclude that popular sovereignty and not mere technical expertise is, finally, the best political technology we have available to us, no matter how expert the experts are.

Acknowledgments

As is the case with any book, the debts owed by this author are deep and multiple. Instead of providing a long list of names, however, I need to give special thanks to three men and two organizations. First, I need to thank the Earhart Foundation of Ann Arbor, Michigan, which provided, between 1988 and 2002, two grants that relieved me from the need for summer teaching. During the first grant period I wrote the first half of the book (Chapters 1–4), and during the second grant period I wrote the second half (Chapters 5–8). It is difficult to exaggerate the impact of this efficient, open, gentle, and effective grant process. Without these grants, this book would not have been written. Between 1980 and 2002, Liberty Fund of Indianapolis, Indiana, involved me in a number of colloquia that allowed me to discuss with varying combinations of the finest academic minds in America texts by Plato, Aristotle, Cicero, Bodin, Althusius, Montesquieu, Hobbes, Milton, Locke, Sidney, Rousseau, and Tocqueville, among others; and to discuss constitutionalism as expressed in more than one hundred specific constitutions written between 1800 and 2000, in North America, South America, central and western Europe, and Asia, as well as such constitutional concepts and principles as popular sovereignty, separation of powers, natural and civil rights, rule of law, parliamentary government, civil society, and constitutional amendment. Liberty Fund afforded me what amounted to a second education. For this continuing education I am deeply grateful.

Charles Hyneman first set me to the study of state and national constitutions in the autumn of 1965. He continued to serve as my mentor on this and related topics until his death in 1984. As Hyneman set me off on my quest, Vincent Ostrom began my education in public choice theory and principles of institutional development, an education that continues to the present. In 1978 Daniel J. Elazar first set me to examine covenantal theory in particular and federalism in general. From then until his death in 1999, Daniel Elazar was a constant friend and colleague whose teachings on constitutionalism are reflected throughout this book. Although any mistakes must be accorded my own, whatever may flow from this book that is useful and original must be considered a synthesis and extension of the work of three men on whose shoulders I stand and to whom I dedicate this book. Finally, and far from least, and for more than will fit here, I would like to give my deepest thanks to Linda Westervelt, my wife, compatriot, and coconspirator.

Principles of Constitutional Design

I

Constitutionalism

An Initial Overview and Introduction

A Recurrence to Fundamentals

Thomas Jefferson is famous for his notion that every generation should engage in revolution to preserve the blessings of liberty. The notion of "revolution" in use then, contrary to ours today, did not connote a violent break with the past but a thoughtful evolution away from the present. The early American state constitutions spoke of a "frequent recurrence to fundamental principles" as the bulwark of freedom and constitutional government. The framers of the United States Constitution included an amendment process at the end – not as an afterthought, but as the embodiment of this frequent recurrence to fundamentals, this permanent (r)evolution.

"Recurrence" does not mean "the reestablishment of" or "adherence to original intention." The recent debate over the intentions of the American founders has been far from sterile, but that discussion is not what is meant here. Rather, "recurrence to fundamental principles" involves the action of going back mentally and in discourse to recapture the principles that inform and animate our constitutional system, to reconsider these principles in the light of altered circumstances and commitments, and either to reaffirm in contemporary language and symbols what still speaks the truth to us or to alter and then ratify formally modifications or additions to these principles.

We stand in need of such a recurrence in part, ironically, because our political system seems to have triumphed in the face of a half-century struggle with our political antithesis – the nondemocratic, anticonstitutional Soviet Union. However, the long struggle with communism has warped our own constitutional democracy in ways that have yet to be analyzed and left us with a political vocabulary that is too often descriptively inaccurate and theoretically misleading. In short, our very ability to engage in the kind of discourse needed for a recurrence to fundamental principles is impeded by the imprecision of terms that success has brought. In part this results from inattention, but it also results from the assumption that, because we knew what we did not like about our Cold War adversary, we had a clear idea of what we had been defending. However, soviet communism is so far removed from constitutional democracy that what stands in opposition is everything from noncommunist authoritarianism to the virtual anarchy of radical laissez-faire government.

The demise of communism has brought with it not only the need to reassess our own constitutional democracy but also a resurgence of constitutional democracy elsewhere that can be studied for use in our own conversation. In the widespread recurrence to fundamental principles throughout eastern and central Europe, as well as in other parts of the world (especially Latin America) where the end of the Cold War allows such recurrence to proceed relatively free of external meddling in internal affairs, we are witnessing the kind of revolution Jefferson envisioned. For example, discourse elsewhere on the nature and importance of civil society has led to a renewed discussion in the United States about the decline in civil society and the manner and extent to which we should alter civic education in the United States.

Books and articles concerning constitutionalism and constitutional design have begun to proliferate, and the generation of new comparative schemes for categorizing political systems is a growth industry. There is also a resurgence in the literature declaring the demise of the nation-state. The overall picture that emerges is a twenty-first century with more and more democratic nation-states linked by world markets in capital, goods, and labor that make democratic nation-states less and less relevant. One thesis to be implicitly argued is that the contrary is true. The continued growth of world markets hinges precisely on more effective local control by constitutional democracies. Put another way, recent economic difficulties in Asia underscore the importance of rule of law and transparent political and economic processes in addition to institutions of popular sovereignty, as opposed to political corruption, arbitrary or authoritarian government, or centralized elite decision making. Rule of law and popular sovereignty virtually define constitutional democracy. In the long run international markets and the continued health and spread of constitutional democracy are intertwined. Even technological innovations associated with computer networks depend upon, as well as enhance the spread of, constitutional democracy.

One way of dramatizing this linkage might be to reproduce an e-mail message I received sometime during the past fifteen years.

> Apologize for slow response – electricity off and on every day. Cannot attend your conference because it is difficult to travel, and I must stay with the family in case more serious violence spreads. There is shooting in the streets at night, and people have been disappearing. Construction and repairs have stopped, money seems to have fled, and delivery of food is a problem. There is almost nothing moving in or out of the city.

This person and his family are now safe in another country. Was he keying the message from Somalia, Eritrea, Indonesia, Uganda, Panama, southern Mexico, Sri Lanka, Bosnia, Zaire, Haiti, Cambodia, Sierra Leone, Peru, Afghanistan, Burma, Colombia, Chile, Brazil, Moldavia, Venezuela, Algeria, Armenia, Azerbaijan, Ethiopia, Argentina, Nigeria, Iraq, Armenia, Kuwait, Tadjikistan, Yemen, Sudan, Albania, Bulgaria, Nigeria, Angola, Nicaragua, Zaire, Congo, Rwanda, Chechenya, Kosovo, Lebanon, or Kashmir? It could have been from any of these places, but it was in fact from another. That there are still so many possible places left that fit the description in the e-mail message, even after the lengthy list, is a measure of how wildly premature are the assumptions of both an automatic, effective sovereign operating everywhere and a benign "world order" replacing the system of nation-states, a world order of international organizations, multinational corporations, free trade, the Internet, and an unrestricted flow of goods, capital, and people.

The breakdown of order in the absence of an effective local power makes trade, financial markets, and even the Internet nonfunctional. Nation-states, or the local equivalent, remain the fundamental requirement for these world markets and networks to function. Indeed, the need for local order has been behind the proliferation of nation-states

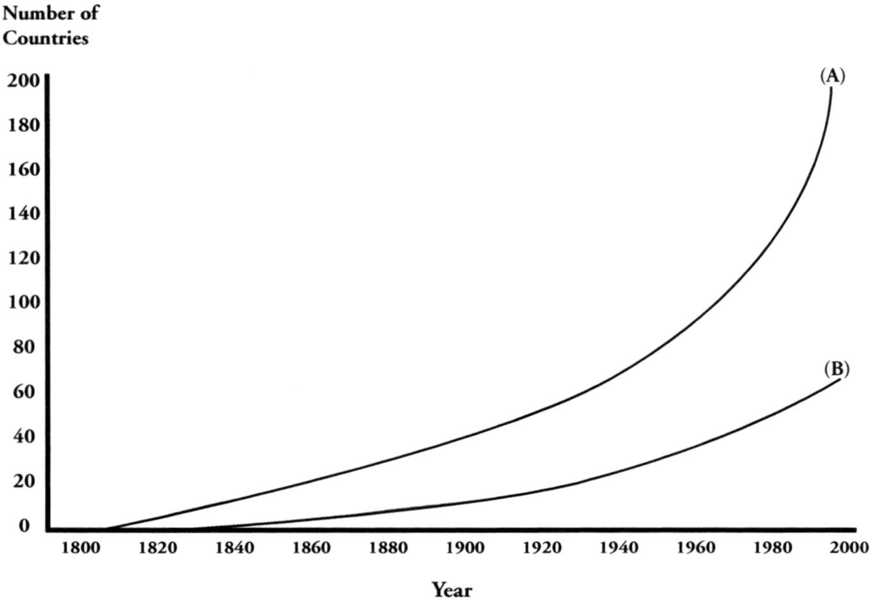

FIGURE 1.1. Approximate number of countries with a written consitution (A) compared with the approximate number of countries having met the requirements to be a constitutional republic (B).

and the framing of constitutions in order to create at least the semblance of what passes for local sovereignty. At the same time, the presence and operation of these international networks create pressures for both effective local sovereignty and, in the long run, the spread of constitutional democracy. The short-lived "Asian model," although at first very successful economically, illustrated the power of these pressures as the countries supposedly embodying this new model found themselves vulnerable to rapid economic shifts in the relative absence of true constitutional democracy.

Consider Figure 1.1. Over the past two centuries, we have moved from a situation where almost no country had a written constitution to one where almost every country has one. A gradual, fitful process from 1800 to 1900 increasingly accelerates after 1900 until it finally slows down as there are fewer and fewer countries remaining without a written constitution. Comparison with the historical curve for constitutional democracies is instructive. The disjunction between the two curves indicates how much more difficult it is to develop a constitutional democracy than it is to adopt a written constitution. Still, it is remarkable how the lower curve tracks the upper one with a lag of one century or less. It is quite possible that once a country writes down a set of rules, even though they are merely window dressing, these rules over time create among the people an expectation of reasonable compliance that amounts to a self-fulfilling prophecy. In day-to-day operations the leaders of nondemocratic countries often use most of their written constitution as a convenient means for coordinating behavior and minimizing inefficiencies. Over time it can be quite natural for a people to ask why 90 percent of a constitution is followed and not the other 10 percent. Perhaps there is a connection between continued economic development and constitutional democracy; or increasing trade between nations is the driving force behind the worldwide recurrence to fundamental principles. Although such speculation rests on unsystematic anecdotal evidence, the similarity between the two curves is suggestive and demonstrates the potential for continued diffusion of constitutional democracy.

What are the prospects for such diffusion? For our purposes here, in order for a nation to be considered a functioning constitutional democracy, it must have achieved the following performance criteria:

1. There is a constitution that is followed rather than ignored.
2. The constitution is based on and supports the rule of law.
3. There are free elections involving essentially all of the adult population.
4. There are two or more competitive parties.
5. There has been at least one peaceful transfer of power between competitive parties, or between significantly different party coalitions, through the free electoral process; or else we are confident that an electoral outcome that would replace the currently dominant party or party coalition would be peacefully accepted.

Although group B countries listed in Table 1.1 have not yet fulfilled these criteria to everyone's satisfaction, they are still viewed by many as constitutional democracies. Events over the past decade in Estonia, Korea, Latvia, Lithuania, Mexico, the Philippines, South Africa, Taiwan, and Uruguay have been especially reassuring in this regard. Within the next decade at least seven nations in group B are likely

TABLE 1.1. *Current Functioning Constitutional Democracies*

Group A: Current major constitutional republics (democracies) ($n = 32$)	
Argentina	India
Australia	Ireland
Austria	Israel
Belgium	Italy
Brazil	Japan
Canada	Netherlands
Chile	New Zealand
Colombia	Norway
Costa Rica	Papua New Guinea
Czech Republic	Portugal
Denmark	Poland
Finland	Spain
France	Sweden
Germany	Switzerland
Greece	United Kingdom
Hungary	United States
Group B: New or renewed constitutional republics (democracies): Probably stable and generally viewed as at or near the performance criteria ($n = 21$)	
Benin	Nicaragua
Bolivia	Panama
Botswana	Philippines
Dominican Republic	Romania
El Salvador	Slovenia
Estonia	South Africa
Jamaica	Taiwan
Korea (South)	Turkey
Latvia	Uruguay
Lithuania	Venezuela
Mexico	
Group C: Current small constitutional republics (democracies): Populations less than 1.5 million ($n = 30$)	
Antigua and Barbuda	Marshall Islands
Bahamas	Mauritius
Barbados	Micronesia (Federated)
Belize	Nauru
Cape Verde	Palau
Cyprus (Greek)	St. Kitts and Nevis
Dominica	St. Lucia
Fiji	St. Vincent and the Grenadines
Grenada	San Marino
Guyana	São Tome and Principe
Iceland	Solomon Islands
Kiribati	Trinidad and Tobago
Liechtenstein	Tuvalu
Luxembourg	Vanuatu
Malta	Western Samoa

to move into group A, and group B will add six or seven countries not now on the list. There is also a good possibility that three or four now in group B will cease to be considered functioning constitutional democracies by anyone. Group C countries are generally considered constitutional democracies but because of their small size are usually ignored by scholars in comparative politics.

Altogether at least sixty-two constitutional democracies with more than 2.2 billion people were functioning in 2000, although one could argue that the actual number is about seventy. The small countries in group C are usually not included in comparative studies because they are likely to skew empirical studies in ways that are not helpful. However, size is not an unimportant variable for constitutionalism where the first rule is to match the constitution to the people and their circumstances. This rule requires that we include the smaller democracies in order to look for tendencies related to size of territory and/or population. It is also helpful to reconsider the countries in group A in this regard. Countries with roughly 5 to 10 million people such as Austria, Belgium, Costa Rica, the Czech Republic, Denmark, Finland, Greece, Hungary, Ireland, Israel, Norway, Portugal, Sweden, and Switzerland probably have more in common with the small constitutional republics in group C than with many of the others in group A.

Nor will it do to ignore the other extreme in size. Countries more than 500,000 square miles in extant or with more than 75 million people have a strong tendency toward federal or quasi-federal structures. For this reason it may be no more helpful to consider France a model for the government of a united Europe than to consider Iceland a good model for France, or the United States for Venezuela. Put another way, is it immaterial for Germany that it is smaller in geographical size than Paraguay; or for Mexico that it is larger in extent than France, Germany, Italy, Britain, and Spain combined; or that the European country with the largest territory (France) would be the eleventh largest country in the Americas (less than half the size of Bolivia); or that Portugal, Switzerland, the Netherlands, Belgium, and Austria are not only all smaller in geographical size than Guatemala, Honduras, and Nicaragua, but also smaller than Cuba? Perhaps none of this matters, and because of modern communications and technology, the problems of governance for Russia, Indonesia, and India in fact do not materially differ from those of Sweden, Italy, Costa Rica, or Ireland – at least not for anything related to size. Perhaps this is the case, but it is unlikely. Invariably, matters of size are subsumed under "diversity" of some sort, which implies, improbably, we can assume that a given set of institutions are appropriate for a Brazil of 20 million or 200 million as long as relative diversity remains constant. The problem here is, given the evidence to be gleaned from human history, it seems highly probable that for a population to increase significantly it requires the introduction of increasing diversity of all sorts, although there are a few continuing exceptions, such as Japan. On the other hand, certain constitutional forms seem tailored for dealing with sensational increases in diversity without significant institutional change – federal systems, for example.

In our recurrence to fundamentals, we will not assume that any variables or aspects of life are immaterial, although initial study may lead us to conclude a greater importance for some than others – and not always the ones we now too easily take for granted. The growing number of constitutional democracies, and the diverse mixture of variables they contain, finally allows us to study constitutional democracy the way Aristotle studied constitutionalism in general. The stage we have recently reached in the history of constitutional democracy not only allows us to study the phenomenon; it requires that we do so. The nation-state is not going away. Every new development cited by those who see a more highly interconnected future world requires the successful functioning of something that resembles the nation-state, and it seems to favor the form of nation-state we term a constitutional democracy. The development of supranational organizations still rests on "local" control by nation-states, whether it be NAFTA or the South American Mercosur. Even the European Union rests on either the continuance of its member nation-states or the creation of one very large nation-state.

General Constitutional Developments since World War II

Although this volume is concerned with the theoretical principles of constitutional design, these principles are not divorced from the actual behavior of constitutional democracies. Later discussion addresses this behavior in a more systematic fashion, but for now a general overview of some trends over the past half century and a look at some of the lessons they hold provide an efficient entree to the discussion of principles.

Growth of Democracy. The growth in the number of constitutional democracies, though definite – from nineteen in 1947 to at least sixty in 2000 – has been episodic. Figure 1.1 creates the impression of a smooth and accelerating increase in numbers, but historically this growth has been characterized by periods of rapid increase followed by long plateaus or declines. The demise of the Soviet Union has produced the most recent upward surge, just as decolonization did in an earlier era. The probability for now is an increase over the next decade to about eighty countries that meet the test of constitutional democracy and then a plateau or perhaps minor decline in the numbers. In general the curve of constitutional democracies has followed the curve for the number of countries with written constitutions, with about a one-century lag, which has recently declined to a half-century lag. Constitutionalism is a difficult if rewarding form of government, and we should not expect significant future diffusion of the form to be rapid or inevitable. Figure 1.1 does imply, however, that if a nondemocracy has a written constitution, there are long-term pressures to democratize the system. A written constitution is a bit like a self-fulfilling prophecy. Still, one lesson to be learned from experience over the past half century is that, even though constitutional democracy is quite secure as we move into the twenty-first century, its spread is neither easy nor certain. The curve of its diffusion looks strong and hopeful, but it has taken more than two centuries of gains and losses to get where we are now.

Diffusion of Institutions and Principles. The diffusion or transference of both specific institutions and constitutional principles over the past half century has been significant. For example, the German electoral system has been widely copied, often with variation; indeed, the German constitutional system has served as a major model. Diffusion of socioeconomic rights has also occurred across Europe and into other parts of the world, along with the spread of federalism and the separation of powers as operative constitutional principles. Such transference does not result from simple copying but rather from the adoption of techniques and principles that effectively address problems and needs found throughout the world. Diffusion of institutions and principles is prima facie evidence that constitutional design makes a difference and that there are connections between institutional design and general political outcomes. In the end, however, the connection is pragmatic and practical, not ideological.

Parliamentary versus Presidential Systems. Nearly all new democracies constituted or reconstituted during the 1970s, 1980s, and 1990s have had elected presidents with varying degrees of political authority. Among newer democracies, true parliamentarism remains largely a phenomenon of the former British Empire. Since World War II, no existing "presidential" system has ever changed to a parliamentary system, whereas a number have moved in the opposite direction. This is evidence not of the inferiority of the parliamentary form but rather of the need for more separation of powers than a true parliamentary system provides. In Britain, the rule of law has been sustained primarily through a political culture that prevented the potential abuses of power inherent in the highly centralized and essentially unlimited power structure of the parliamentary form. The high failure rate of parliamentary government, especially in Africa, results from the absence of the unique and particularistic British political culture. So-called presidential systems have at the same time tended to incorporate institutions of a more parliamentary nature so that the distinction between the parliamentary and nonparliamentary form has become blurred. As a result of this blending, we should not only seek new categories and fresh analytic approaches to comparative constitutional study but also be cautious of research that makes such a distinction as if it were not problematic. One conclusion to be drawn is that constitutional design is not so much the science of finding an optimal form, but the art of mixing the old with the new, which results in an array of possibilities, each blending into the other. Institutional mixes will vary as the mixes of population and circumstances vary, and matching the underlying reality must take precedence over the defense of any given constitutional form as optimal.

Growth of Separation of Powers. A useful way to describe post-World War II institutional trends is as a general move toward a greater degree in the separation of powers. Many of the elected presidents have minimal powers, but their presence has been matched by reducing the ability of parliaments to appoint officials or to revise the constitution without the intervention of some other body. Often the regulation of the electoral system is taken out of parliament's hands as well. An important part of the increase in the separation of powers has been a general emergence of more independent supreme or constitutional courts to supplement the trend toward stronger and/or more divided executive powers. This has been supplemented by the strengthening of upper or second branches of the legislature – that is, a strengthening of bicameralism. In sum, those who have lived under constitutional democracy have, by their decisions for change, underscored the need to be realistic about the dangers of power, and the role of constitutionalism in channeling and controlling power.

Consensual Politics. Constitutional democracies have tended to move away from the majoritarian model of decision making toward a consensual model. The purer a parliamentary system is, the closer it approximates the majoritarian model. Consensual politics puts a premium on deliberative processes with multiple entry points, plus multiple decision points that slow the process down enough to produce legislation that takes into account the needs and wishes of more than a simple majority of the population. This trend underlies the previous one involving the separation of powers and is related to the next two trends. Constitutions need to be viewed more as instruments for achieving general fairness and justice than as instruments for efficiently pursuing specific public policies.

Decline of Unitary Systems. A move away from unitary government toward systems that are federal, confederal, or consociational has been slow but persistent. The European Union is a major example. Unitary systems work best with highly homogeneous populations and less well with the populations that are more heterogeneous. Not only are newer constitutional democracies less homogeneous than older ones, but many older ones are coming to recognize aspects of heterogeneity that were submerged or ignored in the past. The trend away from unitary government is another example of the lesson that the fundamental goal is to match the constitution to the people.

Inclusion of Minorities. Underlying the previous three trends has been a significant trend toward the recognition and inclusion of ethnic, religious, ideological, regional, racial, and indigenous minorities. The mix of institutions used has varied according to the nature of the cleavages. Federalism is most useful for territorially based cleavages. Indigenous and racial cleavages have often been addressed by increasingly more activist or more powerful national courts Bicameralism has been used for regional, ethnic, and religious cleavages. The more cleavages there are, the more complicated the range of institutions brought to bear. The lesson is that constitutions are supposed to aid the moving of conflict from the streets and battlefields to arenas of compromise and persuasion, and not to produce peace per se.

Rights Consciousness. Constitutional democracies have made a general and significant move toward "rights consciousness." Rights consciousness has involved two more or less equal subtrends, involving group and individual rights. In many countries, as in Canada, both subtrends have been intertwined. Longer and more complex bills of rights, more active national courts, and political mobilization through normal politics have all achieved greater prominence. It is reasonable to conclude, at least provisionally, that constitutions produce long-term pressures for identifying remaining injustices and codifying mutually acceptable solutions for these injustices.

Political Mobilization. In country after country, both social justice and political justice, often defined in terms of growing rights consciousness, have been addressed by supreme or constitutional courts. In country after country the net effect of judicial intervention in this regard has been marginal. Instead, social and political justice have been best served most consistently through political mobilization regardless of the content or even the existence of bills of rights. Bills of rights and rights consciousness have served more often than not as the catalyst and justification for political mobilization, and court activity has tended to legitimate rather than effectuate the demands underlying such mobilization. The openness and effectiveness of political institutions for participation thus loom larger than the reform of legal institutions when it comes to addressing the consequences of heterogeneity. There are several possible lessons here. Constitutions, including bills of rights, are in the end only pieces of paper absent popular acceptance and support. These pieces of paper do, however, help to instigate and frame popular political activity. In the end, constitutions rest on popular approval and popular activity. They are not self-enforcing through logical or legal exercises.

Appropriate Electoral Systems. A key participatory institution is the electoral process. It is of considerable interest, then, that historically once a constitutional democracy has initiated an electoral system, that system is rarely changed in any significant way. This implies that no electoral system (e.g., single-member districts vs. multimember districts) has an inherent advantage over another per se. Rather, constitutional framers seem to have been uniformly proficient in successful constitutional democracies at developing electoral systems appropriate to, and accepted by, the relevant population. Again, the lesson seems to be that matching the institutions to the people is more important than pursuing some theoretically optimal institutional design.

Need for Popular Consent. Over the history of modern constitutionalism, the failure rates of parliamentary and presidential systems have been very similar. The situation is even more ambiguous than this statement indicates, because, while commentators frequently are willing to classify a political system as one or the other, most political systems are hybrids of these two polar types so it is difficult to assign blame for failure on specific institutional arrangements. Rather, failure generally has resulted either from sociopolitical factors that made any constitutional arrangement problematic or from a mismatch between institutions and the people they were supposed to serve. One common mistake is to create a presidential system where the executive is the commander in chief of the army that overthrew the old regime. Another is to create a majoritarian parliamentary system for a highly fragmented population. Modern political science has reaffirmed Aristotle's dictum that the constitution must be matched to the people, and a people unready for constitutional democracy will not support any form of it. On the one hand, Aristotle showed us how to abstract general principles from the comparative study of constitutions. On the other hand, his dictum, as well as his abstracted principles, warn us about the limits we face when advising those writing new constitutions. A people will establish a constitutional democracy when they are ready, and the form it takes should have indigenous roots. Ideas and institutions may be borrowed or adapted, but constitutional democracy rests on popular consent for what is familiar and understood and not on some ideal design. Even in those rare instances where a successful constitution was imposed from the outside, as with post–World War II Japan and Germany, there usually has been prior constitutional experience that could be drawn upon, basic social and cultural patterns have been left relatively undisturbed, and the document has been appropriated over time through gradual but complete amendment, whether formally or through de facto usage, by the people living under it. Aside from repeating the lessons drawn earlier, one could add that experience under constitutional democracy shows constitutionalism to be a process rather than a model – a never-ending process that works out, through experience, the changing hopes and needs of the people living under the constitution.

National versus Constitutional Cultures. Experience since World War II has highlighted a persistent, recurring problem with the nature of citizenship in constitutional democracies. Does a common citizenship require a common identity beyond that of citizen? In the old nation-state perspective, where both "nation" and "state" were reified and linked, the answer tended to be yes; however, this links personal identity with the state. Those who refuse to reify the nation or the state think otherwise and say no – citizenship and patriotism do not require nationalism or a strong common identity. Yet citizenship and patriotism do require the passing on of something from generation to generation, and what this "something" is stands at the center of most current constitutional controversies. To what extent does one need to pass on the values of a national culture, and to what extent must one pass on the values of a constitutional culture? In principle, a constitutional culture can encompass several nationalities, or a constitutional culture can be identified with a particular national culture. Or a constitutional culture can be based on the gradual extinction of all national cultures, as some argue happens in the United States. Is it possible to have constitutionalism with no cultural component beyond a constitutional culture, or does this amount to a politics of nonidentity? Concern over the presence of multiple identities in the same political system is not a new phenomenon, but the identification of the political system with a singular nation is a relatively recent invention grounded in Hegelian statism. It is time to at least think about the nature and extent to which nationality and political nationhood may be decoupled.

Socioeconomic versus Group Rights. Finally, it is now respectable to constitutionalize both socioeconomic and group rights, but to what extent is each helpful for the long-term health of constitutional democracies? The former implies that all citizens should be treated the same, and not in a minimal legalistic sense. The latter implies that citizens should be treated differently depending on group or ethnic membership. The theoretical and practical disjunction between the two is too often glossed over. In addition, constitutionalizing socioeconomic and group rights tends to emphasize the role of the state in guaranteeing rights, whereas rights were invented to protect citizens *from* the state. Aside from the possibility that such an emphasis undercuts the actual function of rights, it tends to undercut the ability and motivation of citizens to pursue political outcomes beyond or different from what a constitutionally oriented court might support. Such a tendency short-circuits the role of citizenship per se and seems to view constitutionalism as a set of objectively predetermined outcomes rather than as a process of citizens involved in the working out of mutual hopes and needs through the use of commonly accepted decision-making rules and processes.

The Three General Elements of Constitutionalism

All of the trends, problems, and considerations just outlined point toward the need for a recurrence to original principles – to a deeper and clearer understanding of what constitutionalism means and implies. For example, it is not helpful to confuse constitutionalism with legalism, although the former leads to the latter. Perhaps the place to begin is with the connection between constitutionalism and prepolitical cultural mores. Although constitutionalism necessarily includes the notion of culture, it also transcends culture. "Culture" has been variously used to refer to what others might term "ideology," "shared interests, preferences, or perspectives," "a common set of values," ethnicity," "shared mental states," and so on. The term is here used in a more formal, anthropological sense to refer to a shared set of symbols, used to organize joint behavior for the solving of common problems, that is passed from generation to generation. Cultures are used to create and sustain societies and are historically prepolitical because they were used long before the creation of formalized political systems of any type. Constitutionalism, currently the most complex form of sociopolitical organization, recapitulates the history of human social organization and thus both assumes and uses culture. This recapitulation results in constitutions containing a cultural element, a power element, and a justice element.

The cultural element reflects residual human experience in a prepolitical condition. Humans (*Homo sapiens sapiens*) have for most of their existence evolved culturally rather than biologically. This has given humans a competitive advantage over other species and has led to their accelerating dominance over the rest of nature. Until finally brought under domination by political societies, these culturally organized societies continued until the nineteenth century on all continents as what are now termed aboriginal peoples. What we now term culture is thus so ingrained in the human psyche that it cannot be extirpated from human consciousness without our becoming something other than, or less than, human. Inevitably, constitutions embody, contain, or at least leave significant room for cultural mores and values that are still the fundamental grounding for human social organization.

The cultural element in constitutions has several components or is expressed in a variety of ways. Constitutions, as Aristotle famously told us, define a way of life in general terms by laying out and using as organizing principles the values, major assumptions, and definitions of justice toward which a people aspire. The cultural element is generally found in long preambles, opening declarations, and – more recently – bills of rights. The definition of citizenship or characterization of who belongs to the people or nation that is frequently found in constitutions is also a fundamental expression of the cultural element. In the Mexican Constitution of 1917, the definition of a Mexican is set out at great length along with detailed provisions on the duties of fathers, parents, and so on – a kind of primer on sociocultural mores. One can understand this concern if we remember that after the 1917 revolution that produced Mexico's current constitution there was a concerted effort to define the dominant *mestizo* culture as the basis of nationality in place of the colonially imposed Spanish culture. We also find a high level of explicit cultural content in constitutions adopted by more traditional societies that are recent recruits to constitutional democracy, such as Kiribati, Western Samoa, and Papua New Guinea. As a general proposition one might posit that the stronger the aboriginal presence in a country, the more apparent the cultural content of the constitution will be.

The power element in a constitution is found in institutions for decision making. In a coherent constitution, these institutions for organizing power are rooted in and reflect the culture or cultures of a politically organized people and simultaneously accomplish several things. They identify the supreme power (sometimes called the sovereign), which is always finally determinative; they distribute power in a way that leads to effective decision making over the range of all possible issues; and they provide a framework for continuing political struggle. Significantly, the political struggle often involves competition between cultures that are linked together under a common constitution, whether it be Anglo-Saxon and aboriginal in the case of Canada and Australia or "ethnic" in the broad sense as in the Anglophone-Francophone division in Canada. In essence, the power element structures conflict so that it can be managed politically rather than through violence in the streets.

The justice element is the key ingredient for constitutionalism because most political systems in human history, even though by definition they represented organized power, did not have constitutions until very recently. Constitutionalism as a political technology attempts to marry power with justice. It attempts to do so in a variety of ways. A written constitution, available for reading by any citizen as well as by every political actor, creates a known and "predictable" process of decision making that serves to limit the use of power to settled, agreed-upon procedures. The separation of powers that constitutions often contain limits power by vesting the power to reach collective decisions in multiple hands to prevent arbitrary decisions that would tend to run counter to the prevailing sense of justice accepted by the people and embodied in the constitution.

Power is also limited through specific prohibitions on decision outcomes reached by those in power. These prohibitions are often but not always encoded in bills of rights. Sometimes they are scattered through the constitution proper, such as the prohibition on ex post facto laws in the U.S. Constitution. Because bills of rights often mix prohibitions with long-term aspirations that reflect cultural mores, bills of rights create interesting and potentially troublesome opportunities. If a supreme or constitutional court has the ability to enforce rights, it also has the ability to interpret these rights; and because rights are to a significant degree artifacts of the underlying cultural element, this puts the court in the position of potentially defining or redefining the culture underlying the constitution. This is not perverse per se since the reality of constitutionalism is that political power trumps culture. A problem arises if and when a court is the body to exercise that trump.

Much of formal, legal constitutional law around the world involves courts in the struggle between competing cultures, subcultures, or the interpretation of a unified culture with multiple ideological constructions. Thus, judicial decisions can be deeply controversial in a way that impedes or prevents the implementation or enforcement of judicial decisions. This is a major reason why, as noted earlier, supreme and constitutional courts have not really been the major source of political change since 1945. Court members are almost certainly too embedded in the dominant culture to easily see their way to new and innovative decisions; and when they do, there are too many ways for their will to be thwarted through other political means. We have often seen the phenomenon of a national court enunciating a legal principle that is at odds with dominant cultural mores through the use of dissenting opinions or speculative internal reasoning, while at the same time reaching an overall decision that does not act on that new legal principle but instead affirms the dominant culture. The contracultural reasoning that accompanies the culturally expected decision is a way of floating trial balloons in order to encourage the broader political process to rethink the matter.

In conclusion, these three elements – culture, power, and justice – cohabit a constitution in its various parts and institutions. Any constitution worthy of the name includes all three. On the one hand, a good constitution provides a coherent package for all three. On the other hand, the three elements are inherently "at war" with each other. The cultural element is specific and particularistic, whereas the justice element works from the premise of universal applicability. That is, the rule of law inherent in constitutional processes requires that all citizens be affected alike and to the same degree, while the cultural component rests on distinctions and expectations that are not universal in their implications. The so-called majority-minority problem is one aspect of this disjunction. The power element is restrained by the universalistic rule-of-law element. At the same time power is inclined to respond to popular and particularistic demands from various parts of the population, because future power rests on the distribution of governmental goods and services in a nonuniversal manner. We see this disjunction in, for example, the debate over affirmative action in the United States. The culture-power-justice nexus embodied in a constitution has been most famously examined by Montesquieu. His term "spirit of the laws" is an analytically useful approach to the overall problem, and we turn next to outlining his core contributions to comparative constitutional analysis.

Fundamental Principles and the Spirit of the Laws

As we recur to the fundamentals of constitutional democracy, analysis can develop from comparative empirical analysis, from careful analysis of texts that clarify language and thinking, from the logical analysis of models, and sometimes through simple deduction from prior principles. The incautious reader might conclude that the end product promises to provide a master plan or a set of blueprints that might be applied mechanically to the design of constitutional democracy. Such is not the intent of this study, even if the goal were reasonably possible. Understanding events post hoc, even the understanding of empirical relationships, does not translate in human affairs into highly predictable institutional outcomes. The many reasons for this do not bear lengthy reiteration. There are too many variables, most of which are not susceptible to human control; for the rest, the connections between independent and dependent variables are often so imperceptible and far removed that they cannot be effectively utilized; human attempts to control these variables elicit counter human attempts to thwart or slide past them; and the human ability to create and learn new responses can make formerly important variables irrelevant, and attempts at control counterproductive. The impossibility of the task defined by logical perfection, however, does not render the task unimportant or meaningless. On the contrary, the task is recommended by both its difficulty and its importance.

A pedigree for constitutional analysis, while involving many political philosophers, runs most directly from Aristotle through Montesquieu to *The Federalist Papers*. Recent books have tended to work explicitly from Madison and Hamilton, but it is worth briefly summarizing Montesquieu here, if for no other reason than his approach is most directly supported by constitutional design over the past half century.

Montesquieu began by terming the reconciliation of freedom and coercion as the most fundamental problem of political philosophy. He worked from a conviction that organized political systems are created because they provide not only protection a la Hobbes, but also because they lead to long-term economic benefits not possible in prepolitical societies. In this regard he has some kinship with Locke, but Montesquieu's analysis is broader than Locke's. For one thing, Montesquieu defined the benefits of civil society to include justice explicitly, as well as the possibility of trade and commerce, whereas Locke never mentions justice. For another, Montesquieu recognized that the sovereign power created by humans frequently deprives citizens of the benefits for which it is created. As a result, his analysis focuses more clearly and deeply on the means to limit coercive power, which is another way of saying that Montesquieu was profoundly constitutional in his approach whereas Locke was only incidentally so.

To a significant degree Montequieu is an intellectual heir of Aristotle, but most political philosophers who wrote during the seventeenth and eighteenth centuries had lost Aristotle's realism and empiricism. In his recovery of Aristotle, Montesquieu ends up looking very much like a relativist, but this is not the case. Montesquieu believed that there was no universally applicable solution to the freedom-coercion problem. Instead there are types of solutions such that the reconciliation of might with right must be achieved differently in different cultures and political settings. Any given solution, to be successful, depends on a number of factors. Among others, he identifies geography, climate, the size and nature of the population, the nature of the economy, and the traditions in place – including religion and the existing political culture. Because we can systematically analyze the effects of each, the solution in a given country to the freedom-coercion problem is thus neither arbitrary nor accidental.

To say that there is a nonarbitrary, nonaccidental solution is not to say that there is an ideal one. Under the best of circumstances the solution can only approximate optimality, and to seek either optimality or perfection is to invite inevitable disaster. There is no optimal solution across political systems, or in any particular one, in large part because any successful solution cannot be permanent. It is subject to change by correction or corruption. In his view change is inevitable, and political institutions invariably lag behind social and economic change. As a result, both the content and application of constitutional principles are subordinate to facts, and facts are collected in order to generate and to condition the application of general principles. The principles that emerge are interconnected both logically and empirically. Logically, they illuminate the kinds of structures that are needed. Empirically, they help us to understand the inner logic of the specific set of structures adopted by a people. As a result, we are able to analyze the institutional logic of a political system using principles that transcend particular nations, and at the same time we can analyze the particularistic solution and its underlying, constitutive principles that integrate the society – which he terms the "spirit of the laws." This "spirit" is a composite of what we earlier termed the culture-power-justice nexus, and provides the energy for the political system the way a mainspring or a battery does a watch. Overall, then, Montesquieu is not only the heir of John Locke but also of Jean Bodin and Niccolò Machiavelli. He is a realist and an empiricist.

The analysis of comparative constitutionalism pursued here uses Montesquieu's approach not only because of its elegance or the veracity of the principles he advanced, but because the history of constitutionalism down to the present ratifies the utility and power of that approach. Although his analysis of the effects of climate strike us today as primitive and wrongheaded, he was correct in his general thesis that political power is organized in order to emancipate humans from the blind forces of nature, and that the political freedom that ought to result from man's increasing power over nature is threatened by the very instruments of power through which he organizes to control nature. This thesis led him to a powerful anti-Hobbesian conclusion. Because humans in the state of nature are weak, they are not dangerous to each other. But the creation of civil society makes humans collectively strong, and this newly gained strength produces conflict within and between political systems. In short, the creation of civil society marks the beginning of a possible state of war, and Montesquieu's solution to this possible state of war is a constitutionalism characterized by popular sovereignty and the separation of powers.

Again, though some of his analysis seems time-bound, Montesquieu held that constitutional democracy, which he generally termed a republic, is usually found in the form of a commercial society. Empirically he saw constitutionalism as enhancing what we now term economic development better than any other political form, and the more economically developed a country is, the stronger the pressures generated within the population for republican government. Here he ran into another problem. Economic development leads to the acquisition of vast riches, which in turn leads to greater and greater degrees of inequality. However, republican government (constitutional democracy in our terms) rests on republican virtue and equality. Hence we see the basis for his emphasis on a separation of powers structured so as to address the effects of inequality, and hopefully to redress it to some extent, while at the same time protecting the property of rich and nonrich alike.

Montesquieu did not believe that the constitutional form was the solution to the abuse of power. Rather, successful constitutionalism rested supremely on a political and social substructure that supported constitutionalism, which he termed the "spirit of the laws." Without this underlying political culture, the formal institutions of constitutionalism are moribund. Tocqueville in his *Democracy in America* spoke similarly of the "habits of the heart" that undergird and make constitutional democracy possible. These "habits of the heart" or this "spirit" derives to a significant degree from the way we organize and live our day-to-day lives – hence the importance of economics for Montesquieu. Because constitutional democracy cannot be defined merely in formal institutional terms, Montequieu resisted treating the separation of powers as a dogma and instead looked upon it as an instrument that allowed the population to organize a counterpower to power. Unless a people and their circumstances are such as to allow the creation of constitutionalism, it will not occur. By the same token, if the people do not organize themselves to preserve constitutional government in ways allowed by the separation of powers, constitutionalism will not last.

Conclusion

Constitutional government is not a natural form of political organization but a human artifact that is selected for use because of its beneficial tendencies. We choose to use this human-made tool, this technology, not for itself but for its relative advantage over other political technologies in the pursuit of fundamental human hopes. One can, in a sense, view constitutionalism as resting on natural inclinations, but constitutionalism flows from the human psyche in an attempt to channel and improve human nature. A constitution rests on deeply shared human hopes but not on behavior that, even when considered "natural," is in any sense inevitable. Three hopes in particular justify, animate, and define constitutionalism – the universal human hopes, one might say inclinations, for self-preservation, unfettered sociability, and beneficial innovation. These three animating hopes of constitutionalism are sometimes encoded as life, liberty, and the pursuit of happiness; but rather than being a separable value, liberty is a concept that encodes the triple goal of self-preservation, unfettered sociability, and beneficial innovation.

Constitutional purposes are multiple, and liberty thus has several layers; among various related institutional implications are rule of law, republicanism, and limited government. Rule of law, often associated with equal treatment, was actually developed to minimize arbitrariness, particularly arbitrariness that threatened one's life and livelihood. Republicanism, the belief that one should not be subject to laws to which one has not directly or indirectly consented, rests upon the free interaction of citizens in pursuit of the common good, which both assumes and enhances unfettered sociability. The common good, however, is not unlimited. Rather, republican government in pursuit of the common good has limits, and those limits are defined by human activity that results in beneficial innovation. "Beneficial innovation" is defined as any human invention that enhances or maximizes the probability of humans preserving themselves, developing morally and psychologically, and achieving relative material ease – without interfering with the inclination or ability to innovate further. Beneficial human innovations take many forms, including, but not limited to, such things as medical advances, effective international peace institutions, better teaching methods, more efficient production methods as well as more efficient ways of moving capital to underwrite such methods, faster and less expensive means of communication, advances in architecture and housing development that make human interaction easier in more pleasant settings, technological advances that can be used to free up more time for people to choose activities involving self-expression or personally rewarding joint activities, creative expression in more highly developed art forms, and alterations in the workplace that enhance safety as well as the productive use of the entire personality.

"Beneficial innovation" is not to be confused with a notion of progress where more is always better. Nor is it to be confused with innovation per se. What is beneficial can only be determined by a freely interacting citizenry reflecting on the nature of the citizens' own personal and human needs and hopes. Finally, although a free citizenry can determine whether an innovation is beneficial by adopting or not adopting it, "voting" for or against innovation – whether individually or collectively – must not censure, impede, or discourage future innovation if the system is to remain constitutional and serve the ends for which constitutionalism was invented.

If a constitution is to enhance the self-preservation of all citizens (otherwise why would they submit themselves to it); if it is to enhance the common good, which again implies consideration of all citizens; and if it is to protect the actions of beneficially innovative citizens whom we cannot identify beforehand, and who thus could come from any part of the population; then we must include all as citizens. That is, the constitution's rule of law, consent-grounded republican institutions, and power limitations must extend to all citizens; and the extension to all citizens is called popular sovereignty. Popular sovereignty thus rests at the base of constitutionalism, and that is why any analysis of constitutionalism and constitutional design must begin with an analysis of popular sovereignty.

As a preface to the analysis that follows, it might be noted that popular sovereignty can take one of four broad forms. The first might be termed "direct popular sovereignty," which describes a situation in which a people gather in the same location and make all collective decisions together face-to-face. A second form might be termed "strong popular sovereignty," which describes a situation where there is more or less constant oversight of elected officials by highly participatory citizens using a variety of supervision and consent mechanisms beyond periodic elections. "Weak popular sovereignty," then, describes the general situation where oversight is limited primarily to periodic elections. Finally, one might identify something called "foundational popular sovereignty" as the situation where the citizens are essentially limited to approving the constitutional structure and the rules that define it, as well as the amending of those rules and that structure.

The next chapter begins a sustained analysis of sovereignty and popular sovereignty that will be philosophical, historical, and analytic.

2

Sovereignty

The Reality Addressed by Sovereignty

Constitutionalism and, with it, the design of constitutions rest ultimately on an idea that today is rarely used in political analysis and, when it is, is generally misunderstood. That idea is sovereignty. The disuse into which the concept has fallen, and the misuse to which it is sometimes put when not ignored, impoverishes our political discourse at the very point where it should be the richest and most subtle – at the point where justice and power meet in constitutionalism. Constitutionalism is a human creation that results from the interaction between human nature and the brute facts of social existence in a postneolithic world. One brute fact is the absolute need for some form of order in any organized society; another is the inevitable chaos that results when such order is not achieved. Sovereignty is a human creation, an idea that attempts both to denote the factual necessity of order in human society and to connote a preferred way of relating to that fact. The preferred way of relating to the brute facts of social existence connoted by sovereignty is a constitutional order that marries justice with power in such a way as to tame that power and turn it to the service of a civil society.

Constitutionalism is one way of organizing sovereignty, but not the only way. Other possibilities that humans have tried historically include the identification of the best among them according to some criterion of military prowess or secular wisdom and handing power to them and then their descendants under the assumption that virtue breeds virtue; the use of a religious or priestly caste to watch over, guide, or admonish secular leaders; and the extension of social mores into the political realm under the guise of traditions or some common moral code, perhaps even a common law. One central premise of this analysis is that constitutionalism has emerged as the best technology, the best human invention for organizing sovereignty. Indeed, the word "sovereignty" is itself a part of the political technology that has come to be known as constitutionalism. Any understanding of constitutionalism must therefore include a clear sense of what "sovereignty" denotes and connotes, as well as how it has evolved over the past several hundred years. Before we get to that exercise in linguistic exegesis, however, it will be useful to first lay out in broad strokes how and why the supreme political power for which "sovereignty" is one possible identifier is a topic that must be addressed in constitutional design.

Humans use language to name things that they experience. In addition to being denotative, the words humans devise frequently involve connotations that significantly affect how those using the language relate to the experience that is named. For example, the word for "wind" may imply for some "the breath of God," in which case the wind will take on more than a simple climatological role in the lives of these people. Words are also used to describe things that cannot be seen and are taken for granted until they are missing. "Oxygen" is such a word, as is "sovereignty."

Words are stipulative, and in this sense they are artificialities; but this should not lead us to the erroneous conclusion that because words are artificial that their referents are also always human creations. I can call that green, leafy plant that grows outside my window a "tree," a "furd," an "arbol," or perhaps a "car," but that green, leafy thing will remain there and go on doing what it is doing regardless of what I call it. The word I use for it will be part of a language with other words and a grammar for their interrelated usage. I can use this language to imply a number of relationships between me and that "furd." However, although the relationship implied by the name I give this green, leafy thing may change what I do in relation to it, my relationship with it – whether my actions toward it are placatory, admiring, indifferent, dominating, or destructive – will not alter the existential fact of the "furd." It is simply there and does what it will do regardless of my name for it.[1]

The example of a "brute fact" used here comes from physical nature – the realm studied by biology, chemistry, physics, and the other hard sciences. But brute facts also exist in the realm of the social sciences. In effect, any aspect of human life that does not rely on artificial creation by humans, any aspect of human life that will occur without our willing it to, and despite any wish we may have to deny its existence, is a fact with the same status as the brute facts of the physical world. Human institutions result from, and are responses to, such brute facts. The need for nourishment is a brute fact of human existence. Humans, faced with this brute fact, use the possible sources of nourishment in their immediate environment, and invent ways of preparing food. Groups of people develop sets of food preparation techniques that are called cuisines. The variety of invented cuisines does not negate the brute fact that we need to eat. That we develop a need for prepared food as opposed to eating carrion is a second-order need that results from the interaction of other facts: we need to eat, humans easily invent new behavior, and humans have the natural ability to coordinate complex behavior to produce cuisines. Once the benefits of innovation in food preparation are experienced, it becomes close to impossible to not use these innovations. Political institutions, like cultural ones, teach us to want nonnatural experiences with a strength that approaches a need.

Political, social, and cultural institutions are human inventions or innovations. An institution is defined by a set of rules and expectations understood and followed by the relevant actors. These rules do

[1] The discussion here moves quickly through a theoretical minefield with little or no development of some important philosophical underpinnings. Because my project is the explication of a theory of constitutionalism rather than the defense of a metaphysical or epistemological position, I can only point to others who together develop what I consider to be the essential underpinnings for my assumptions and theoretical approach. For an explanation of the overall approach, see Larry Arnhart, "The New Darwinian Naturalism in Political Theory," *American Political Science Review* 89, no. 2 (June 1995): 389–400. On the relationship between social construction and the world of "brute facts," as well as the nature of human institutions, see John R. Searle, *The Construction of Social Reality* (New York: Free Press, 1995). On the relationship between persons, institutions, and communities, see Philip Selznick, *The Moral Commonwealth* (Berkeley: University of California Press, 1992).

not exist independent of human will the way a tree does, but institutions do result from human experience with brute facts of existence. Humans do not live according to unconscious tropisms like trees, or simple instincts like animals, but can choose to behave in ways that have a large element of unpredictability to them. Put another way, humans can invent behavior. This fact is the basis for what we often term liberty or freedom. It is also the ground for human institutions, because without this innate inclination for innovative behavior there would be neither the need to coordinate potentially diverse behavior nor the ability to do so. Therefore, institutions, although not natural in the form they take, are natural in that their existence is an expression of human nature. The existence of human institutions can be considered a second-order brute fact. Institutions will exist whether we want them to or not; the possibility for, and inclination toward, creating institutions is grounded in human nature, and the need for institutions results from nature at large. Without the coordinated behavior produced by human institutions, we cannot compete with other species or survive the conditions of nature to the extent we have. Humans have learned how to transform themselves from just another struggling species into one that increasingly dominates all other species. The natural need for survival has been translated into the learned need to reduce the dangers to survival progressively by dominating that environment through human invention.

It is well recognized, even obvious, but generally forgotten, that humans derive a competitive advantage over other species through the coordinated behavior that results from culture, society, and political organization. Humans have learned to "evolve" through the creation of institutions at a much faster rate than can occur in the rest of nature through genetic evolution. Humans at first used this comparative advantage to defend themselves against predatory species and to survive the challenges posed by nature, but eventually they used this advantage to dominate nature in general. One can argue that the process of humans learning to dominate nature has gone too far, but one cannot argue that this process has not occurred.

To summarize the major propositions to this point: humans share with other species the intense desire to survive as long as possible; humans tend strongly to prefer their own species to others; and humans share, as humans, the ability to learn new ways of doing things (innovate) and to pass on this new knowledge. The first of these three facts is the basis for what we experience as self-preservation in its crudest manifestation and self-interest in more developed form. The second fact is the basis for our social inclinations and thus for the willingness to coordinate behavior. The third fact is the basis for innovation, and thus for the ability to create institutions. Powerful inclinations in all humans for self-preservation, sociability, and innovation serve to condition human natural freedom and lead us to choose some actions over others and to coordinate rather than act as unconnected individuals.[2]

Humans learn that rule-governed sociability has profoundly positive consequences for self-preservation. Indeed, the evolution of culture leads to societies with larger and larger numbers of humans as the competitive advantage plays out over time in nature. At some point, coordinated behavior requires more specialized institutions, which we now call political. This development results from the endless ability of humans to learn, and thus to learn to want and "need" things promised by more effectively coordinated behavior; the need to deal with conflict between societies as they grow to collide with each other over natural resources, preferred geographical settings, and conflicting rules of coordination; and the need to deal with the internal conflict that results from the friction of large numbers – especially in the distribution of benefits and the inculcation of rules, the antisocial behavior of members seeking comparative advantage by breaking the rules, and the need to control or moderate social pathologies that result from higher-density living patterns. At some further point, coordination requires peacekeeping, the enforcement of rules, and more sophisticated mechanisms of decision making than can be accomplished through daily face-to-face discourse.[3] In short, natural and unchangeable human inclinations lead

[2] These extremely strong tendencies in human nature do not preclude exceptions. Humans are known to commit suicide, to engage in antisocial or criminal behavior, and to become hermits. In an evolutionary context these contrary examples, although recurrent, tend to be self-limiting because they are not conducive to successful propagation. In a nonpejorative sense these individuals become the losers in long-term human development, and the competitive advantage of humans over other animals also holds true for those humans able and willing to coordinate behavior over those who can not or will not. History is not made by criminals, suicidal individuals, or hermits, but by men and women who can induce coordinate behavior.

[3] The study of communities by historians, anthropologists, and other social scientists reveals that no cultural group has ever reached 200,000 members without developing specialized institutions of coordination that we can clearly term political. With

to the eventual need for political institutions, which in turn requires a supreme enforcer of coordination if there is to be successful coordination at all. Thus is born political power, and with it comes the hope that power can continue to serve the ends that led to its need – freedom, individual self-preservation, sociability, and continuing beneficial innovation.

The term "sovereignty" has tended to be associated with the nation-state, but this masks the generality of the phenomenon. Somalia during the early 1990s lacked a supreme political power to enforce coordination among the warring factions and clans, but within each faction or clan there was a supreme power that enabled each to act in human history as an organized, effective entity. Thus, contrary to the words of some newscasters, Somalia was not an example of chaos, but of a name for an entity that at that time lacked a supreme power to enforce coordination. Without this coordination there really was no Somalia, only a name for a nonfunctioning entity. The same can be said for Bosnia in the 1990s – the absence of a supreme power effectively makes Bosnia a name without a referent in the real world. Instead, there are smaller entities, each with its own respective supreme power, vying to become the supreme coordinator of something that could be called Bosnia. Organized behavior of humans acting in groups requires some way of saying "this is what we will do" and having the group's members act together in that way. Whether the group is an extended family, a clan, a town, a nation-state, or an empire is merely a matter of the "span of control" involved.[4]

relatively few exceptions political institutions develop by the time a society reaches 5,000 to 10,000 members, unless the society is quite isolated from contact with other societies. Indeed, political institutions seem necessary to reach even this number, or at least to maintain a society this size, since the comparative advantage of political institutions leads to the defeat and absorption of the politically unorganized by the politically organized.

[4] The argument here is intentionally at variance with that of F. H. Hinsley, who grounds his analysis of sovereignty on the emergence of the nation-state. That the concept of sovereignty is logically and empirically independent of the nation-state is implicit, but unnoted, in Hinsley's own analysis when, he says that sovereignty exists when "no final and absolute authority exists elsewhere"; see *Sovereignty* (New York: Basic Books, 1966), p. 25. A second, somewhat revised edition was published with the same title in 1986 by Cambridge University Press. Because there is no alteration in the analysis, the first version is used here. For those in favor of world government to end wars between nation-states, this necessarily amounts to a world sovereign. Sovereignty

The examples used thus far seem to imply that the supreme power always rests on the direct, successful application of force, which is not the case. More often than not coordination takes place without the use of force and violence, although the threat of such use may be more or less explicit – even in the instances where supreme power rests on consent. In this discussion we are working toward an understanding of why the use of "sovereignty" is a preferred descriptor for this supreme power rather than others, and one major reason is that "sovereignty" implies the minimal use of force and violence and, thereby, minimal injustice. The main points here are three:

1. Without a supreme power, successful human coordination cannot take place, and we are left open to domination by the nature around us.
2. Without coordination with a sufficient span of control by a supreme power, humans are left open to the threat of domination and violence to a far greater degree than is the case with such coordination – that is, we are better off with a supreme power than without one.
3. The use of a "sovereign," properly understood, allows the creation of a supreme power that minimizes violence and injustice.

Human nongenetic evolution leads to the creation of a supreme power, an entity that will have the final say concerning matters of coordination. This supreme power is the sine qua non of political institutions and is a second-order brute fact that becomes an unavoidable reality. It is a reality we like because of the fruits of coordination it can give, but at the same time we fear for its ability to deny those fruits and thwart those human inclinations that led to its creation. Complex societies with emerging political institutions have straightforward and natural pathologies – the failure to maintain order, the destruction of liberty, the undermining of sociability, and the halting of beneficial innovation. Because the latter three pathologies can all result from the first, the greatest temptation is to create a central power that is too strong. The possibility that a supreme power can produce one or more of the pathologies just mentioned is the reason why the necessity for a

would be worldwide in its span but would still exist even without nation-states. In the same way, entities smaller than nations can exhibit sovereignty.

supreme power carries with it an equally strong requirement for some means of restraining, controlling, or directing it in beneficial directions. Although the notion of a constrained, supreme power may seem more than a little paradoxical, the various facts of human nature play out in such a way that the paradox is now a permanent fact of life. The bottom line is still that, without a supreme power, coordination breaks down.

The basic literature is in agreement on these fundamental points. As Bertrand de Jouvenel puts it:

> Two preoccupations will always obsess the minds of men who reflect on politics. First, in any organised society or state, there must be a supreme authority which all admit. This authority mobilises the subjects in the event of danger from without, and quells and appeases internal disputes. The state of a country in which there is no authority able at need to issue commands and get them obeyed is one of misery, desolation and ruin. At certain times persons of an authoritative temper become completely obsessed by the vital need for a sovereign, and by the need for him to be an absolute sovereign if he is to quell disputes. This obsession gets to the point at which they overlook the second problem presented by sovereignty. A legitimate sovereign is necessary – that is the first point. But, secondly, he must command nothing which is not legitimate, and not every order which issues from a legitimate source is legitimate.[5]

F. H. Hinsley says in a similar vein:

> The concept of sovereignty... is not in terms of history or in terms of political science a concept which may properly be used to explain – let alone justify – whatever the state or the political society does or may choose to do. It is a principle which maintains no more than that there must be a supreme authority within the political community if the community is to exist at all, or at least if it is to be able to act as its character and circumstances require it to do.[6]

These representative quotations use the implicit language of sovereignty in their respective definitions when they refer to "authority" rather than "power." If power is the ability of some person or entity A to get some person or entity B to do something that B would otherwise not do, authority usually implies power that rests on the assent,

[5] Bertrand de Jouvenal, *Sovereignty: An Inquiry into the Political Good*, trans. J. F. Huntington (Chicago: University of Chicago Press, 1957), pp. 200–201.

[6] Hinsley, *Sovereignty*, p. 219.

consent, or agreement of those over whom it is exercised.[7] The strong tendency for theorists to use "authority" when discussing sovereignty is recognition that to speak of a supreme power as a sovereign is to alter our expectations of that supreme power, and thus to change the rules within which power operates. The word "sovereign" has historically carried a double connotation that virtually requires the use of "authority" when describing it. On the one hand, sovereignty implies supremacy in respect of power while, on the other hand, it simultaneously implies supremacy in respect of excellence such that the supreme power is characterized by superior qualities that make it better than the normal supreme power, usually in a moral sense. A sovereign has supremacy in decision making, but a sovereign is also supposed to surpass others of its kind – for example, happiness as the sovereign of goods, justice as the sovereign of virtues, and Arthur as the sovereign of knights. It is of more than passing interest that this dual implication of sovereignty has, when it is operationalized as popular sovereignty, strong implications concerning the characteristics of the population that is functioning as sovereign. These implications will occupy much of the discussion in the next chapter.

"Sovereignty" is one of several terms I might use to describe the reality of ultimate or supreme power. The term I use will not change the fact that supreme power exists, but it will tend to structure my expectations, and thus my responses to supreme power. The term I use may well affect whether I even notice the phenomenon. Part of the argument here is that it makes a great deal of difference whether we use "sovereignty" as opposed to "absolute power," or "power," for the simple reason that the historical linguistic network is such that the implications of "sovereignty" can change my behavior and the behavior of others in ways that are extremely beneficial for us all. Put another way, even though we cannot destroy the reality that these words denote, we can choose words within a working vocabulary such that we create alterations in that reality by our relationship to it. Because some realities are more in accord with our shared human nature, or make us happier, or have more beneficial results for those mixed up with that reality, it then makes sense for us to prefer or seek the creation of that

[7] This definition of power is based on the classic formulation by Robert Dahl, "The Concept of Power," *Behavioral Science* 2 (July 1957): 203.

better or superior reality. Because words and the ideas related to them can have consequences for the choices we make, political theories using these words and ideas can lead us to create different institutions for dealing with the reality of political power, and thus we are able, to an important degree, to determine how political power works itself out. In sum, given the fact of a supreme political power, it is worth asking what difference it makes if we view it as sovereign.

The Genesis of "Sovereignty": Before Bodin

The term "sovereignty" expresses the idea that there is a final and absolute power somewhere in the political community. From the beginning it also implied the idea that this final authority was somehow limited, about which we will have more to say in a moment. That there must be a final and absolute power somewhere in the political community was generally taken for granted by most political theorists before Jean Bodin, although medieval Europe was characterized by a complex struggle between the church and secular authorities over this very question, and Bodin's work was part of the final effort that led to the demise of the medieval "two sword" arrangement. Published in 1576, Jean Bodin's *Six Bookes of a Commonweale* contains the first systematic analysis of sovereignty in Western political thought. Although discussions of sovereignty usually begin with Bodin's work, it is helpful to spend a little time on what came before in order to better understand his contribution.

Classical political discourse did not use the term "sovereignty" because it is rooted in medieval French; however, the idea was still expressed in somewhat different terms before Bodin wrote for the simple reason that the problem addressed by sovereignty is as old as politics.

> As every political society possesses some political institution, however primitive, so every system of rule, however undeveloped, rests on some method of legitimation of the ruler and some pattern of accountability that the ruler observes. For it is in this way [the observation of a pattern of accountability] that rule has ever distinguished itself from mere political power. Sovereignty is a concept by which men have sought to buttress older forms of legitimation and accountability or on which they have hoped to base new versions of these means by which power is converted into authority. Its [sovereignty's] function

> in the history of politics has been either to strengthen the claims of power or to strengthen the ways by which political power may be called to account.[8]

Bodin's rendering of the concept emphasizes the claims of power while downplaying, yet retaining, the inevitable claims for limiting power that the term also implies. Hobbes and Grotius fall into the same general camp. Others, like Althusius, Philippe du Plessis-Mornay, Spinoza, Locke, Sidney, Rousseau, and Constant fall into the camp of emphasizing the claims for limiting power while retaining the inevitable claims of supreme power contained in the concept. Despite differences in language, customs, and institutions that separate us from ancient and medieval political thought, whenever we encounter pre-Bodin discussions in which there is an attempt to marry supreme power with institutions and practices that limit the operation of that supreme power, we are in the presence of a discussion about what amounts to the concept efficiently conveyed by "sovereignty."

Aristotle captured the paradoxical double thrust of sovereignty – a supreme power that is limited – as well as the inclination to ground the limits in some transcendent order when he suggested that superiority in the political community should be vested in the rational principle embodied in laws handed to men by the gods rather than in any person or persons in the community. Aristotle's formulation, as codified by Cicero in the idea of natural law, became the standard formulation until supplanted by the modern positivist view of law making. Aristotle's view supported the idea that law is found, not made, and thus the sovereign is automatically limited by this higher law. Christianity would gloss this position by declaring God the one and only true sovereign, so that his representative(s) on Earth were always bound by his will. Aristotle also set in motion the thousand-year attempt to link political supremacy with virtue when he argued that the ideal form of government, the best in an absolute sense, would be one in which all citizens were good men and the rulers were the *aristoi* according to a standard of perfection. Because he recognized earthly regimes could aspire to this ideal but never reasonably expect to approach it, he suggested a variety of means to rein in the dangers of tyranny toward which supremacy tended. Aside from admonishing his readers to seek

[8] Hinsley, *Sovereignty*, p. 25.

men of virtue to fill offices, he also advised the use of a mixed regime as the best constitutional design possible, given human nature. We see here the precursor to divided but coordinated power that in the modern world is codified as separation of powers and checks and balances. His doctrine of the mixed regime complemented the marrying of virtue with power, as well as his notion of a higher law limiting the actions of the supreme power. These three approaches continue to be the primary means for limiting the supreme power to produce what we now call a sovereign.

Aristotle's initial formulation of the solution to political power is suggestive in other ways. Although he was emphatic in his opposition to democracy as a degenerate form of government, this resulted from his stipulating that democracy should refer to the rule of many for their class good. He also stipulated that the rule of the many for the common good should be termed a polity, and the polity is what we seek in the modern world when we attempt to create democracy in our understanding of the term. Aristotle's mixed regime created a set of political institutions that together held supreme power. Because these institutions together were the supreme power, and together they included all of the classes within the community, Aristotle's mixed regime stands as a precursor to popular sovereignty. His ability to conceptualize a limited supreme power that was grounded in the broad population required that he first have a notion of a limited supreme power. It is no accident that the first person essentially to articulate a concept of political sovereignty was also the first to develop the theory of constitutionalism. A community organized around an effective but limited supreme power is the essence of constitutionalism. It is also no accident that Aristotle, in thinking deeply about the best way to organize constitutional government, concluded that the polity should be erected on the broadest definition of citizenship that could be justified under the particular circumstances. The idea of constitutionalism was born not only in association with the implicit formulation of sovereignty but also in association with popular sovereignty in embryo.

The idea of sovereignty implicit in Aristotle was worked out institutionally in the ancient Roman Republic. Under the Republic all magistrates enforced the law in the name of the *populus Romanus*. In the same way, *imperium* denoted a power to rule conferred by the Roman people on specific individuals, who then became public officials in the service of the people. Although the very broad (for its time) definition of citizenship was still too restrictive by our standards to serve as the basis for popular sovereignty as we now know it, the Roman people under the Republic still served as something functionally equivalent. Students today are bewildered by the Roman system of multiple offices in the Republic that seemed to provide no clear political superior. For example, the chief magistrate was known as the consul, but there were two consuls, not just one, with the idea that they would check each other and prevent a return to prerepublican monarchy. There were at first two, and then later four praetors. The *praetor urbanus* decided cases involving citizens, while the *praetor peregrinus* decided cases involving foreigners. There were two quaestors charged with the treasury, and later four when the office was opened to the plebians. There were multiple aediles in charge of roads, games, public buildings, and other public utilities. Finally, there were two tribunes elected by the popular assembly who could veto any decrees of the magistrates. The multiple magistracy did not reflect ignorance about sovereignty but instead revealed a rather sophisticated understanding. The creator is always greater than that which is created, and by making the various magistrates creatures, at least in theory, of the *populus Romanus*, the Roman Republic effectively declared the people as a whole to be sovereign. Furthermore, because every magistrate had at least one other person with an equivalent title or similar power, and the various civic powers were divided between at least a dozen people, no one could claim anything that looked like the supreme power.

At the same time the concept of the people as a supreme power was itself circumscribed in ways that are in line with the limits implied by sovereignty. For example, the law in republican Rome was not supposed to rest on the will of the people but on the higher morality that Cicero identified as the natural law. This subservience of the people's will to a higher law, commensurate with Aristotle's notion that a higher law that limits human will is supposed to be found and not made, was expressed and supported both culturally and institutionally. Those charged with making, interpreting, or enforcing the law had this higher-law doctrine inculcated through socialization. To supplement these internalized norms there was an evolving set of institutions that simultaneously linked the magistrates with the *populus Romanus* and limited the ability of the *populus Romanus* simply to get whatever it willed.

When the city of Rome deposed its last king in approximately 509 B.C., it established, along with its double consul system, a council of elders called the Senate, which was to advise the consuls, and a periodic assembly of the people organized according to family and religious memberships known as the *comitia curiata* – also as a means to advise the consuls. The *comitia curiata* never developed much power, however, and was supplanted over time by another assembly of the people, the *comitia centuriata*. This second assembly was composed of all men of military age (the committee's title effectively means "the people in arms") and, until 287 B.C., elected the chief magistrates and approved the laws submitted to it by the Senate. Because the military was dominated by those who could afford chariots, horses, and armor, the *comitia centuriata* was always dominated by the wealthier classes. The constant struggle between patricians and plebians led eventually to the formation of another assembly, the *comitia tributa*. This assembly was the successor to the *concilium plebis* (the council of the plebians, or poor), after a general strike by the plebians in 471 B.C. had led to its creation as a body to elect the tribunes, who in turn were supposed to veto decrees seriously at odds with plebian interests. In 287 B.C. the name of the *concilium plebis* was changed to *comitia tributa*. Prior to 287 the *concilium plebis* would meet not only to elect the tribunes but also to talk over political matters so as to advise the tribunes. This unofficial debate became increasingly influential until it reached the point where resolutions of the *concilium plebis* could have the force of law if they voted on matters that had first been submitted to them by the Senate. Also, the tribunes had the power to ask for the advice of the assembly through a vote, which was called a *plebiscitum*, or plebiscite as we call it today. In 287 B.C. the *comita tributa* inherited these powers.

On paper, republican Rome had a system of popular sovereignty in which the sovereign was limited both by a notion of a higher law and an upper house (the Senate) to impede the will of the people expressed through a lower house, the *comita tributa*. In fact, the highly aristocratic Senate dominated the mix through its election of all the magistrates except the tribunes, the ability to co-opt the tribunes with the promise of future election to a well-paying high office, and the ability to manipulate many members of the *comita tributa* through bribery, social patronage, and threats. Still, the Senate was itself denied supreme power by the very real impediments of a lower house and the tribunes elected by this lower house, which stood as roadblocks to Senate capriciousness, as well as the doctrine of the *populus Romanus* and the idea of a higher law. Furthermore, the multiplicity of magistrates impeded the enforcement of arbitrary senatorial will.

In sum, the Roman Republic was not democratic, but it was profoundly constitutional, and the effective use of an implicit doctrine of sovereignty stood at the center of its constitution. Constitutionalism can therefore be based on a doctrine of sovereignty that is not necessarily popular, at least not in the sense associated with what is called "strong democracy." The Roman Republic strained institutionally toward Aristotle's mixed regime or "polity," and Aristotle's polity was defined by a set of institutions that, while not making the majority of average citizens the dominant voice, did require that all classes of citizens have a voice in the creation and enforcement of laws. We might term this the commonwealth model of popular sovereignty, where the inclusive common good is pursued through a mix of institutions that protects the interests of all parts of the population, but the various parts of the population are not equal in their ability to affect the final outcome. The Senate in republican Rome can also be seen as an approximation of the kind of parliamentary sovereignty typical of Britain until the reformation of the electoral system in the nineteenth century. As with the British Parliament, the Roman republican Senate was effectively the supreme power, but one that was also hemmed in by both a legal doctrine and an institutional design that divided, balanced, and limited political power. Regardless of how democratic or aristocratic the Roman Republic was, its institutions embodied the essential paradox of political sovereignty. The institutional blueprint of the Roman Republic virtually defined the ideal of sovereignty for more than a thousand years of European history.

One can view the Middle Ages as dominated by the struggle for sovereignty. With the breakdown of the Roman Empire during repeated barbarian invasions, supreme power went to whoever could establish local order through force of arms. The fragmentation and localization of political power in Europe severely diminished the span of control of political units, and the seemingly endless warfare and arbitrary rule that resulted once again did not so much indicate chaos and the absence of sovereignty as much as it reflected a span-of-control problem, and thus an endemic struggle to structure sovereignty more effectively. One can view the gradual pacification of Europe and the eventual, fitful rise of the nation-state as an evolutionary process to discover a span of control that met the dual requirements of sovereignty – an effective, supreme power that could monopolize force within its boundaries, as well as a supreme power limited enough to prevent it from becoming itself a threat to the population for which it provided order and safety.

Local supreme power enforced by arms remained problematic unless a sufficient span of control could be achieved to muster sufficient force either to turn back or to defeat and absorb the barbarian clans. The solution seized upon was a feudal system in which a complex arrangement of fiefdoms allowed the coordination of many localities in a common defense. Often the barbarian leaders were themselves involved in the feudal network as a means of tying barbarian clans to a given place and ending the threat of their nomadic depredations. A gradual and complicated process of consolidation then began as what amounted to local sovereigns started to vie with each other for a greater span of control through the elimination of local competitors. Modern Europe emerged from the process. This difficult and slow process that worked from the bottom up was greatly complicated by a division between religious and secular power that went back to the onset of the Middle Ages and virtually defined the major problems of political theory during that thousand-year era. The consolidation eventually went beyond nation-states to include empires, but an equilibrium seemed to be reached after World War I that excluded units larger or smaller than nation-states until the emergence of the European Union. The European Union is, for the moment, still a loose confederation of what remain nation-states, and if the union is successful the end result will be a nation-state. A successful European Union requires the emergence of a common sovereign, whereas its failure leaves intact the smaller sovereignties. Sovereignty has been the central question in European politics for fifteen centuries, and it remains so today.

Many historians date the beginning of the Middle Ages to the second sack of Rome in A.D. 455. There is no clear and certain date for the onset of the roughly thousand-year period, but it is clear that less than forty years after the second sack of Rome Pope Gelasius I had formulated a doctrine known as the "two-sword" theory that would ground all discussion of sovereignty until the writings of Bodin. The two-sword theory argued for two equal earthly powers in Christendom with different spheres of responsibility. Religious authorities, with the pope at the apex of the church, were to have supremacy in spiritual matters, whereas secular authorities, with the emperor at the apex, were to have supremacy over the rest. Neither earthly authority was sovereign; rather, God was sovereign. Therefore, both of the supreme magistrates on Earth were supposedly bound by God's will as revealed in Scripture and through reason. Where God's will did not command, earthly powers were free to construct as need be.

This rather neat theoretical solution retained the essentials of sovereignty. God is the supreme power, but through the Old and New Testaments we know that he voluntarily limits his omnipotence through a covenant with humankind that allows for human freedom to say yes or no to his grace. God's will is seen not as capricious but as following a pattern contained in the natural law, which includes freedom for humans. The two-sword theory may satisfactorily justify the simultaneous operation of two earthly, coequal authorities to a population that is Christian, but it did not answer, even for believers, the question of what constituted the proper definition or limits for each sphere of authority. When disagreements arose over the practical application of the two-sword theory, who was to make the supreme decision as to which authority governed? Medieval politics in Europe revolved around a series of controversies that were particular manifestations of this central question of sovereignty. That the system worked at all is testimony in part to the relative weakness of both emperor and pope in a highly fragmented and localized power structure. The system also worked because pope and emperor were interdependent in a number of ways, especially before A.D. 1100.

For example, the Roman emperor Constantine in A.D. 313 granted religious freedom to Christians throughout the empire, and in 314 he convened a synod at Arles to regulate the church in the West, thereby inventing the ecumenical council. In 325 he convened and presided over the famous Council of Nicaea, which dealt with the troubles over Arianism. Even before the Middle Ages began, then, the emperor was involved in resolving religious as well as secular conflicts. The papacy had no great reputation at this time, but as the empire declined in political power, the pope inherited some of the emperor's position as symbol and defender of civilization. Several popes such as Julius I, Innocent I, Leo I, Gregory I, and Martin I distinguished themselves in dealing with the barbarian invasions and managed to obtain lands as a result of this defense. Most notably, in A.D. 756 Pepin the Short, Charlemagne's father, gave the papacy large tracts of land that became the Papal States. With this Donation of Pepin, the pope became a powerful lay prince as well as an ecclesiastical leader. In the turmoil of late eighth-century Europe, Charlemagne sided with the pope in wars over conflicting claims, and in A.D. 800 Pope Leo III crowned Charlemagne Holy Roman Emperor. Charlemagne had in the preceding years unified the Gauls and conquered the Saxons, as well other tribes, and had thereby re-created a large portion of the Roman Empire in western Europe. Leo III could claim some superiority over the empire since the crowner is presumably the creator and therefore has supremacy over the created. Ironically, Leo at once sponsored the empire and sanctioned the creation of a state, which, as the Holy Roman Empire, was to become the chief competitor with the papacy for sovereignty.

The power of the two competing earthly sovereigns waxed and waned as a result of periodic corruption, political intrigue, and the varying ability of the major actors. In 1122 the Concordat of Worms between Pope Calixtus II and Emperor Henry V ended a long-term struggle over investiture and restated the Galasian doctrine of the two swords, with no clearer definition of which sword ruled when there were competing claims. Much inventiveness went into legal and theological arguments supporting the superiority of one sword over the other, and virtually every major political thinker from William of Ockham and John of Salisbury to Marsilius of Padua had the problem of sovereignty implicitly at the center of his work. The symbolic struggle between pope and emperor increased in importance as the two positions increased in power during the high Middle Ages. By the time Bodin arrived on the scene it was clear that order and progress demanded that one side had to win. Bodin picked neither.

This is not to say that Bodin lacked a preference. He clearly supported the secular power, but not the emperor, the king. Perhaps he saw that the span of control that the emperor needed was too large to bring under sovereignty, and thus was an impractical goal. Certainly he understood that the nation-state was coming into its own as the primary political actor in Europe for the simple reason that the nation-state could produce the level of internal order and foreign exclusion that sovereignty implied. In his scheme of things the pope was just another prince ruling over his own nation-state, and the emperor was devolving into just another king, albeit with an exalted title. In sum, Bodin saw clearly that the traditional discourse concerning supreme earthly power was characterized by conceptual confusion born of false hopes and a failure to recognize the new European order on the horizon.

Bodin's Theory of Sovereignty

Bodin was not simply an apologist for kingly power. Like Machiavelli before him, and Hobbes afterward, Bodin attempted to develop a more realistic, empirical, and conceptually coherent view of politics. In a certain sense he was describing events more than prescribing them, although at the same time he had some shrewd and helpful advice to give the king – much as Machiavelli attempted to provide clear-eyed advice to his prince. Bodin's discussion of sovereignty therefore proceeded at three levels. First, he attempted to clarify the concept of sovereignty and then develop a theory of sovereignty that could be used by anyone, regardless of his political inclinations. In this respect, he was a political theorist. Second, he mapped out the different possibilities for the placement of sovereignty and thereby produced a new catalog of possible regimes and their characteristics. In this respect, he was a political scientist describing the catalog of political systems that he saw around him in terms of his new, empirically grounded theory. Third, he was a political partisan advocating the rule of kings as an antidote to the confusion and potentially dangerous political struggles he saw swirling around Europe. Too often he is interpreted at only this third level. His real contribution lay in developing a theory that could be used by anyone – pope, emperor, king, or commoner.

Although Bodin was analyzing the present and looking to the future, he did not abandon completely medieval political thought but built upon it. Most important, he framed his entire theory with the conventional medieval premise that God is above all earthly powers and is thus the only true sovereign. Also, in keeping with medieval theology he worked from the premise that sovereignty was alienable, and thus God could alienate sovereignty to the extent that an earthly power could be sovereign locally, that is, on Earth, while God retained His status as true sovereign. Bodin departed from medieval thought in his conclusion that God could allow multiple sovereigns on Earth, thus breaking with the assumption of universality that the Stoics, Roman natural law, Augustine, and the major medieval thinkers took for granted. This raised a fateful question: If God could assign multiple earthly sovereigns, to whom should it go? During the seventeenth century the king, Parliament, and the people would contend for the honor, but as far as Bodin was concerned sovereignty was a fact that could reside in any of these entities, although in only one at a time in a given political system. Bodin's analytic neutrality has led some commentators to conclude that he was inconsistent in his idea of sovereignty. There are difficulties with Bodin's presentation, but inconsistency is not one of these, even when he was expressing his preference for resting sovereignty with the king.

Bodin lays out his essential position at the opening of chapter VIII, entitled "Of Sovereignty."

> Majesty or Sovereignty is the most high, absolute, and perpetual power over the citizens and subjects in a Commonweale . . . that is to say, the greatest power to command . . . so here it behooves [us] first to define what majesty or Sovereignty is, which neither lawyer nor political philosopher has yet defined; although it be the principal and most necessary point for the understanding of the nature of a Commonweale.[9]

First of all, "majesty" and "sovereignty" are treated as equivalent terms, an equivalence that is pregnant with implications. Majesty is rooted in the Latin term *majestus*, which was used in classical Rome to signify the power and dignity of the people, especially with respect to offenses against it. *Majestus* was the primary attribute of the *populus Romanus* and was thus the Latin equivalent of the modern term

[9] Jean Bodin, *Six Bookes of a Commonweale* (1576), book I, chap. VIII, from the 1606 English translation, as edited by Kenneth Douglas McRae (Cambridge, Mass.: Harvard University Press, 1962), p. 84. Spelling has been modernized from the original text so that, for example, soueraigntie becomes sovereignty, vnder becomes under, certaine becomes certain, and commaund becomes command.

sovereignty, as Bodin correctly puts it. In medieval Europe, however, majesty was used to describe the greatness and glory of God, a usage that can be found in the works of Chaucer, Malory, and Milton, to use examples from those writing in England. Literary use paralleled that of theology and philosophy in which *majestaticus* technically described the glorious presence or inhabitation by God. By implication, then, to describe someone as possessing majesty was to say that in some sense God was present in that person. One can see how, in the struggle between pope and emperor, language gave the pope a certain edge, but by crowning the emperor the pope passed this majesty from God onward and also confirmed his own majesty. If he did not crown the emperor, the pope left open the possible claim that the emperor could crown himself, which happened on more than one occasion, and the pope would thereby lose political leverage. By the time Bodin wrote, the premise of God's sovereignty, combined with the idea that rulers were designated by God and thus ruled through his favor, had resulted in the implicit notion of divine right that would be explicitly codified during the century after Bodin, most famously in England by Robert Filmer in his book *Patriarcha*.

By linking sovereignty with majesty Bodin called up and built upon two thousand years of tradition, but, as the difference between Roman *majestus* and medieval *majestaticus* implied, where sovereignty naturally should fall was not clear. Bodin took this potential weakness and turned it into a strength by declaring there was no natural designate of God's sovereignty. Sovereignty lay with whoever could successfully claim he possessed the essential character of sovereignty – a power that is "most high, absolute, and perpetual." A few lines later Bodin says:

> We have said that this power ought to be perpetual, for that it may be, that that absolute power over the subjects may be given to one or many, for a short or certain time, which expired, they are no more than subjects themselves: so that while they are in their puissant [mighty] authority, they cannot call themselves Sovereign princes, seeing that they are but men put in trust, and keepers of this sovereign power, until it shall please *the people or the prince* that gave it to them to recall it; who always remained leased thereof. For as they which lend or pawn unto another man their goods, remain still the lords and owners thereof: so it is also with them, who give unto others power and authority to judge and command, be it for a certain time limited, or so great and long

time as shall please them; they themselves nevertheless continuing still leased of the power and jurisdiction, which the other exercise but by way of loan or borrowing.[10]

Whoever can enforce their claim is sovereign, but this sovereign can "put in trust," "pawn," "loan," or "lease" the execution of sovereignty to some agent or agents who act under the authority of the sovereign. The agent(s) has absolute power; the agent does not have most high and perpetual power. Bodin thereby draws a distinction between the holders of sovereignty and the executors of sovereignty. The distinction seems tailor-made to use with popular sovereignty, for which he initially seems to argue.

But let us grant an absolute power without appeal or control to be granted by the people to one or many to manage their estate and entire government: shall we therefore say him or them to have the state of Sovereignty, when as he only is to be called absolute sovereign who next unto God acknowledges none greater than himself? Wherefore I say no sovereignty to be in them, but in the people, of whom they have a borrowed power, or power for a certain time, which once expired, they are bound to yield up their authority. Neither is the people to be thought to have deprived itself of the power thereof, although it have given an absolute power to one or more for a certain time... the Sovereignty still remaining with the people.[11]

Despite this and other statements of popular sovereignty, there are also just as many statements that seem to assume that the prince or king is the sovereign on his own. Also, recall that in the initial quote from his text Bodin said that an executor of sovereignty remained so until he was replaced by the "people or prince." This dualism is not peculiar to Bodin. Otto Gierke refers to a "double majesty" perspective that was typical of medieval ambivalence toward kings.[12] One notion held that kings had authority from God such that the positive law of the king must be accommodated to natural law but was otherwise not limited in his authority when acting as a true sovereign. A second notion, which supplemented but did not serve as an alternative or competitor to the

[10] Ibid. (italics added).

[11] Ibid., p. 86.

[12] Otto Gierke, *Natural Law and the Theory of Society, 1500–1800*, trans. Ernest Barker (Cambridge: Cambridge University Press, 1934), pp. 43–45, 54–55.

first, was the proposition that the king derived his power by grant from the people. On the one hand, this meant that the king could be viewed as above positive law, for he makes it and gives it its coercive power; on the other hand, the people can make a law by custom that has more weight than the ordinances of the prince. In theory, then, the king should voluntarily abide by human law as well as follow the natural law. However, the essential points made by Bodin at this point are that, first, sovereignty can be seen as vested in any entity that can maintain the claim; and, second, sovereignty resides in whoever grants fiduciary power to the executor of sovereignty. The first point speaks to the nature of sovereignty, while the second speaks to how one identifies the sovereign. He repeats the second point again in a way that reinforces the first: "... who never gives so much power unto another, but that he always keeps more unto himself; neither is he ever to be thought so deprived of his sovereign power, but that he may take unto himself. So that Sovereignty is not limited either in power, charge, or time certain."[13]

Sovereignty resides in that entity whose power is not limited in extent or time, whereas any entity whose power is limited in extent or time is not sovereign, even though, as Bodin has made clear, the executor of sovereignty, although limited in some sense, is still as executor temporarily absolute. The sovereign is thus seen as having some of the essential attributes of God, who is after all the model for sovereignty as well as the only true sovereign. For this reason, supporters of popular sovereignty will in later years say that the voice of the people is the voice of God. But we should not be distracted by Bodin's cautious circumlocutions. What he is working up to is the very Hobbesian notion that sovereignty on Earth belongs to whoever can make the claim good. Successful social organization requires a supreme power, and this supreme power can be discovered by tracing back grants of power to the entity that stands behind them all. We may call this supreme power a sovereign in the hopes of keeping it in the service of the common good, but that does not change the fact that in the end there will be a supreme power. Bodin is here stating what he thinks is a fact grounded in necessity – there must be a supreme earthly power – and then telling

[13] Bodin, *Six Bookes of a Commonweale*, p. 85.

us how to empirically locate that supreme power. The implications of this neutral, empirical stance turn out to be straightforward, but stark. The sovereign "must either be by the good liking of him that gave the power, or else by force: if by force, it is called tyranny; and yet nevertheless the tyrant is a sovereign: as the violent possession of an intruder is in nature a possession, although it be contrary to the law, and they which had the possession before are so thereof disseised."[14]

Sovereignty is a characteristic possessed by whatever entity does possess it – that is, the ability to enforce order and coordination. There is no "natural" earthly sovereign, which is why Bodin speaks of both the people and the prince as potential sovereigns. Furthermore, just as God, the model sovereign, has alienated part of his sovereignty to an earthly sovereign who is to act in accordance with his will, and in effect be the earthly executor of God's sovereignty, so too earthly sovereigns can partially alienate their sovereignty to executors who temporarily wield absolute power in the name of the earthly sovereign.

But because the earthly sovereign is but God's executor, and there is no natural entity in which sovereignty must necessarily be vested, earthly sovereignty is capable of being completely alienated, presumably if the earthly sovereign feels unable, or is unwilling, to act as the supreme power. Bodin thus explains that a sovereign people may turn to monarchical sovereignty.

But what shall we then say of him to whom the people have given absolute power so long as he lives? In this case we must distinguish: if such absolute power be given [to] him purely and simply without the name of a magistrate, governor, or lieutenant, or some other form of deputation; it is certain that such a one is, and may call himself a Sovereign Monarch; for so the people have voluntarily disseised and despoiled itself of the sovereign power, to seal and invest another therein; having on him, and upon him transported all the power, authority, prerogatives, and sovereignty thereof; as if a man should by pure gift deliver unto another man the property and possession that to him [the giver] belongs; in which case such a perfect donation admits no conditions.... But if the people shall give all their power to any one so long as he lives, by the name of a magistrate, lieutenant, or only to discharge themselves of the exercise of their power; in this case he is not to be accounted any sovereign, but a plain

[14] Ibid., p. 87.

officer, or lieutenant, regent, governor, or guardian and keeper of another man's power.[15]

This passage is interesting and important for a number of reasons. First, it implies that earthly sovereignty always begins in the people. Second, it explains the obvious fact that there are sovereign monarchs. Third, it implies that there is always a covenant, compact, or agreement of some sort at the beginning of each regime. Fourth, it indicates that the content, terms, or conditions of this original agreement are crucial. Finally, it implies that there are good reasons why a people might want to alienate their sovereignty completely. As to the last implication, although Bodin never tells us explicitly what these reasons might be, implicit in all of his text is the notion that we are better off with a sovereign than without one, and a people may designate a sovereign monarchy in order to produce the order that for some reason they cannot by themselves produce. Put another way, an organized people may be able to wield sovereignty effectively, but a disorganized people may not be able to do so and are better off throwing their support to a prince who can impose order rather than living with the disorder. Otherwise, it can be expected that a sufficiently organized people may want to retain sovereignty to pursue not only order but also the commodious life and other common ends that first brought them together. At this point, Bodin looks to have worked himself to a position not much at variance with that of Hobbes. Although there has been no explicit discussion of a state of nature, an original compact or covenant among the people themselves, and then a covenant with the monarch ceding temporary or permanent power, Bodin's argument sets the stage for Hobbes. Here we have clearly stated the first aspect of sovereignty – absolute, enforceable power. A few pages later Bodin restates the first essential aspect of sovereignty – the need for absolute power – but then he immediately, unlike Hobbes, provides an extended discussion of the other face of sovereignty when he tells us that every earthly sovereign, however it comes into being, is inherently limited in a number of ways. These limits are not automatic or certain, but they are inherent in the term "sovereign," and together provide us with a way of clearly distinguishing sovereignty from an unlimited supreme power, at least in words.

[15] Ibid., p. 88.

> This so great a power given by the people unto the king, may well be called absolute and sovereign, for that it have no condition annexed thereunto, other than is by the law of God and nature commanded.[16]

> But as for the laws of God and nature, all princes and people of the world are unto them subject: neither is it in their power to impugn them, if will not be guilty of high treason to the divine majesty, making war against God.[17]

All sovereigns, even those to whom a people have permanently ceded their power, are still limited by the laws of God. That these laws of God seemed in practice to be effectively inoperative was the very reason that later theorists felt more comfortable retaining sovereignty in the people as a means of giving force to natural law. However, a sovereign is a sovereign, and popular sovereignty still faces the problem that the people can ignore God's law as well. Initially it was assumed that popular sovereignty is much more difficult to activate than monarchical sovereignty, and therefore inherently less dangerous. It was also assumed that popular sovereignty would be more or less episodic, expressing itself primarily in the selection of its agents, and therefore the agents of popular sovereignty were the ones who needed their everyday actions limited. Hence, constitutions were created initially to specify the limits placed by the people on the executors of their will, and only later as a means of placing public limits on popular sovereignty as well. Only as the evolution of constitutionalism reached this latter phase do we encounter the idea that constitutions should embody the natural law – or, not necessarily the same thing, the laws of nature.

Also, from the very beginning Bodin is implying that the sovereign, whoever it is, is limited by those ends for which a sovereign is established. The opening sentence of the first quotation placed sovereignty in the service of the "commonweale." We have become used to reading this as "commonwealth," especially since Locke, who seems to imply that only wealth or property is held in common. However, the original meaning of both words implied much more – something more along the lines of common good. "And forasmuch as we have before defined a Commonweale to be the right government of many families,

[16] Ibid., p. 89.
[17] Ibid., p. 92.

and of things common among them, with a most high and perpetual power: it resteth to be declared, what is to be understood by the name of a most high and perpetual power."[18] Bodin does not speak of sovereignty outside the context of a commonweale, and thus what constitutes "right government" and "things common" among many families is an essential part of what is meant by sovereignty. Without sovereignty there is no commonweale, and without the commonweale there is no sovereignty.

The opening line of Bodin's book defines a commonweale as "a lawful government of many families, and of that which unto them in common belongs, with a puissant [mighty] sovereign."[19] On the same page he distinguishes a commonweale based on lawful and rightful government from all other "assemblies," which he terms "robbers and pirates." His explication makes clear that many or most so-called governments are little more than piracies. Commonweales are formed by the joining of many families for the provision of life's necessities as well as for the provision of lives that are "commodious" and better than might be had outside of a commonweale.[20] A commonweale does more than enhance our ability to meet material needs. It allows the pursuit of common projects that cannot be pursued, or perhaps even conceived, by isolated men, and in the process of pursuing common projects the relationship between the men involved is transformed.

> Now when the master of the family goes out of his own house where he commands, to entreat and traffic with other heads of families, of that [which] concerns them all in general, he then loses the title of master, head, and lord, to be a companion equal and fellowlike with others, leaving his family to enter into a city, and his domestic affairs to entreat of public; and instead of a lord calls himself a Citizen, which is no other in proper terms than a free subject holding of the sovereignty of another man.[21]

This "free subject" is a "citizen," who is also a subject, because "some small part of his liberty [is] diminished by the majesty of him to whom he owes abeyance."[22] Citizens can be born into a commonweale or naturalized into it. Naturalization consists in voluntarily subjecting

[18] Ibid., p. 84.
[19] Ibid., p. 1.
[20] Ibid., p. 5.
[21] Ibid., pp. 46–47.
[22] Ibid., p. 48.

oneself to the common sovereign.[23] What defines a commonweale, however, is not the common sovereign per se, but the common laws passed under the authority of the sovereign. Note that this definition is neutral with respect to what entity serves as sovereign, and though Bodin preferred a king, the definition leaves open popular sovereignty as an option. Unlike the medieval theorists who defined a sovereign in terms of a set of privileges, Bodin shifts the definition of a sovereign to a single criterion that is the same everywhere – the sovereign is the one with the power to make laws. A nation-state is therefore defined by a common set of laws, and a commonweale by a set of laws made by a sovereign with respect to citizens.

The concept of a citizen who is also a subject requires further discussion in order to prevent confusion on an important matter that has been held in abeyance since the opening discussion on the advantages of coordinated behavior. Too often today the term "coordination" will automatically be read as equivalent to "directed." The implicit pyramid model in which those at the top tell those further down what to do and not do is precisely what is not connoted by "coordinate." If entity A says that entity B will drive on the right-hand side of the road, and will drive on road X today to deliver a message given him by person C, this is an example of directed behavior. If, on the other hand, entity A says that all persons will drive on the right-hand side of the road but leaves up to those affected by this rule to decide when and where they go, as well as for what reason, this is an example of coordination. Rules of coordination apply generally to all actors, not to specific ones; enhance rather than restrict the range of action; and structure a process of combining and recombining that is open-ended because those engaged in it mutually adjust actions that are spontaneous and individually motivated. This is what Bodin means by everyone being a subject vis-à-vis the sovereign but citizens with respect to each other. We are all subject to the laws, and Bodin defines the lawgiver as sovereign; we are free and equal as citizens to pursue our nondirected ends within the space that is defined by and enhanced by the laws – the rules of coordination – put in place by the sovereign.

Hobbes will generate a concept of Leviathan, a supreme power that is directive and threatens to extinguish the public realm of freedom

[23] Ibid., p. 49.

within which citizens operate. This potential for the supreme power to become Leviathan is attacked by the concept of sovereignty. A sovereign is absolute in the application of power but limited in the matters over which it can be absolute. A sovereign coordinates and does not direct. A sovereign creates a public space for the operation of citizenship and does not threaten this space with extinction. Supreme power is the reality we inevitably face in a postneolithic world. Sovereignty describes a kind of supreme power that we can choose, but which must be created and sustained through advanced human invention.

The distinction between "direction" and "coordination" helps us to understand why Bodin saw the sovereign to be, at least in theory, limited to those means of coordination appropriate to citizens as opposed to mere subjects. When people think of themselves as citizens, as opposed to merely subjects, they have expectations about how they should be treated that lead to their resisting laws from the sovereign that are inappropriate in terms of being too directive, too restrictive, or less than general in their application. Thinking of a supreme power as a sovereign, and thus of oneself as a citizen, then becomes an important self-executing means for limiting the supreme power.

Bodin also sees the sovereign as limited by *legis imperii* – laws that concern the form of government. These general laws are particular to each commonweale and consist of prohibitions on actions that would undercut or tend to destroy the sovereign. In the case of France he cites the prohibition on female succession to the throne and prohibition of any action that would alienate any part of the public domain. Both rules are essential to the continued existence of the particular sovereign of France. The first helps assure orderly transmission of sovereignty, and the second safeguards the sources of revenue needed in order for the sovereign to perform his duties.

Finally, Bodin attempted to strengthen the force of natural law by deriving from it two specific limitations on all sovereigns. First, a sovereign is bound like any and all humans to keep his promises, which usually include those made by his predecessors. All civilized order, said Bodin, rests on "the keeping of faith and the performance of covenants." Bodin then suggests that the sovereign can minimize these restrictions by not explicitly promising to maintain the laws of previous sovereigns when he or it is installed. Since at least 1219, with the adoption of the Golden Bull, it had become common for the investiture of king and emperor to include in the ceremony just such a promise to uphold and enforce existing laws made by previous sovereigns. Bodin's advice to the king that avoiding this oath during investiture would give him a freer hand can also be viewed as advice to the citizens not to overlook the inclusion of this investiture oath. Theoretical principles worthy of the name can be used by anyone of any political faction, and this is a good example.

A second limitation rested on the principle commonly derived from natural law by philosophers and jurists that "every man shall have his due." Bodin used this natural-law principle to construct an impressive defense of the sanctity of private property and placed it firmly outside of governmental control or regulation. Among other things, Bodin argued that this precept precludes taxing property owners without their consent. He suggested that in France the Estates General was the proper mechanism for conveying this consent, but because in France at that time the Estates General did not have any authority independent of the king, the prohibition on taxation without consent was more theoretical than real. The same principle enunciated in Magna Carta became in England the basis for common-law limits on the monarch and eventually contributed importantly to the development of parliamentary supremacy. Whether Bodin saw this constitutional possibility is not clear, although if someone had suggested the king-in-parliament formulation of sovereignty that was adopted by Britain in the Glorious Revolution of 1688–1689, he might have agreed that this is what he meant. Regardless, Bodin was able to derive at least two clear limiting injunctions from natural law beyond the unconvincing "appeal to heaven."

The sum total of these limits we would today rightly view as inadequate safeguards against tyranny, but they are listed here to illustrate the manner in which Bodin continues the tradition of having the term sovereign automatically include limits on the supreme power. When we consider Bodin's earlier statement that even a tyrant, if he has de facto supreme power as a result of the force of arms, is still a sovereign, his view of sovereignty looks quite similar to that of Hobbes. Sovereignty, established to attain ends not attainable without the coordination that such supreme power makes available, looks much like a "beast" that needs taming. To those not accustomed to take for granted God's retribution in the next world as a realistic limit on sovereignty, the concept looks to need a great deal more development.

Those writing immediately after Bodin worked to develop his idea of popular sovereignty more fully, but popular sovereignty is no more self-executing than any other means of taming power. For this reason future development of sovereignty theory focused more and more on the development of constitutional means that were self-executing once put into place. In the short run, Hobbes was to restate Bodin's theory in a way that not only clarified Bodin's first face of power, but also, by divorcing sovereignty theory completely from medieval assumptions, pointed toward the terrible possibilities inherent in sovereignty and clarified the need for much stronger secular institutions to prevent a sovereign from degenerating into an unlimited supreme power – a Leviathan.

The Hobbesian Gloss on Bodin

Hobbes, unlike Bodin, is still widely read today, so there is no need to explicate his argument to the same extent. The discussion here is limited to what Hobbes contributed to our understanding of sovereignty, as well as the challenge he left to others.

Part II of his *Leviathan* entitled "Of Commonwealth" begins with the famous chapter XVII, "Of the Causes, Generation, and Definition of a Commonwealth." Hobbes begins by rejecting natural law as relevant to sovereignty. "For the laws of nature (as justice, equity, modesty, mercy, and (in sum) doing to others as we would be done to) of themselves, without the terror of some power to cause them to be observed, are contrary to our natural passions, that carry us to partiality, pride, revenge, and the like. And covenants without the sword are but words, and of no strength to secure a man at all."[24] Hobbes goes on to say that if the natural law were operative and self-executing, there would be no need for government in the first place "because there would be peace without subjection."[25]

Because of natural human passions, and because the natural law is not self-executing on Earth, "it is no wonder if there be somewhat

[24] Thomas Hobbes, *Leviathan*, ed. Edwin Curley (Cambridge: Hackett, 1994), p. 106.
[25] Ibid., p. 107.

else required (besides covenant) to make their agreement constant and lasting, which is a common power to keep them in awe, and to direct their actions to the common benefit."[26] Hobbes has the individuals who would constitute the people of a commonwealth covenant with each other to confer the power each has in a state of nature to a common power. This common power he calls Leviathan, which he deems a "Mortal God" (the idea of God is still the model for the sovereign).

And in him [Leviathan] consisteth the essence of a commonwealth, which (to define it) is one person, of whose acts a great multitude, by mutual covenants one with another, have made themselves every one the author, to the end he may use the strength and means of them all, as he shall think expedient, for their peace and common defence. And he that carrieth this person is called SOVEREIGN, and said to have Sovereign Power, and every one besides, his SUBJECT.[27]

Hobbes differs from Bodin in giving the sovereign a name – Leviathan. This term has been used to connote a beast (often a huge sea serpent), or a man of enormous power. The name Leviathan, however, is rooted in a Hebrew word for Satan.[28] It is tempting to see Hobbes as using the name to connote the link between a fallen nature and the need for a supreme power to rein in that nature. It is also interesting to note, as many have, the frontispiece to the original edition of *Leviathan*, supposedly designed by Hobbes himself. It depicts a huge man wearing a crown gazing out onto a peaceful and productive countryside over which he towers. This man, presumably the Leviathan, is composed of thousands of little men compacted into the giant figure. Some see the diminution of individual men into a mass of undifferentiated, dependent beings. Others see a Leviathan that has no existence independent of the people who compose it. Hobbes does say that Leviathan always rests upon consent either voluntarily given in its creation, or post hoc by conquered people who choose to submit rather than leave.[29] Hobbes also holds out at least the logical possibility of popular sovereignty when he says, "For elective kings are not sovereign, but ministers of the sovereign; nor limited kings sovereigns,

26 Ibid., p. 109.
27 Ibid. (emphasis in original).
28 See Isaiah 27:1.
29 Hobbes, *Leviathan*, p. 131.

but ministers of them that have the sovereign power."[30] The first would seem to refer to the people, and the second to a parliament, but both may refer to a parliament.

Regardless, Hobbes says on page 109 that the people who covenant to create Leviathan may bestow sovereignty "upon one man, or upon one assembly of men, that may reduce all their wills, by plurality of voices, unto one will." The name thus implies not only the bestial power of the sovereign but also the singularity of its will – which, it turns out, can be expressed through the will of those with the most votes in a parliament. Hobbes in this regard has said no more or less than Bodin. Both men speak of domestic peace and common defense as the primary purpose for the supreme power. Hobbes's reference to everyone as "subjects" vis-à-vis Leviathan would seem to be at odds with Bodin's distinction between a citizen and a subject. However, in the very next passage Hobbes draws essentially the same distinction.

> The attaining to this sovereign power is by two ways. One, by natural force, as when a man maketh his children to submit themselves and their children to his government, as being able to destroy them if they refuse, or by war subdueth his enemies to his will, giving them their lives on that condition. The other is when men agree amongst themselves to submit to some man, or assembly of men, voluntarily, on confidence to be protected by him against all others. This latter may be called a political commonwealth, or commonwealth by *institution*, the former, a commonwealth by *acquisition*.[31]

Men united in a political commonwealth through voluntary consent Bodin would call citizens, whereas those in a commonwealth by acquisition he would call subjects. However, Bodin would not disagree with Hobbes's statement as written. As noted earlier, Bodin argues that "free subjects" who are citizens are also subjects, because in a commonwealth every citizen has his liberty diminished to a small degree by the majesty of the sovereign.[32] In other words, Bodin saw all men in a commonwealth as subjects vis-à-vis the sovereign, and citizens with respect to each other. Hobbes, too, sees those who consent to Leviathan as subjects vis-à-vis the sovereign. The normal interpretation sees Leviathan as ruling, at least potentially, all aspects of life, and thereby providing no space for the exercise of citizenship with respect to each other.

[30] Ibid., p. 123.
[31] Ibid., pp. 109–110 (emphasis in original).
[32] Ibid., p. 48.

TABLE 2.1. *Comparison of Rights of the Sovereign*

Bodin	Hobbes
1. Exclusive power to make laws	1. Exclusive power to make laws
2. Exclusive power to make war and peace	2. Exclusive power to make war and peace
3. Sole power to appoint magistrates	3. Sole power to appoint magistrates
4. Power to hear last appeals	4. Ultimate judge of legal controversies
5. Power of pardon	5. Power of pardon (included in no. 4)
6. Due liege, fealty, and homage	6. Position prevents accusation by subjects of injury
7. Coining of money	7. Position prevents punishment by subjects
8. Regulation of weights and measures	8. Power to determine honors and rank
9. Exclusive rights of taxation	9. Judge requirements for internal peace
	10. Determines acceptable opinions and doctrines
	11. Power to determine rewards and punishments
	12. Consent required before power can be transferred to another

Certainly there seem to be few limits on Leviathan, and resolution of this point would seem to be crucial. Both Bodin and Hobbes provide lists of what sovereign power entails. A comparison is instructive (see Table 2.1).[33]

The first five powers are the same, but then Bodin's general prescription against dishonoring the king becomes in Hobbes's hands an immunity from accusation and punishment, as well as a power to determine how much anyone should be honored, including, presumably, those acting as and for the sovereign. Although Hobbes's formulation looks stronger, we cannot tell for sure because Bodin does not elaborate on

[33] Bodin laid out and discussed the powers of the sovereign in *Six Bookes of a Commonweale*, book I, chap. 10, pp. 153–182. Hobbes summarized the powers of Leviathan in *Leviathan*, p. 128, and discussed in detail in part II, chap. xviii, pp. 110–115. The powers are listed in the order in which Bodin gives them, and those listed by Hobbes are matched as best they can be for the sake of comparison, and thus his are not in order.

this power. From what he says elsewhere, it would seem that his intent is virtually identical, and if given the chance, he would probably alter his list to match that of Hobbes in this case. The major divergence comes in the comparison between the last three powers on Bodin's list and the last four on Hobbes's list. Bodin makes the sovereign the coordinator of the economic marketplace, leaving economic activity to the free activities of citizens whose private property, as was noted earlier, remains sacrosanct.

Hobbes, on the other hand, includes four general powers that potentially make the sovereign totalitarian. Economic matters are subsumed under the sovereign's powers, but also anything and everything that creates domestic conflict, including opinions and ideas. Here Hobbes generates the true potential of sovereignty, and Bodin, if pressed, would probably agree that, as far as power goes, the sovereign can potentially do all of these things. However, Bodin is sensitive to the second face of sovereignty, the need to limit power, and perhaps not as imaginative or logically relentless as Hobbes. Perhaps religious and political turmoil was not as desperate in sixteenth-century France as the situation Hobbes experienced during the seventeenth century with the Thirty Years' War on the continent and the Civil War in England. A more desperate, chaotic situation may have prodded Hobbes's imagination beyond Bodin's formulation. In any event two things are clear. Hobbes enunciates more clearly the potential power of the sovereign, and he provides little if anything in the way of limits on sovereignty.

The only available limit seems to be the natural human fear of death on which sovereignty is initially grounded. He says that a covenant not to defend myself from force with countervailing force is void. That is, even though a man can make a covenant to the effect "unless I do so and so, kill me," he cannot make one that says "unless I do so and so I will not resist when you come to kill me." As Hobbes puts it, the danger of death by resisting is "the lesser evil." We can imagine widespread resistance to executioners sent by a tyrant, with the resisters killing the executioners and then deposing the sovereign. The resisters become the new sovereign, just as the former sovereign would remain so if its agents were successful.[34] Sovereignty for Hobbes becomes merely a fact that

[34] This characterization of a possible scenario is taken from Mulford Q. Sibley, *Political Ideas and Ideologies* (New York: Harper and Row, 1970), p. 352.

someone holds supreme power. Instead of constitutional limits, Hobbes seems to see only contending factions seeking sovereignty in potentially constant warfare unless the supreme power combines overwhelming force with enough good sense and mercy to minimize resistance. Bodin's anemic limits look good by comparison, but the inability of Hobbes to see the possibility that such limits could be extended and made effective supremely lay in a fundamental difference – the replacement of Bodin's natural-law analysis with a law-of-nature analysis in which Hobbes sees a nature without God or any higher law to instruct us that there is more to human life than fear of death.

Hobbes described a state of nature in which life is "solitarie, poore, nasty, brutish, and short" that could only be ended with a covenant grounded in fear of death and dismemberment. Bodin also spoke of an original agreement establishing the sovereign, but his original agreement rested on the hope for a better, more commodious life. That Bodin did not see a hellish state of nature, but a fallen human nature that could lead to violence and injustice breaking out at any time, certainly helps explain why Bodin may have been more positive about the beneficence of government, or at least the lower likelihood that it might have to be repressive. Bodin and Hobbes described the basic beast of supreme power. Each gave it a name. Bodin called it a sovereign, and Hobbes called it Leviathan. Each name describes a version of supreme power that creates expectations, and each set of expectations has the potential for creating a certain kind of supreme power. Hobbes showed us the full logical and empirical potential of this supreme power. Bodin indicated to us how the beast might be tamed through constitutionalism.

Bodin and Hobbes: Their Implications and Legacy

There are various reasons for us to engage in the kind of textual "archaeology" being used here. One is to excavate alternative concepts to use in understanding and dealing with timeless political problems. In effect, the history of political thought is a storehouse of ideas that can be brought to bear on contemporary politics. Another reason for the exercise is to clarify these alternatives and the language that describes them. Bodin and Hobbes together provide us with a language and system of categorization that, when combined with some well-accepted additions gleaned from later theorists, allow us to describe and analyze

TABLE 2.2. *Definitions of Various Regime Types*

Power	The ability of entity A to get entity B to do something that B would otherwise not do
Authority	Power that is viewed as legitimate by those over whom it is exercised, usually because the exercise of that power is in some fashion based on the consent of those over whom it is exercised
Supreme power	A singular entity with power that is unlimited in extent, absolute in its exercise, and in principle perpetual
Leviathan	A supreme power that is authoritative because it rests on consent; that has no function beyond maintaining internal order and excluding external invasion; and that has no limits to the orders it may direct beyond the violence that will be elicited by attempts to kill those over whom it has power
Sovereign	A supreme power that is authoritative because it rests on consent; that in addition to maintaining order coordinates behavior through laws designed to advance common ends; and that is limited by the need to enhance and not thwart those ends for which it was created; by the characteristics of those who created it; by prohibitions on actions that would undercut or tend to destroy the sovereign, including the breaking of promises;[a] and by the requirement to protect private property[b]
Popular control	A situation where a people effectively united into a singularity constitute the supreme power such that nothing occurs without their consent
Popular sovereignty	A situation where popular control is limited by the same means and for the same reasons as any sovereign
Constitution	The covenant that contains the limits that convert a supreme power into a sovereign
Constitutionalism	A set of attitudes shared by relevant actors that the supreme power should be limited, that is, should be a sovereign; that there should be a covenant which lays out the means for limiting the supreme power; and that the covenant should be enforced and obeyed

Monocracy	A political system where an individual is the supreme power
Constitutional monocracy	A political system where the sovereign is an individual, monarch or otherwise, limited by a constitution made operational by constitutionalism[c]
Oligarchy	A political system in which the supreme power is vested in the hands of a relatively small part of the population organized in terms of a party, class, family, and the like
Constitutional oligarchy	A political system where sovereignty is vested in an oligarchy limited by a constitution made operational by constitutionalism
Democracy	A political system characterized by direct popular control
Constitutional democracy	A political system where sovereignty is vested in the people who exercise this sovereignty directly, and who are limited by a constitution made operational by constitutionalism
Republic	A political system where an elected legislature is the executor of popular control
Constitutional republic	A political system where an elected legislature is the executor of popular sovereignty
Tyranny	The thwarting of essential human inclinations and/or the specific hopes and needs of a given people resulting from an uncontrolled supreme power

[a] This is a special instance of its authoritative nature since authority rests on consent, consent rests on a promise to fulfill the covenant, and therefore failure to keep or enforce a particular promise negates all promises, including the one which created the sovereign.

[b] This is a particular instance of the first limitation listed (the need to enhance), since one of the common ends that led to the creation of the sovereign was the hope of each consenting entity to protect his property.

[c] The presence of a constitution but the absence of constitutionalism renders a system of one man rule a simple monocracy.

political systems in terms of a theory of sovereignty. The basic terms of this language and categorization schema are presented here in Table 2.2 for use in later analysis.

Today we use the term "democracy" to denote what is more properly termed a "republic," and perhaps most properly termed a "constitutional republic." In this book an attempt will be made to use these terms according to the definitions laid out in Chapter 1. Until recently these distinctions were well understood and were generally used in political science literature. Later empirical analysis of cross-national polities will illustrate why we should continue to take this theoretical and definitional legacy seriously.

Part of Bodin's overall theoretical contribution was to emphasize that the most fundamental characteristic of a sovereign was the ability, some said the right, to make laws. If a sovereign establishes a commonweale, and a commonweale is defined by a set of citizens governed by a common set of laws, then the requirements for a common set of laws determine the necessary characteristics of a sovereign. A sovereign must be a single entity, or there will be conflicting laws. A sovereign must be absolute in the sense of having no competitor, or the laws will not be enforceable. A sovereign must be perpetual, or the laws will be mutable and therefore unstable and unpredictable. A sovereign must be limited, or there will be no laws, because there will be nothing beyond the sovereign's changing, capricious will.

Bodin's theory of sovereignty had a number of important implications for practical politics. He provided a way of defining the nation-state – any geographical area sharing the same laws enforced by a sovereign who could successfully maintain internal order and exclude any and all competing powers. This produced a way of conceptualizing relations between nation-states, which in turn allowed the creation of rules of conduct in international relations. Although Hugo Grotius would become famous for providing the initial, definitive theory of international relations, Bodin initiates such a theory in a lengthy discussion of the differences between a treaty, a defensive alliance, and a confederation. He also discusses how to think about the conduct of war in a long discussion at the end of the book.

Also important, by moving to sovereignty theory Bodin recast how we can categorize governments. Whereas before an aristocracy was defined by virtue and rule by the wealthy, now sovereignty is placed in the hands of a few no matter what their characteristics. Bodin kept the Aristotelian typology of political forms – monarchy, aristocracy, and democracy – only now government is defined simply in terms of the number of hands in which the supreme power is placed. This removed ethical and normative considerations from descriptions of regimes, made possible comparative empirical analysis, and moved political theory to consider actual regimes rather than ideal ones. Bodin rejected all discussion of ideal political systems and focused future analysis on how political systems, their institutions, and political actors really operated. In this sense Bodin was closer to Machiavelli than to any medieval political thinker.

Using Bodin's logic, we can even clearly conceptualize and understand political forms that Bodin had trouble dealing with. For example, Bodin rejected the utility of a mixed regime and felt that a federal system was either not possible or merely a smokescreen for the sovereign. With a robust concept of popular sovereignty, we can now view a mixed regime, federalism, and separation of powers in Bodin's own terms. In each case we push beyond the multiple executors of sovereignty to the entity that is "most high, absolute, and perpetual," the people. The people are now viewed as a single entity created by a covenant, a single entity that is the "greater force," and thus the supreme power. The people, through the constant and endless replacement of members as they die with new members as they are born, are perpetual. And finally, the covenant as constitution creates a self-limiting people with all of the necessary characteristics of a true sovereign. This popular sovereign can then distribute pieces of its power to a variety of agents acting in its name. Institutional arrangements like separation of powers, mixed government, and federalism are thus like multiple pipelines of power sent to various agents acting in the name of the popular sovereign.

Bodin himself spoke of the people as a possible perpetual singularity using the generational-replacement argument, as well as speaking of the people as a possible supreme power. At one point, he says flatly that any entity that can enforce its will over all other contenders – and he specifically mentions the people as a possibility – has the characteristics of a sovereign. Bodin had all the elements in his theory for popular sovereignty but did not put them together as a serious contender vis-à-vis monarchy.

Although Bodin is rarely read today, for at least a century after its publication *Six Bookes of a Commonweale* was one of the most widely read and cited works in political theory. Bodin's influence during the seventeenth century was immense. Along with Machiavelli and Hobbes, Bodin helped propel political thinking into the modern era. The strengths of Bodin's analysis allowed thinkers like Grotius and Althusius to make their contributions, while the weaknesses of his analysis induced Hobbes to develop a purer, even more powerful analysis of the first face of sovereignty. The Hobbesian formulation, however, did not eclipse Bodin for the simple reason that Hobbes showed in sharp relief at least one clear superiority in Bodin's theory – the need for explicit, self-executing limits on the sovereign if it was to be properly termed a sovereign and not merely an arbitrary supreme power. Bodin also indicated the ease with which popular sovereignty and constitutionalism could be harnessed to this task.

3

Popular Sovereignty

The Relationship of Popular Sovereignty to Sovereignty

It must be made clear at the outset of this chapter if we are to make sense of the term "popular sovereignty" that a "popular" sovereign is still a sovereign and therefore a supreme power. Popular sovereignty is sometimes treated as a "God word" – one that seems to be immediately clear and descriptive of an unqualified good. If analysis of the term is to proceed fruitfully, however, one must remember that popular sovereignty is by definition both a supreme power and one that is limited. An analysis of popular sovereignty is therefore a logical extension of an analysis of sovereignty, because any theory of popular sovereignty first requires a clear and useful concept of sovereignty. By the same token, rejecting the notion of sovereignty as somehow time-bound, no longer relevant, or merely mythical entails conferring the same status on popular sovereignty as well. This in turn implies the rejection of constitutional democracy and constitutional republicanism and brings into question constitutionalism of any sort. If one does not like the term "sovereignty" and prefers to use a different vocabulary to describe a limited supreme power, the shift in language will not alter the fact that we are still talking about the same thing. Like the green, leafy thing outside my window, the limited supreme power will continue to exist and function. Those who would like to change the language need to show the advantages that will result. Otherwise, using historically grounded terminology has the decided advantage of allowing us to tap into and understand the various analyses used by sovereignty theorists who first identified and struggled with the problem, and we can stand on their shoulders accepting and rejecting what we wish.

To recapitulate a bit, a sovereign is a supreme power that is limited in some way in the extent of its powers or by the means available for the exercise of that power. The primary means of limiting a supreme power is to tie it to a regular, publicly sanctioned process of law making, law enforcement, and adjudication. It is still, however, a supreme power. In principle, a sovereign can assign penalties of death, dismemberment, and all lesser penalties unless specifically excluded by the limits that make it a sovereign rather than a simple supreme power. A sovereign, as a supreme power, may be prohibited from using a death penalty, but in principle and in fact this is a penalty available to the sovereign, and one that will be used, unless excluded by the original covenant that makes the supreme power a sovereign. Those opposed to the death penalty may do so on many grounds, and there are good ones, except to argue that a sovereign has no inherent ability to do so as a sovereign. A sovereign may do, and in fact will do, whatever is not excluded by the limits established by the original covenant, or later excluded by the amendment process established by the original covenant.

An amendment process, by using a decision-making procedure equivalent to that used for adopting the original covenant, is essentially a recovenanting. Changes in a political system that do not use the formal amendment process – for example, through a court decision – do not limit the sovereign, popular or otherwise, and a court's decision may be discarded through a "normal" (i.e., noncovenantal) process. One of the greatest temptations in a constitutional system is to "constitutionalize" everything in an attempt to render the matter settled and beyond further change. Another temptation is to avoid or finesse the amendment process in order to achieve changes without the requisite level of consent. Both of these constitutional pathologies have long-term consequences for system stability, a matter to be discussed at length in a later chapter.

The original covenant can be amended to alter the prohibitions on the sovereign if, and only if, the decision-making process that leads to the alteration returns to the same level of consent that was used to establish the original limits on the sovereign. The need to return to the original covenant results from a peculiar but obvious aspect of sovereignty – all limits on a sovereign are self-limits. Bodin, like the sovereignty theorists before him in medieval Europe, used as his model the Judeo-Christian God as described in the Torah or Old Testament. In this view, God is by definition omnipotent, which means unlimited in power. The omnipotent God creates a universe bound completely and in detail by his will. However, God chooses to create a corner of freedom in the universe when he creates humans with the ability to say yes or no to his will. This voluntary self-limiting of his power makes God a sovereign rather than a simple supreme power, and he becomes the model for a voluntarily self-limiting sovereign on Earth.

God limits himself for his own reasons, which need not concern us here, but earthly sovereigns limit themselves for reasons that are understandably human. A man who conquers a people can rule as a simple supreme power, or even a tyrant, but then faces the inevitable fact that those over whom he rules will use their natural inclinations for liberty, self-preservation, sociability, and beneficial innovation as the grounding for opposing the operation of the supreme power. As a result, the ruler's life is made difficult, dangerous, and unpleasant. His position depends on the continued cooperation of a number of men who will enforce his will through violence; however, the continued support of these violent men is itself a problem, because they will continue to do so only to the extent they regard the ruler's orders as legitimate. Rulers learn that they can, by extending the sense of legitimacy to the broader population, make their own lives more secure, more pleasant, and less arduous. Almost all rulers by conquest, and certainly the rational ones, inevitably seek to create broadly accepted legitimacy for their rule.

Machiavelli was the first to realistically codify the process of legitimation. He advised the prince to engage in violence at the very beginning of his rule in order to eliminate any competitors around which contending counterpower might organize. He advised killing off competitors from the indigenous aristocracy immediately along with their families. He then advised the prince to be ready to use any force necessary to maintain his position, but to also avoid interfering unnecessarily in the lives of the people. Among other things, he advised the prince to keep and enforce existing laws and not to interfere with the property or women of his subjects. After a while, he argued, by maintaining peace, order, and lawfulness without harming the people needlessly, the prince's rule will come to be accepted as legitimate. A successful prince would be one who could walk among the people rather than remain walled up in some fortress. Thus did Machiavelli at great length and in considerable detail lay out the kinds of self-limits a supreme power needed in order to become legitimate, and thereby a sovereign, as well as the benefits of such self-limits – not the least of which was enduring fame.[1]

As an effective political theorist of the modern school, Machiavelli was codifying what a conqueror would empirically tend to do anyway. His admonitions amounted to a systematic analysis of what would result in an effective process of legitimation as opposed to one that would fail. That his advice would lead to a prince acting in accord with the limits set out by Bodin for a sovereign acting in accord with natural law is not an accident. Nor is it an accident that the remaining powers available to a legitimate Machiavellian prince, after limiting himself out of self-interest, resemble those Bodin outlines as available to a sovereign. Using history and experience as the basis of empirical analysis, both men tended to bring the social coordination by a supreme power in line with the brute facts of human existence. Also, Bodin was greatly influenced by Machiavelli.

Machiavelli's ultimate goal was the creation of a stable sovereign that rested on the consent of the people – what he termed a republic. Bodin and Hobbes also sought the creation of a stable sovereign grounded in popular consent. Together they were engaged in the project of creating government that would be effective in maintaining order as well as be in accord with fundamental human nature. Part of this human nature was the ability and tendency for extending beneficial innovation. By implication, the modern project in political theory involved the development of a more systematic, empirical basis for grounding political stability in order to enhance material "progress." All three theorists seemed to understand that this required matching

[1] The more compact, more famous, and sometimes misunderstood version of Niccolò Machiavelli's advice is contained in his book *The Prince* written in 1513. The more developed, detailed, and complete version is contained in *The Discourses on the First Ten Books of Titus Livius*, which Machiavelli finished writing in 1519. Any references to Machiavelli are based on the Modern Library Edition, which contains both works in the same volume and was first printed in 1950.

the government to the people, and that the most effective means of matching involved some form of popular consent. Popular consent implied what we now call popular sovereignty, and sovereignty of any sort implied a set of attitudes that we now call constitutionalism. What constituted popular consent, and what this consent actually entailed, thus became the key theoretical problem for political theory in general, and constitutional theory in particular.

Toward a Definition and Typology of Popular Sovereignty

Consider the following definitions of "popular" from the *Oxford English Dictionary*.[2]

> Generic definition: Affecting, concerning, or open to all of the people; as opposed to a particular class
> Definition 1: Devoted to the cause of the people
> Definition 2: Prevalent or current among, or accepted by the people generally
> Definition 3: Studious of, or designed to gain, the favor of the common people
> Definition 4: Approved by the people; based on the consent of the people

The generic definition, in the context of sovereignty, tells us that a political system characterized by popular sovereignty is one where sovereignty affects, concerns, and includes everyone. However, the next four definitions together lay out a typology that helps us understand the major contending positions on popular sovereignty. It makes a great deal of difference whether something is devoted to the cause of the people, in accord with popular opinion, designed to gain the favor of the people, or specifically approved by the people.

Definition 1 implies the weakest form of popular sovereignty and seems to be close to what Hobbes had in mind. Once established, the sovereign is assumed to be performing the job intended for it in the manner intended, but there is no way for the people to certify that this

[2] These definitions are taken from the *Oxford English Dictionary*, but they have been arranged and numbered to assist the analysis.

is or is not the case. In terms of a robust theory of popular sovereignty, we are asked to assume the very thing that needs to be established. Furthermore, once an agent is selected, sovereignty is permanently given away by the people. The agent of popular sovereignty becomes the actual sovereign, and popular sovereignty is no more than a transitional condition. From our own experience, it is difficult not to think of Marxist regimes that used this notion of popular sovereignty and the kind of politics that resulted.

Definition 2 is essentially the position defended by Bodin. When the agent of popular sovereignty is created, the agent promises to preserve and uphold the rules and customs already generally accepted by the people. The popular sovereign becomes generally inactive, but it can bind its agent or agents to uphold and enforce new customs that the people might evolve. One can imagine highly homogeneous, traditionalistic societies as being most comfortable with such a notion of popular sovereignty, and many still-traditionalistic societies currently have constitutions that reflect the Bodinian perspective. While Bodin defined this version of popular sovereignty, there are variations of it that approach definition 3. Some of its proponents – including Althusius, Bellarmine, and Suarez – place such a heavy emphasis on the power of the people over their agents that one is surprised they do not take the obvious step of explicitly making an elected body of representatives the apex of government. Kingly rule was still so much a part of normal expectations that their arguments usually turned more on the ability of the people to commit tyrannicide than on regularizing popular sovereignty through elected legislatures. Still, the cumulative impact of these theorists was to develop a sense of popular sovereignty so strong that it was easy, almost inevitable, for many theorists to take that next step.

Definition 3 is an even stronger form of popular sovereignty and is close to what Blackstone defended as undergirding parliamentary government. However, the common law as evolved in Britain expresses something closer to the second definition. To the extent common law in a country becomes primarily the sum total of parliamentary decisions, that country is institutionalizing a purer form of the third notion of popular sovereignty; and to the extent parliament shares its rule as the source of common law with the courts, we have a blend of the second and third notions.

Some may argue that when a constitution declares parliamentary sovereignty, it is by definition either enshrining the third notion of popular sovereignty, or perhaps not establishing any form of popular sovereignty at all. In answer to the first contention, it would seem prudent to follow Bodin's recommendation and look below the surface to trace power back to that entity which creates the rest. If the institution of parliament is created by the people and/or rests on actions by the people in order to exist and operate, then the people are de facto sovereign and parliament its de jure agent. Any parliament that is composed of persons elected by the people, and subject to removal in future elections, would appear to be merely the agent of a greater power. Indeed, it is the certainty of future elections that leads parliament to "be studious of the favor of the people." The key characteristics of this sense of popular sovereignty are that the people elect representatives on a regular basis but are otherwise inactive, except to judge the actions of their agents in future elections. Representatives are left free between elections to pursue the common good without prompting from the people. The result is usually termed "trustee representation," because legislators are, like trustees of a trust fund, supposed to use their own judgment in pursuit of the broad goals and principles that are laid out in the document establishing the trust.

The last notion of popular sovereignty is the most robust. It supports what some term "strong democracy," or participatory democracy, and produces what is usually termed "delegate representation" in its weakest form and direct democracy in its strongest. Delegates are agents who are supposed to represent those for whom they are delegates as if those represented are actually present.[3] Under the delegate theory, the people can and will be active in instructing their representatives and expect a high level of congruence between public opinion and public policy. The

[3] The best summary analysis of representation remains Hanna Fenichel Pitkin, *The Concept of Representation* (Berkeley: University of California Press, 1972). Her analysis reflects the ambivalence we have come to feel toward popular control when she notes the paradox of representation that characterizes modern democracy. On the one hand, we expect a representative to act as if those who are represented are in effect present, a position congruent with the delegate theory and thus of the fourth and strongest version of popular sovereignty; while at the same time we expect the representative to act better than the constituents would if they were present, which is congruent with the trustee theory of representation, and thus with the somewhat weaker third model of popular sovereignty.

majoritarian principle is stronger than is the case with the previous version, and attention to minority rights is accordingly weaker. The pure form would have all legislation passed by the people gathered together, or perhaps in referenda.

For the sake of simplicity we will term the first version of popular sovereignty the Leviathan Model; the second, or Bodinian, version we will call the Traditionalistic Model; the version that rests on elected agents acting according to the trustee theory of representation we will call the Constitutional Republic Model; and the strongest form, whether based on the delegate theory of representation or on referenda, will be termed the Constitutional Democracy Model. When it comes time to further differentiate political systems and their respective constitutions, we will find the analysis focusing primarily on Constitutional Republics and noting Traditionalistic and Constitutional Democratic elements that are included in the mixture. Few political systems will be found to approach a pure type. From this point on, what has been termed "constitutional democracy" out of deference to common usage will be termed a "constitutional republic" in keeping with the analysis laid out here. The former term will be reserved for a limited direct democracy, and the latter for a limited government that uses elected representatives. We can then speak of the relative strength of the democratic principle in any given constitutional republic.

Before we begin to unravel the various ways in which popular sovereignty can be embodied in a constitution, it will be helpful to return to the original development of a theory of popular sovereignty to explicate in greater depth and with more precision what popular sovereignty implies, and why it turns out to be the most efficient and effective means for matching a government to its people.

The Historical Development of Popular Sovereignty

Jean Bodin published his *Six Bookes on a Commonweale* in 1576. Thomas Hobbes published *Leviathan* in 1651. Between 1570 and 1700, the competing theories of popular sovereignty that we today take for granted were defined, developed, and explicated in depth. Even a partial listing of the important works that contributed to popular sovereignty theory besides those of Bodin and Hobbes would have to include François Hotman, *Francogallia* (1573); Theodore Beza, *Du droit des Magistrats* (*Right of Magistrates*, 1574); Philippe du Plessis-Mornay, *Vindiciae contra tyrannos* (*Defense of Liberty against Tyrants*, 1579); Richard Hooker, *The Laws of Ecclesiastical Polity* (1597); Juan de Mariana, *De Rege et Regis Institutione* (*On Kingship and the Education of a King*, 1599); Francisco Suarez, *De legibus, ac Deo legislatore* (*On Law and God the Lawgiver*, 1603); Johannes Althusius, *Politica* (1603); Robert Cardinal Bellarmine, *The Power of the Pope in Temporal Affairs* (1610); James Harrington, *The Commonwealth of Oceana* (1656); George Lawson, *An Examination of the Political Part of Mr. Hobbs His Leviathan* (1657) and *Politica Sacra et Civilis* (1660); Benedict [Baruch] de Spinoza, *Tractatus Theologico-Politicus* (1670); John Locke, *Two Treatises of Government* (1690); and Algernon Sidney, *Discourses Concerning Government* (1690).

In addition to these better-known works, other political tracts written by men little known today, but who had considerable impact on the thinking of their contemporaries, developed the theory of popular sovereignty to its highest level. In seventeenth-century England, the Levellers substantially contributed to this development, although their doctrine failed to catch hold in England.[4] Harrington, Locke, and Sidney synthesized the best of their ideas into coherent, though less radical theories. Among the more noteworthy in this movement, we can identify Henry Parker, *Contra-Replicant* (1643); Richard Overton, *A Defiance against All Arbitrary Usurpations or Encroachments* (1646); John Lilburne, *Englands Standard Advanced* (1649); Isaac Penington Jr., *The Fundamental Right, Safety and Liberty of the People* (1651); and Henry Vane, *A Healing Question* (1656).

Perhaps more important than their cousins in England, because their ideas and political institutions took root and became the dominant perspective, theologically based thinkers in colonial America combined advanced thinking on popular sovereignty with successful design of political institutions grounded on the concept. There were many proponents of a highly participatory version of popular sovereignty at work in the American colonies.[5] The more prominent

[4] See, for example, the discussion in Edmund S. Morgan, *Inventing the People: The Rise of Popular Sovereignty in England and America* (New York: Norton, 1988).

[5] The creation of institutions of popular sovereignty in the British colonies of North America, and the extent to which the constitutionalism it engendered was based on

among them were Richard Mather, *Church-Government and Church-Covenant Discussed* (1643); Thomas Hooker, *A Survey of the Summe of Church-Discipline* (1648); Roger Williams, *The Bloudy Tenant of Persecution for Cause of Conscience* (1644); and William Penn, *A Brief Examination and State of Liberty Spiritual, and The Frame of Government of the Province of Pennsylvania in America* (1682). It is notable that these men were frequently responsible, as Penn was, for the creation of consent-based government that embodied popular sovereignty. Thomas Hooker was involved with the framing and adoption of The Fundamental Orders of Connecticut (1639), and Roger Williams with the Acts and Orders (Rhode Island, 1647), both of which established highly democratic representative governments. Penn's Pennsylvania began as the most democratic of the colonies and continued to be the most democratic state with the most robust sense of popular sovereignty after the American Revolution.

Excluding the Levellers, we can list each of these men according to which one of the four models of popular sovereignty they supported.

Leviathan Model, in which popular sovereignty is temporary and transitional: Thomas Hobbes

Traditionalistic Model, in which the people are superior to and therefore create the king: Johannes Althusius, Robert Cardinal Bellarmine, Theodore Beza, Jean Bodin, Richard Hooker, François Hotman, Juan de Mariana, Franciso Suarez, Philippe du Plessis-Mornay, and Benedict Spinoza

Constitutional Republic Model, in which the people erect and judge a supreme legislature: James Harrington, George Lawson, John Locke, Richard Mather, William Penn, and Algernon Sidney

Constitutional Democracy Model, in which the people are directly active and participatory: Jean Jacques Rousseau, Thomas Hooker, and Roger Williams

covenant theology, is a large topic that can only be summarized here. For more extensive discussion, see Donald S. Lutz, *The Origins of American Constitutionalism* (Baton Rouge: Louisiana State University Press, 1988); Joshua Miller, *The Rise and Fall of Democracy in Early America, 1630–1789* (University Park: Pennsylvania State University Press, 1991); and Barry Alan Shain, *The Myth of American Individualism: The Protestant Origins of American Political Thought* (Princeton, N.J.: Princeton University Press, 1994).

Although we have grouped these thinkers, there is considerable variation within a given group. Althusius, Bellarmine, and Suarez defended a more developed, stronger sense of popular sovereignty than did Bodin, even if they did not draw what we would today consider the logical conclusions of their respective theories. Harrington, Lawson, Locke, and Sidney are listed in alphabetical order, but the same order describes their respective closeness to the second and fourth definitions of popular sovereignty. Sidney came closest, marginally, to Constitutional Democracy, and Harrington was closest to the Traditionalistic version.

Before moving on to discuss the Constitutional Republic and Constitutional Democracy models, the diverse group of theorists collected under the Traditionalistic label needs to be examined more closely. This category is defined by a continued attachment to monarchy, and the consequent lack of emphasis on a legislature as the primary agent for popular sovereignty. Still, working within what seems to us today as a restricted range of institutional possibilities, the Traditionalists developed modern popular sovereignty theory to a level for which we usually credit people like John Locke. Two men in particular, Mornay and Althusius, are worthy of our attention.

Philippe du Plessis-Mornay was the first to use covenant theology as the grounding for popular sovereignty, and his formulation not only solved the problem of how to create an organized singularity out of a people who could then act independently; it also imported into popular sovereignty an inherent egalitarianism that would lead to the highly democratic expectations we now take for granted. Althusius took Mornay's insight and developed it into the first comprehensive political theory based on covenant theology.[6] Mornay begins by rejecting Bodin's cultural basis for the people's supremacy: "And now we say

[6] Althusius refers frequently to Mornay, and Mornay took his basic idea from Heinrich Bullinger's *De testamento seu foedere Dei unico et aeterno* (*The One and Eternal Testament or Covenant of God*, 1534). Bullinger's work is available in English as the second part of a book by Charles S. McCoy and J. Wayne Baker, *Fountainhead of Federalism: Heinrich Bullinger and the Covenantal Tradition* (Louisville, Ky.: Westminster/John Knox Press, 1991). A slightly abridged translation of Mornay's *Vindiciae* can be found in Julian H. Franklin, trans. and ed., *Constitutionalism and Resistance in the Sixteenth Century* (New York: Pegasus, 1969). The Frederick S. Carney translation and edition of Althusius's *Politica* has recently been reprinted by Liberty Press (Indianapolis, 1995).

that it is the people that establishes kings, gives them kingdoms, and approves their selection by its vote. For God willed that every bit of authority held by the kings should come from the people, after Him, so that kings would concentrate all their care, energy, and thoughts upon the people's interests."[7]

Mornay cites as his authority for this proposition Deuteronomy 17:14–15. Deuteronomy, which along with Genesis contains the most explicit, sustained discussion of covenant in the Bible, especially in its application to political organization, would become the standard text for those theorists establishing a religious basis for a strong sense of popular sovereignty. Mornay combines biblical exegesis with logical analysis.

And since no one is born a king, and no one is a king by nature; and since a king cannot rule without a people, while a people can rule itself without a king, it is clear, beyond all doubt, that the people is prior to the king and that kings were originally established by the people.[8]

Since kings, then, are created by the people, it seems to follow that the people as a whole is greater than the king. This is an implication of the term itself, since one who is created by another is considered his inferior.[9]

Mornay compares the people to the owner of a ship of which the king is not the captain but the pilot. The people is also likened to a river that it is perpetually renewed so that unlike a king it never dies. Mornay in this fashion establishes that only the people as "a corporate entity" possess the defining characteristics of a sovereign – absolute, unlimited, perpetual power. Men create kings, he says, for their own advantage, and

they would not have surrendered their natural liberty, which they prize like any other animal, had they not anticipated great advantages. The formost of these is the guarantee of justice by the king.... When the people began to feel the need for equal laws, they were prepared to accept them from a just and honorable individual. But men like that are scarce, and the outcome was very often different. In most cases the only semblance of law was the discretionary power of the king, which spoke differently to different persons. This was the point at which learned men, together with the other magistrates, invented laws,

[7] Philippe du Plessis-Mornay, *Vindiciae Contra Tyrannos*, as reproduced in Franklin, *Constitutionalism and Resistance in the Sixteenth Century*, p. 158.

[8] Ibid., p. 160.

[9] Ibid., p. 161.

which were to be the same for all. Henceforth the first obligation of the king was to be the guardian, minister, and protector of the laws.[10]

Because not all eventualities can be predicted, the king has some discretion to supplement the laws from time to time, drawing upon natural equity. But to protect against kings doing violence to the laws, the "people appointed notables as associates of the king."[11] A king receives the law from the people when he takes his coronation oath. An oath is by definition a covenant, since a covenant is any agreement to which God is a party or a witness. Mornay calls it a "compact" and says that "In all legitimate governments a compact is always to be found."[12] The people in turn take an oath not to obey the king, but to obey the crown, which is defined as a legitimate and therefore limited king. The king cannot make law. Laws are made by an assembly that has deliberated and approved them. Mornay then defines law as reason freed from passion and says that to be subject to a king without the law is the same as being subject to a "beast." The image of an illegitimate king as a beast has important theoretical implications as we learn in a striking passage a few pages later.

> In the first place, nature instructs us to defend our lives and also our liberty, without which life is hardly life at all. If this is the instinct of nature implanted in dogs against the wolf, in bulls against the lion, in pigeons against the falcon, and in chickens against the hawk, how much stronger it must be in man against another man who has become a wolf to man. To fight back is not only permitted, but enjoined, for it is nature herself that seems to fight here.[13]

Any man who acts out of passion rather than the reason embodied in law is a beast, and potential prey must be expected to resist like any other beast. If the bestial grounding for Hobbes's Leviathan is clearly prefigured here, Hobbes's solution is not. As Mornay says in an earlier passage, absolute power is virtual tyranny, and no human being can exercise it, nor can any sensible man want to have it. Yet the great benefits to be derived from a supreme power lead men to create it, and the same reasons that lead to the creation of a supreme power lead to its limitation as well. The king is limited, but the fountain of law, the

[10] Ibid., p. 169.
[11] Ibid.
[12] Ibid., p. 181.
[13] Ibid., pp. 187–188.

people, is a supreme power also capable of acting like a beast. Mornay's implicit solution is to separate the supreme power, the people, from those who make laws, the assembly and other magistrates. Enforcing the law is separated from the assembly and put in the hands of the king. The separation of powers works to the extent the people are relatively inactive.

The covenant or compact through which legitimate power originates rests on the natural "instincts" of humans as animals. Although Mornay says that the people can rule themselves without a king, he does not discuss any covenant among the people that would remove them from what is clearly a state of nature and create an organized, singularity termed "the people." Their status as an organized entity, as far as his theory goes, is assumed. The notion of a foundational covenant witnessed by God is implicit, but the nature and implications of that covenant are not discussed. Mornay evidently assumed that his readers would be familiar with covenant theory as first explicated by Bullinger and reiterated over the years into a commonplace by 1579. The implications of covenant for political organization are many and powerful. Mornay's reference to its implicit egalitarianism is an example, but it is left to others to develop the synthesis fully.

Prominent among these others was Johannes Althusius. Infrequently read today, Althusius was highly regarded and widely cited during the seventeenth century. His *Politica* was apparently written as a detailed rebuttal of Bodin, much the way Locke and Sidney wrote in rebuttal of Filmer. Bodin is specifically mentioned many times by Althusius, invariably in the negative. Yet Althusius could not have written his treatise without Bodin's theory, and in the end the two do not end up that far apart.

Althusius viewed society as virtually flooded with covenants. The Latin word for covenant is *foedus*, from which we derive the term federalism. Althusius was a compleat covenant theorist not only because he used covenant as the most fundamental tool for the creation of a popular sovereign but also because his "complete sovereign" was erected on a federal structure much as the United States was originally created by the people of thirteen states. Althusius speaks of a "universal association," which he also terms a "polity," a "commonwealth," or a "realm," built up from many smaller associations that have a prior existence. There are many "private, natural, necessary and voluntary societies" that go into the forming of families, cities, and provinces, which in turn are the building blocks for the commonwealth. The people thus are organized for action prior to the creation of a commonwealth, but they are initially organized into a number of smaller natural peoples rather than into a single people. These smaller units constitute themselves into a "universal association" for common ends. "The bond of this body and association is consensus, together with trust extended and accepted among the members of the commonwealth. The bond is, in other words, a tacit or expressed promise to communicate things, mutual services, aid, counsel, and the same common laws (*jura*) to the extent that the utility and necessity of universal social life in a realm shall require."[14]

The use of terms like consensus, tacit and express consent, and utility, when combined with his concept of federalism, mark Althusius as the fountainhead of much of modern political theory. To speed our analysis along, and to connect him efficiently with both previous and later consent theorists, we let him speak in his own words.

> Such are the members of the realm. Its right is the means by which the members, in order to establish good order and the supplying of provisions throughout the territory of the realm, are associated and bound to each other as one people in one body and under one head. This right of the realm (*jus regni*) is also called the right of sovereignty (*jus majestatis*).... What we call this right of the realm has as its purpose good order, proper discipline, and the supplying of provisions in the universal association.... Therefore, the universal power of ruling (*potestas imperandi universalis*) is called that which recognizes no ally, nor any superior or equal to itself. And this supreme right of universal jurisdiction is the form and substantial essence of sovereignty (*majestas*) or, as we have called it, of a major state. When this right is taken away, sovereignty perishes.... The people, or the associated members of the realm, have the power (*potestas*) of establishing this right of the realm and of binding themselves to it.... Without this power no realm or universal symbiotic life can exist.[15]

[14] Frederick S. Carney, trans., *The Politics of Johannes Althusius* (Boston: Beacon Press, 1964), p. 62. Carney's translation is of the third edition of Althusius's book published in 1614. That the book was in its third printing after only eleven years, especially in the context of the early seventeenth century, is testimony to its popularity and wide readership.

[15] Ibid., pp. 64–65.

Much of what underlies the theoretical propositions on sovereignty introduced in Chapter 1 are here efficiently laid out by Althusius in relatively few words. He then describes sovereignty as indivisible, incommunicable, and interconnected so that "whoever holds one holds them all."[16] Althusius attacks Bodin for saying that sovereignty is above the law and perpetual, and he implies that Bodin meant above natural law. Bodin, of course, said just the contrary. Althusius then says neatly what took Bodin many pages to articulate. "Universal power is called pre-eminent, primary, and supreme not because it is above law or absolute, but in respect to particular and special subordinate power that depends upon it, arises and flows from it, returns in time to it, and is furthermore bound to definite places."[17]

Like Bodin and other sovereignty theorists, Althusius notes that while supreme in a particular place and time on Earth, the sovereign and its agents are still limited by and inferior to natural law and divine equity. The sovereign people and their agents are also limited by the fundamental law of the realm, *the lex fundamentalis regni*, and the terms of the covenant. These limits are basically the same as those laid out by Bodin. Althusius also says later that a king is mortal, whereas the universal association is immortal, and therefore perpetual, as Bodin argued.[18] Althusius was not the first or the last to use a straw man in order to make his key points. The irony is that while Althusius is attacking Bodin, we who can look back over subsequent political theory and recognize that he is actually arguing against a fifteen-year-old Englishman who will not publish his major work for another half century – Thomas Hobbes.

Althusius repeatedly notes that the supreme power, or sovereign, is also by definition limited by those ends for which the universal association was originally organized. These ends are "order and the utility and advantage of the people." Prominent in the definition of utility is the supplying of economic goods. Order is necessary for economic activity to occur, and the protection of economic activity is the ultimate reason why men form a sovereign. Bodin's list of sovereign powers also

[16] Ibid., p. 66.
[17] Ibid., p. 69.
[18] Ibid., p. 117.

clearly indicated that the sovereign is supposed to provide the order and universal laws required for economic activity to proceed. Like Bodin, Althusius sees economic exchange as part of the voluntary, private activity of society, and not subject to direction from above. One important difference between Althusius and Bodin is the way Althusius emphasizes the subordination of the king to the people.

> But by no means can this supreme power be attributed to a king or optimates, as Bodin most ardently endeavors to defend. Rather it is to be attributed rightfully only to the body of a universal association, namely, to a commonwealth or realm, and as belonging to it. From this body, after God, every legitimate power flows to those we call kings or optimates. Therefore, the king, princes and optimates recognize this associated body as their superior, by which they are constituted, removed, exiled and deprived of authority.... For however great is the power conceded to another, it is always less than the power of the one who makes the concession, and in it the pre-eminence and superiority of the conceder is understood to be reserved.[19]

As he says later, the magistrate is called supreme only because he exercises the supreme power of the realm of which he is temporary minister.[20]

Statements like the ones quoted from Mornay and Althusius became common intellectual currency during the period 1570–1700 in political theories written in France, Britain, the British colonies in North America, Switzerland, the Netherlands, Spain, and various political entities in what is now Germany. The striking connection among this disparate literature was the extent to which it was based on religious principles and, except in Spain, on the emerging covenant theology of the more radical Protestant sects. The relevance of covenant theology for popular sovereignty is not a matter of mere historical interest. Just as Christian theology grounded the basic development of popular sovereignty in Bodin and the others who developed the Traditionalistic Model, covenant theology grounded the development of the Constitutional Republic and Constitutional Democratic models. Indeed, without covenant theology these more developed models probably would never have emerged in Europe and America, just as the absence of

[19] Ibid., pp. 67–68.
[20] Ibid., p. 115.

covenant theology elsewhere in the world helps explain why popular sovereignty is a European-American invention.

The Constitutional Republic Model

Mornay and Althusius, working from Bullinger's comprehensive codification of covenant theology, took sovereignty theory to the brink of the Constitutional Republic Model. Working from the same theological assumptions, Richard Mather developed a detailed design for church government, which, when applied to the New England theocracies, institutionalized a very strong Constitutional Republic Model that verged on constitutional democracy. Mather argued that church communities rested on the voluntary consent of equals. Equality rested on the equal ability of all humans to say yes or no to God's grace, and therefore upon their moral indistinguishability. His plan for church government was essentially Aristotle's conception of a mixed government, which blended monarchy, aristocracy, and democracy. In Mather's view, Christ represented the monarchic element, the church elders represented the aristocratic element, and the church members the democratic element. Popular consent had a central though circumscribed role in church government. In practice, the minister rendered most church decisions, but the people were supposed to ensure that the elders, who selected and oversaw the minister, abided by scriptural rules in their administration. No significant action was to be taken without popular consent. The elders could be viewed as a legislature closely controlled by the people. Such an arrangement came close to the Constitutional Democracy Model because popular consent was active rather than passive. In effect, the Constitutional Democracy Model is distinguished from the Constitutional Republic Model in the following way. Constitutional republicanism adheres to the injunction, As long as we do not say no, you may assume tacit consent and proceed, whereas constitutional democracy works from the injunction, Until we expressly say yes, you do not have our consent and may not act. In theory, Mather's political system assumed the latter injunction, but the arrangement of institutions resulted in the former injunction describing actual practice.

As the number of nonchurch members increased in New England communities, a de facto separation of church and state occurred.

Thomas Hooker and Roger Williams codified this split and made covenant theology the explicit grounding for civil government. Popular sovereignty still rested on a theological characterization of human nature, but now popular consent, mixed government, and the political covenant were secular in application. As long as the population generally believed in biblically based religion, there was no need to seek a secular grounding for these political institutions. Also, the covenant basis for political communities assured that popular control was actually popular sovereignty, because the sovereign people were limited by the laws of the actual sovereign, God.

As powerful as these ideas were, and as efficacious the political institutions they produced, the continued dominance of religious assumptions was not tenable in the face of continued immigration and waning devoutness. Civil government in America, despite continuing impetus toward a democratic model, devolved toward the less rigorous Constitutional Republic Model and gradually came to require a theory of popular sovereignty grounded on secular principles. By 1776 that secular grounding was essentially borrowed from John Locke, although Locke's theory was put forward primarily by Protestant ministers who correctly saw that the same institutions generated by covenant theology could be justified by Lockean theory in the context of a covenantal society. They were correct in their institutional analysis, but Locke's theory was in fact a competitor to the religious strain of thought with considerably different implications in the long run.

Locke's theory is well known and need not occupy us for long, but the implications for popular sovereignty must be explicated. First of all, the equality undergirding popular sovereignty is for Locke the result of our equally strong inclination toward self-preservation, and our equal ability to calculate what does or does not conduce to preservation. However, because this basic equality leads to each person becoming the judge and executor of the law of nature, self-preservation, his or her basic equality eventually devolves into an equal ability to harm each other. In this regard he is little different from Hobbes. Whereas Hobbes saw a bloodthirsty human nature, however, Locke saw an essentially neutral, minimal human nature that took on differing characteristics depending on the particular demands made by the individual's environment. In the original state of nature, humans are cooperative and trusting of other humans. The primary threat comes from nature. Humans living at the subsistence level have nothing to steal and no reason to hurt each other. The state of nature is a state of natural liberty guided by the law of nature. The law of nature, which is summed up by the natural inclination for self-preservation, has no moral content as does natural law for Bodin. Instead it is composed of inevitable human inclinations – today we might term them innate behavioral tendencies. In the state of nature we therefore find a strong inclination toward individual self-preservation, a natural condition of liberty, and an inclination toward sociability when our "own self-preservation comes not in conflict."

Locke also sees a natural inclination for innovation, which results in the introduction of agriculture, and then the invention of money. Unfortunately, innovation, which has initially beneficial consequences, also has other, unintended consequences. The mix eventually turns the state of nature into a constant state of warfare. The solution to the new, reflexively generated human environment, is the innovation of a civil society created by a social compact. The social compact is a point where the natural inclinations for liberty, self-preservation, sociability, and innovation come together and are simultaneously satisfied. Civil society is the culmination of these natural tendencies, as well as the means for extending their satisfaction in a coordinated, beneficial manner.

On the one hand, civil society seems to be a human artifact rather than a natural condition, as Aristotle saw it. On the other hand, Locke's theory of human history seems to make civil society an inevitability resting on natural tendencies. Contrary to what some critics like David Hume had to say, there is no need for Locke to prove that a state of nature ever existed or that there was an actual social compact. From the point of view of rational actors already living in civil society, and understanding the natural, empirical inclinations of humans, Locke's state of nature need be nothing more than an act of the imagination to conjure up what would happen if we dissolved civil society. What we would do in such a situation is create a social compact under the terms Locke describes, for the reasons he gives. And what he describes is no more or less than what non–social contract theorists like Bodin say we do when we write and adopt a constitution.

Locke's experiment in thought, like that of Mornay, Althusius, Lawson, and Sidney before him, is to uncover and describe the essence of constitutional government grounded in popular sovereignty. Human equality no longer has a theological grounding, although a Deist could say that God made humans with these empirically observable inclinations before retreating into some corner of the universe. Political power is not limited by God's natural law, as Bodin had it, but by the law of nature – which can be the result of divine will, evolution, or anything else one chooses to read in as the cause. It is no wonder that ministers in the eighteenth century could become the primary conduit of Locke's thought into American political thought, or that the first state constitutions and the Declaration of Independence could use Locke's terminology and refer to "nature and nature's God." The strength of the position is that natural rights rest on what humans are inclined to do anyway – we simply describe these inclinations as rights. One can view Locke's theory as an early version of John Rawls's "original position." Under conditions of liberty, equality, and insecurity, humans will naturally choose civil society as Locke describes it. Locke's secularized view of popular sovereignty also has the clarity and strength of Hobbes's theory. At the beginning of the Second Treatise, in section 3, Locke identifies political power in terms that make it recognizable as supreme power: "Political power, then, I take to be a right of making laws with penalties of death, and consequently all less penalties, for the regulating and preserving of property, and of employing the force of the community, in the execution of such laws, and in the defence of the common-wealth from foreign injury; and all this only for the common good."[21]

Bodin would not quarrel with anything in this sentence, except for Locke's meaning of "right." Any sovereign must first be a supreme power in the manner Locke describes. Nor would Bodin and the other traditionalistic theorists of sovereignty disagree with Locke when he says later in paragraph 96 that the community must act with one will, and that will is determined by the majority because it is "the greater force": or when Locke says in paragraph 139 that "even absolute power, where it is necessary, is not arbitrary by being absolute, but is still limited by that reason, and confined to those ends, which required it in some cases to be absolute." Locke also paraphrases earlier traditionalistic theorists in paragraph 149 when he speaks of governmental agents having a "fiduciary power" from the people who are the

[21] See any edition of John Locke, *The Second Treatise of Government*, chap. 1, par. 3.

"supreme power." The primary difference between Bodin and Locke lies in Locke's limiting the supreme power by rights that amount to the majority's natural, self-executing human inclinations with no moral content. In effect, whatever the majority does, for whatever reasons, is a matter of right. While this means the majority can prevent arbitrary rule by its agents in government, it also means that the majority may not be easily subject to limits, although Locke provides us with some hints in this regard.

Locke sees the government, and therefore the majority behind it, as limited by the ends for which government was established. The presumption here seems to be that no majority would allow a government to engage in actions contrary to what is implied by self-preservation, liberty, sociability, and beneficial innovation. That is, those in the majority would protect the deep interests of the minority in the process of protecting their own interests. In the real world, however, we see that this is often not the case, so the majority's being limited by "that reason" which led to government in the first place might mean that the majority, composed of rational actors, will not permit the introduction of a policy that severely hurts individuals in a minority because the principle involved in the policy might be turned against members of the majority in the future. A rational-actor perspective is suggested at many places in the text – for example, in paragraph 13 when he says, "for no rational creature can be supposed to change his condition with an intention to be worse." Perhaps, but the fact remains that Locke gives us good reason to suppose he has solved the problem of arbitrary government, but not what is now termed majority tyranny.

Part of the difficulty, undoubtedly, is that Locke's civil society is, in comparison with the civil society projected by religiously grounded sovereignty theorists, rather anemic. Liberal theory has often been charged in recent years with failing to create a sense of community built around commonly held, society-enhancing values. Locke may be open to the same charge, although it is more likely that his strong majoritarianism may instead result in the imposition of majority values on dissenting minorities. That is, Locke's apparent lack of concern with community values that might serve as a limit on majority actions or could result in a community that lacked commonly shared values; or else, if there are any values, the majority could shove them down everyone's throats. As a dissenting Protestant in England, it is doubtful

Locke would be inclined to support any "moral majority," especially in light of his later essays on religious toleration. Locke simply does not address the problem in any explicit way here.

What Locke does is support popular sovereignty of a kind that makes the monarch, Parliament, and all other governmental agents subordinate to popular will. If Locke was an apologist for Parliament in its struggle with the crown, and thereby a proponent of what came to pass in the Glorious Revolution, his theory unfortunately renders "parliamentary sovereignty" a nonconcept. Parliament is not sovereign, the people are, and Parliament becomes at most the primary filter for popular opinion – an agent of popular will that may, through its deliberations, clarify and soften the supreme power of the people into a true sovereign.

It is fair to say that while Locke was a constitutionalist, there is almost nothing in his theory about constitutional design. The best that can be said is that he seemed to advocate a separation of powers by placing different functions of the political process in different hands. The people were to have the constitutive power but not the policy formulation power, which was placed in the hands of agents. The majority exercises the supreme power of the people only after the government has been dissolved, he says in paragraph 149; however, he also holds out in paragraph 154 the probability that the people will also act periodically in elections, which implies that at each election the government is at least symbolically dissolved. This minimal separation of powers is perhaps supplemented by a natural division of powers into the legislative, executive, and federative. Yet Locke says in paragraph 148 that, although the latter two are quite distinct, "they are hardly to be separated, and placed at the same time, in the hands of distinct persons." If this theoretical distinction does not necessarily result in separate agents, the distinction between legislative and executive powers is likewise cast into doubt in this regard. None of the major secular theorists provide much in the way of specific constitutional methods for limiting or hemming in popular will. Ironically, though we today look to the likes of Locke for theories of popular sovereignty, most of the constitutional mechanisms we now use around the world for limiting popular will so as to turn it into popular sovereignty were developed by religiously grounded theorists of popular sovereignty, whether Protestant or Catholic.

The Constitutional Democracy Model

Covenant theology did result in some attempts to create constitutional democracy, particularly in colonial North America, but the most prominent theory of this type also belongs to the secular strain in sovereignty theory. Jean Jacques Rousseau is the most prominent among these secular thinkers, and it is worth a brief discussion of his theory to appreciate the difficulties inherent in creating popular sovereignty using the Constitutional Democracy Model.

Rousseau looks at first to be reasonably similar to Locke. Civil society, by aggregating the sum of personal forces, ensures self-preservation, which Rousseau terms the first law of human nature;[22] preserves liberty by transforming natural freedom into civil freedom;[23] reconstitutes sociability among people who, in a state of nature, found such relationships subordinated to relationships between things;[24] and produces greater utility for each individual, the only reason, Rousseau says, for alienating any natural freedom.[25] Whereas Locke saw humans as naturally equal, however, Rousseau says humans are equal only because the contract makes them so, and the contract makes them so because everyone gives his entire self.[26] Also, whereas Locke saw superior force as defining what is right, Rousseau says that force can never create right.[27] The social contract substitutes right for force, which leads him to conclude that majority rule, rather than resting on its being the greater force, is instead a convention established by the contract with no inherent basis in right.[28] Popular sovereignty is conditioned on the replacement of force by right.

Rousseau is therefore dealing with the very question on which Locke is silent – is there a standard of right that is not only independent of force but also objectively true? Rather than attempting to lay out the limits to action by a supreme force that results in its transformation into a sovereign, as did Bodin, Rousseau defines a process that will uncover

[22] Jean Jacques Rousseau, *On the Social Contract*, ed. Roger D. Masters, trans. Judith R. Masters (New York: St. Martin's Press, 1978), pp. 47, 52–53.
[23] Ibid., p. 56.
[24] Ibid., p. 50.
[25] Ibid., p. 47.
[26] Ibid., p. 53.
[27] Ibid., pp. 48–49.
[28] Ibid., p. 52.

what is right in every instance. That which is objectively true is called the general will. Seeking the general will rather than particularistic goods determines the characteristics of the process. The process itself, as well as the general will the process uncovers, constitutes the limits on supreme power. The result is popular democracy resting on the strongest version of popular sovereignty – no law is enacted except by the unanimous consent of a constantly participatory people.

The people are a supreme power that no longer needs to use force, because the process of seeking the general will transforms them into a morally connected entity that cannot do harm to those not in the majority. Those not in the majority automatically recognize the moral force of the majority's conclusion precisely because the majority is seeking the general will and not enforcing its own will in pursuit of its own interests. Majority rule is a convention, therefore, with no particular force since, as Rousseau says, "what generalizes the will is not so much the number of votes as the common interest that unites them" (those in the minority and in the majority).[29] As long as the majority (and the minority) is seeking the general will, the people are acting as a sovereign. If they instead make decisions based on particularistic ends, they are acting merely as a supreme power, what Rousseau terms an "absolute power."

Rousseau's vision of a sovereign as a limited supreme power is consistent with the usage of all other sovereignty theorists. Furthermore, he is clear that even though the popular sovereign does not need to use force in reaching its decisions, it is still a supreme force with "absolute power over all its members."[30] While this, the first face of sovereignty, is necessarily part of popular sovereignty, why is absolute power still necessary if right has replaced force? The answer is that in any community there will always be a few who will not pursue what is right and will instead pursue particularistic ends rather than the general will. These individuals Rousseau terms rebels and traitors, and absolute power must be used on these individuals to preserve the community. The penalty for such actions is death. Rousseau's logic is that, because in the social contract everyone consents to pursue the general will so as not to become the victim of a murderer, one has consented to be

[29] Ibid., p. 63.
[30] Ibid., p. 62.

killed if one turns into a murderer. Every person has thus consented to have the collective force used against him if he becomes an "enemy" to the community by failing to pursue the general will. The answer to the problem, then, lies in creating such a strong sense of community with such homogeneous values that the political problem supposedly solved by the general will is in fact solved by effectively eliminating the moral diversity on which the problem usually rests. If this sounds like a very strong form of political correctness, it is apparently the price to be paid for a highly participatory popular sovereign. Among other things, it explains the need for the civil religion that Rousseau later describes. It also explains the need for the censorial tribune that uses censorship of ideas to preserve the mores underlying the constitution.[31] A proper socialization with highly communitarian content is a necessary part of the overall solution, as is continuous monitoring of ideas expressed by the citizens.

Another essential part of the solution is that while the people are deliberating they do not talk to each other and thereby do not activate associations of citizens based on partial or particularistic interests. It is surprising how little attention the secondary literature gives to this need for the absence of communication. Rousseau in effect tells us that, in order to discover the general will, citizens must police their thoughts even after they have been highly socialized to community values. Citizens are not supposed to communicate during the deliberation process, but what about between bouts of deliberation? Is it reasonable to expect that citizens who have been communicating about their particularistic attachments on a regular basis can forget about these conversations when called upon to act as legislators? Obviously not, so we are left to wonder if, in order to seek the general will, political discussion outside of the citizen legislature must cease as well. This certainly solves the problem of protecting free speech since there will no longer be any politically relevant speech.

One could make the argument that Rousseau's ideal citizen in civil society strongly resembles the solitary human in the original state of nature – no consciousness of self, no speech, no strong attachments to any particular humans, and no connections to things (property). One does not have to read Rousseau this way in order to recognize

[31] Ibid., book IV, chap. VII.

how difficult it would be to achieve the conditions necessary for the general will to be pursued. Without the general will, Rousseau's vision posits an even greater danger of majority tyranny than Locke's. With the general will, Rousseau's vision generates a convincing picture of a complete popular sovereignty, but one subject to Rousseau's own conclusion about democracy – "If there were a people of Gods, it would govern itself democratically. Such a perfect government is not suited to men."[32]

If one establishes a political system in which all decisions are to be reached by the people directly, and the limits on the people result primarily from a universally shared set of "correct" attitudes, it follows that any constitution describing the system will lack institutional limits of any sort. The constitution Rousseau implicitly describes is largely limited to ensuring that the executive can do nothing more than enforce the policies reached by the people-as-legislature. There is discussion of a legislator whose job is to frame the question put to the people, but who is otherwise prohibited from using either coercion or persuasion during the deliberative process. The constitution for Rousseau's Constitutional Democracy will therefore be brief and minimalist in content. Rousseau does speak of an extraconstitutional body called the Tribunate. The job of the Tribunate is to veto or block actions contrary to the constitution created by the social contract and thereby preserve the terms of the agreement. However, because similar institutions elsewhere have grown too powerful, he suggests making the Tribunate an episodic body with limited duration that meets only infrequently. Because the Tribunate is not actually part of the constitutional structure, the people can convene it as they wish without impairing the constitution. How this body would block anything during the long periods when it is off duty is left to the reader to imagine.

Rousseau lays out the problems of a strong Democratic Constitutionalism grounded on the strongest version of popular sovereignty so clearly that few have been willing to design such a system. Instead,

[32] Ibid., p. 85. This page lists the conditions needed for a successful democracy and concludes that these conditions are virtually impossible to achieve or maintain. Comparison with the conditions needed to produce a people capable of seeking the general will, which Rousseau lays out on page 74 in particular, and in book II, chapters VIII–X in general, shows these conditions to be identical with those for a successful democracy.

those engaged in constitutional design have preferred using some form of the Constitutional Republic Model that holds out the promise of institutional limits on a popular sovereign composed of fallible humans.

Constitutionalism and a Fallible Human Nature

"Strong democracy," or what is here called popular control of government, rests on a very positive view of the natural tendencies of humans in large groups, which in turn rests on a very positive view of human nature. The stronger the democracy that is proposed, the more positive the view of human nature required to sustain the proposal. A complementary perspective is that the more pessimistic one's view of human nature, the more inclined one is to support elitism. A very negative view of human nature inclines one toward very weak democracy and toward what can be termed "strong elitism." The set of attitudes that has historically undergirded and defined constitutionalism eschews both extremes when considering human nature and rests instead on what can be called a belief in human fallibility plus the "redemptive" possibilities of political institutions.

A belief in human fallibility is relatively neutral in its estimation of human nature but recognizes that, while there are "bad" individuals, the major problem with humans is that they miscalculate their own interests and how to achieve them, both as individuals and in groups. Put in the terms of this analysis, even though humans naturally seek the morally neutral goals of individual survival, liberty, sociability, and beneficial innovation, they are often mistaken about how to achieve them. There are several reasons for this. As James Madison points out in *Federalist Papers* 10, humans inevitably must act under conditions of imperfect information and on the basis of communication resting on a tool, language, that is frequently, by nature, ambiguous.[33] Consequently, humans are always in the process of learning from their

[33] The analysis of Madison here is derived in part from Vincent Ostrom's excellent work *The Political Theory of the Compound Republic: Designing the American Experiment*, 2nd ed. (Lincoln: University of Nebraska Press, 1987). I have altered his analysis somewhat and introduced a slightly different terminology, in order to address more directly the topic under discussion here.

mistakes and successes. Also, the natural inclination toward liberty, because it does not lead easily to self-limiting behavior, frequently results in actions and proposed innovations that, under conditions of incomplete information and the inherent limits of language, are not always conducive to the ends they seek. Put another way, perceived short-term interests often conflict with the long-term interests. There is even, says Madison, a certain quality of irrationality in human activity such that perceived conflicting interests among humans sometimes rest on the most "fanciful" premises. However, because humans are not inherently evil, antisocial, or ill-willed, once experience shows us how to match means to ends more effectively, we are willing to sacrifice our perceived short-term interests in order to advance toward what he calls "the permanent and aggregate interests" of humans in general, and our people in particular.

This belief does not require us to assume a human nature naturally inclined toward beneficence and charitableness, but it does require that there be a human nature in the sense of more or less universally sought human goals, as well as a basic rationality defined in terms of both a tendency to seek more rather than less of these natural human goods and an ability to match means to ends appropriately. Cooperativeness thus rests on a realization that our general long-term interests are similar and a willingness to forgo short-term relative advantage in favor of our long-term interests once the relationship between the two becomes clear. Constitutionalism rests on a basic belief in human rationality but also a distrust of human passions that interfere with rational calculations. The Madisonian model, and all constitutionalism, rests on institutions that are supposed to prevent simultaneously the implementation of "passions" by any part of society, but especially by those who hold positions of power and create sufficient delay for the relationship between personal interests and the permanent and aggregate interests to emerge. Once this relationship is clear, humans will tend naturally to choose those policies which are in line with the reasons for institutions of coordination initially – individual survival, liberty, sociability, and beneficial innovation.

Any given political interest may or may not turn out to be in the permanent and aggregate interests for the reasons just cited; therefore, every interest must be treated equally and invariably subjected to the same test through fair institutions effective at creating sufficient delay for long-term interests to be identified. At the same time, these institutions of delay should not be so effective that they prohibit deliberative majorities from reaching decisions and enforcing their wills. In this sense, political institutions are "redemptive," because they allow us to continually, and marginally, overcome not a "bad" human nature but one that is prone to fallibility. The demands, wishes, and hopes of every interest are thus in the form of a hypothesis: "If you do as we suggest, we will all be better off in the long run." The essential neutrality with which every interest must be treated in a constitutional system also explains why constitutional systems based on popular sovereignty must rest on rules of coordination rather than on rules of command. No one must be allowed to be a judge in his own case, and "command systems" allow this to happen. At the same time, everyone must be allowed to determine their own interest, and to consider how that narrow interest is linked to the permanent and aggregate interests. Both aspects of constitutional neutrality are grounded in and commensurate with individual survival, liberty, continued sociability, and beneficial innovation.

If popular sovereignty is a principle upon which to ground the coordination of many people pursuing common long-term interests through the mutual accommodation of short-term interests, then the characteristics of that self-governing people would seem to be crucial for successful coordination. Different peoples, despite their common human goals, differ in their characteristics in terms of history, geographical and social contexts, and habits of mind and action. Therefore, the rules of coordination that have a high probability of success will vary from people to people, which returns us to the fundamental Aristotelian notion that a constitution must be matched to the people.

Assuming a natural diversity among peoples and their respective circumstances, and assuming the need to match a constitution to the people and their circumstances, lead us to expect a wide variety of institutional designs among constitutional republics. A simple parliamentary-presidential dichotomy will thus hide more than it reveals when analyzing popular sovereignty. We will spend a later chapter discussing in detail what it means to match a constitution to the people, but at this point the discussion will move forward more fruitfully if we turn to explicating an operational definition of popular sovereignty that will both lay out the constitutional elements that define the concept and allow us to engage in an empirical analysis.

Toward an Operational Definition of Popular Sovereignty

According to Saint Augustine, God is in the details. If God is the true sovereign who serves as the model for the earthly sovereign, then we find God in his earthly guise in the details of a constitution that creates popular control and then transforms popular control into popular sovereignty. That is, the first thing we should be able to discern from a constitution is the location of sovereignty, an expectation consistent with the first principle of constitutional design – create a supreme power. One problem with constitutions is that frequently they contain hortatory statements concerning sovereignty that are not reflective of the facts of sovereignty underlying the political system. It is necessary, therefore, to follow Bodin's dictum and search for the supreme power in the sum of the details in a constitution.

When we conduct such a search for the supreme power, it is necessary to read the document in its entirety and consider the total effect of its various interlocking provisions. We must be able both to identify and to evaluate the relevant provisions, which in turn requires that we have some provisional method for combining what we find into a reasonably meaningful conclusion. Our specific concern in the rest of this chapter is to devise a means for identifying the relative presence of popular control and then of popular sovereignty. In Chapter 1 we defined democracy as "a political system characterized by direct popular control." Popular control, in turn, is a situation where the people are the supreme power. In its pure form, the people gather together in the same place and pass all laws, and nothing is done by government until and unless such direct, popular authorization occurs. This pure form rarely occurs in the real world, so we are left with devising some way of estimating the degree to which this condition is approximated. We do so here by developing an Index of Popular Control, which permits a summary of the cumulative effect of relevant constitutional provisions toward approximating popular control.

A sovereign, however, is a limited supreme power, so popular sovereignty is popular control limited in some way. A Separation of Powers Index will be constructed in the next chapter based on the cumulative effects of provisions designed to turn popular control into popular sovereignty. Why we term this a "Separation of Powers" Index will be fully explicated in that chapter. The attempt to "quantify" popular control, and then popular sovereignty, does not in principle produce a clear result for the simple reason that observers will differ on what constitutes enough popular control to qualify a political system as democratic, as well as on the level of limits needed to transform a popular supreme power into a popular sovereign. Nevertheless, such an exercise will provide us with the means, in principle, to compare the relative level of popular sovereignty in various political systems and to focus our attention on the details that make a difference rather than continue to make global, relatively unanchored judgments as we do now. The following elements are relevant provisions for an Index of Popular Control:

1. The entity that writes or designs the constitution
2. The entity that approves or adopts the constitution
3. The entity that proposes revisions or amendments
4. The entity that approves or adopts revisions or amendments
5. The presence of a statement identifying the supreme power
6. The proportion of directly elective offices at the national level
7. The average frequency of national elections
8. The decision rule used to determine electoral winners
9. Requirements for officeholding
10. The availability of popular referenda for policy initiation, for adopting public policy, and/or for recalling elected agents
11. The size of the legislature in relation to the population (and, thus, constituency size)

Constitutionism was earlier defined as a set of attitudes shared by relevant actors to the effect that the supreme power should be limited, there should be a covenant that lays out the ends and means for limiting the supreme power, and the covenant should be enforced and obeyed. Those who use the index will have to make an informed judgment about the extent to which constitutional provisions are actually followed in the face of incentives to do otherwise. There is no way around such a judgment, since otherwise the limiting provisions in the text of the constitution have no real force. Political systems vary in the probability that constitutions will be followed, so the answer cannot be a simple yes or no.

The Index of Popular Control rests on the fundamental assumption that popular control is defined by a majoritarian principle, not one of unanimity. Buchanan and Tulloch, among others, argue persuasively that it is often preferable to use extraordinary majorities rather than simple majorities in order to minimize what political economists call externalities or external costs, which is their way of saying unwanted or undesirable consequences.[34] Rational political actors, defined as those who maximize benefits and minimize costs, frequently would rather bear the additional decision costs that extraordinary majorities require in order to protect some vital interest or value. Although this may be good constitutional theory, it is not helpful for a theory of popular control because it allows a minority to block proposed legislation and thus determine the outcome. When it comes to popular control a majority is always preferable to a minority, which drives us toward simple majority as the preferred decision rule for popular control. For this reason, the Popular Control Index weights an extraordinary majority less than simple majority in terms of its contribution to popular control. If the people are to be heard, it makes more sense in terms of popular control for them to be heard positively through a simple majority than negatively through a blocking minority. The relative weight assigned to each possible institution is based on its relationship to a simple majority of the people being able to determine the outcome.

This assumption explains the absence of certain electoral system variables. Much has been written about the superiority of proportional representation because it minimizes the "disproportionality" between the number of votes cast for a political party and the number of seats that party obtains in the legislature. However, it is unclear whether such proportionality, although intuitively in line with a sense of fairness, contributes to popular control. The point of popular control is that the people have the supreme say, especially in the selection and control of their agents. Proportionality ensures that all major opinions are represented in the same ratio within a legislature as they occur within the general population, but while this contributes to a

[34] James M. Buchanan and Gordon Tulloch, *The Calculus of Consent* (Ann Arbor: University of Michigan Press, 1962).

fair discussion, it contributes nothing to majority rule. It may, instead, hinder majority rule by producing such hard-and-fast divisions in the legislature that majorities are difficult to form, or else by tending to produce "deals" behind closed doors that end up leaving out the very minority opinions that proportionality had ensured a place in the legislature to begin with. There is also the well-documented tendency for multiparty systems produced by proportional representation to tend toward two party blocs that approximate a two-party system, which renders suspect the supposed advantages of proportional representation. If proportional representation is so good at representing popular opinion, why do systems using it move away from its purer form and toward a system of two umbrella parties that is characteristic of non-proportional systems?[35] Theorists frequently argue that proportional representation enhances the legitimacy of legislative decisions, but it has to be noted that two-party systems result in political systems that are at least as stable as those based on a multiparty system, indicating at least equivalent legitimacy. Also, "legitimacy" is a term associated with popular sovereignty rather than popular control, and therefore is more in the nature of limiting popular control than enhancing it.

At the same time, there is nothing inherent in a two-party system that makes it a better method for popular control than a multiparty system. One could argue that the "first past the post" plurality rule in an electoral district is closer to majority rule than a proportional representation approach, but we are concerned here with popular control that is systemwide, not district-specific. In conclusion, for these and other reasons constitutional provisions that establish one kind of electoral system rather than another are not considered important for creating or defining popular control. As long as there are fair elections that allow popular control of those elected, we will consider all electoral systems as equivalent. Although electoral systems are an important means of matching a particular form of government to the characteristics of the people, no one has ever shown that proportional representation and multiparty systems are better or worse at creating and preserving popular control as it has been defined here. Single-member districts that are compact, contiguous, and contain approximately the same number of

[35] For further discussion, see Arend Lijphart, *Electoral Systems and Party Systems* (Oxford: Oxford University Press, 1994), pp. 143–144.

voters seem to produce about the same overall responsiveness to popular opinion in the United States that proportional representation does, for example, in the Scandinavian countries.

It also needs to be pointed out that few constitutions contain provisions describing the electoral system, and most of these are couched in general, vague terms. Put most simply, those who design constitutions generally do not consider the form of the electoral system a constitutional matter – at least in terms of proportional representation versus single-member districts. On the other hand, the constituency of the second house of the legislature is always laid out in the constitution, as is the executive's constituency.

One possibly important variable for popular control is the internal dynamics of a legislature. Critics of proportional representation argue that, by making clear legislative majorities unlikely, it leads to bargaining behind closed doors that may thwart popular will. However, if that problem were limited to multiparty systems, we would see systems of popular control moving away from proportional representation. An interesting fact is that once an electoral system is put in place, no matter what kind it is, a people will rarely change to another that is very much different.[36] This also argues for a rough equivalence among electoral systems with fair elections as far as popular control is concerned.

Some have argued that the size of the legislature is an important variable for popular control. James Madison argues, for example, that if a legislature is too small it will tend to be dominated by one or a few strong personalities, whereas one that is too large will require organization by a tight leadership that will also tend toward a kind of legislative oligarchy.[37] A system of popular control would therefore move toward a legislative size that is large enough to make it responsive to popular opinion but not so large as to become dominated by a legislative oligarchy. Interestingly, research does reveal a tendency in legislative size, but instead of moving toward the singular moderate size, constitutional republics tend toward the cube root of their respective populations.[38]

[36] Ibid., p. 52.

[37] Ostrom, *The Political Theory of a Compound Republic*, pp. 92–101; and Alexander Hamilton, James Madison, and John Jay, *The Federalist*, ed. Jacob E. Cooke (Cleveland: Meridian Books, 1967), pp. 374, 395.

[38] Rein Taagepera, "The Size of National Assemblies," *Social Science Research* 1 (1972): 385–401.

The larger the population, the larger the legislature. The size of the legislature does seem to be an aspect of popular control, primarily because the larger a legislature vis-à-vis the population, the smaller the constituency size, and the closer the relationship between representatives and their respective constituencies. Presumably, the closer this relationship, the stronger the incentives for representatives to respond to popular opinions and sentiments. We will therefore use the cube root of a nation's population as our baseline and adjust the overall Index of Popular Control by the extent to which its lower legislative house diverges from the cube root rule.

The cube root phenomenon is an interesting case of where those who design constitutions unconsciously struggle toward a similar sense of what is fair and workable in a constitutional republic. The overall tendency is for legislatures to increase in size as a population grows larger, but at a declining rate vis-à-vis increasing population – that is, the size of the average constituency grows larger at an increasing rate. We can surmise several things. First, given a choice, those who design constitutions for constitutional republics prefer the smallest constituency to representative ratio that is practicable. As populations get larger, designers become increasingly sensitive to the problem of overly large legislatures and allow constituency size to increase at an increasing rate. In the end, however, a certain population size is reached where any reasonable constituency size produces a legislature that is simply too large to prevent the legislative oligarchy phenomenon. Madison would view these large legislatures as no longer "moderate" in size, and Robert Michels would invoke the Iron Law of Oligarchy. This raises the question of the extent to which large constitutional republics can sustain sufficient levels of popular control, although as we will see later, bicameralism, federalism, and other institutions can be used to compensate for the problem.

The preceding discussion is an attempt to clarify the basis for including or excluding legal-constitutional provisions in the index. The matter of how to weight each possible provision is more difficult to explain or justify. For purposes of discussion, as well as for grounding an initial analysis, Table 3.1 lists the weights assigned to each possible variation. The total weight assigned to each element of the index implies its relative importance vis-à-vis the others. Thus, for example, the frequency of elections (a possible maximum of 2.00 points) is twice as important

TABLE 3.1. *An Index of Popular Control*

Element and Variation	Weight Assigned to Specific Outcome
Constitution written by	
Elected convention	.85
Legislature	.25
Constitutional court	.10
Body appointed by legislature	.10
Body appointed by executive	.00
Executive	.00
Constitution adopted by	
Referendum – absolute majority	1.00
Referendum – plurality	.85
Elected national convention	.50
National legislature	.25
Majority of state conventions	.50
Majority of state legislatures	.25
More than 65% of state conventions	.65
More than 65% of state legislatures	.40
Constitutional court	.00
Appointed legislative commission	.00
Appointed executive commission	.00
Executive	.00
Revisions proposed by	
Referendum – absolute majority	1.00
Referendum – plurality	.85
Elected national convention	.50
National legislature	.25
Majority of state conventions	.50
Majority of state legislatures	.25
More than 65% of state conventions	.65
More than 65% of state legislatures	.40
Constitutional court	.00
Appointed legislative commission	.00
Appointed executive commission	.00
Executive	.00
Revisions approved by	
Referendum – absolute majority	1.00
Referendum – plurality	.85
Elected national convention	.50
National legislature	.25
Majority of state conventions	.50
Majority of state legislatures	.25
More than 65% of state conventions	.65
More than 65% of state legislatures	.40
Constitutional court	.00
Appointed legislative commission	.00

(*continued*)

TABLE 3.1. *(continued)*

Element and Variation	Weight Assigned to Specific Outcome
Appointed executive commission	.00
Executive	.00
Specific statement assigning sovereignty	
To the people	.35
To a national, elected legislature	.00
To the constitution	.10
To the nation (*Das Volk*)	.10
To the state	.00
To an elected executive	.00
To a nonelected executive	.00
To a political party	.00
Proportion of directly elective offices at national level	
All directly elected	1.50
All except judiciary	1.00
All except executive	.75
Only the legislature	.50
Average national election frequency	
Annual	2.00
Only legislature annual	1.50
Biennial (average)	1.25
Every 3rd year (average)	1.00
Every 4th year (average)	.75
Every 5th year (average)	.50
Every 6th year (average)	.25
Every 7th year (average)	.15
More than 7 years (average)	.00
Decision rule to determine electoral winner	
Half + 1 of all citizens	1.25
Half + 1 of all registered	1.00
Half + 1 of those voting	.75
Plurality of those voting	.50
Requirements for officeholding	
Citizenship, residency, and age	1.00
Party nominees only	.50
Property ownership	−.25
Belong to specific party	−3.00
Specific class or caste	−3.00
Initiative, recall, and/or legislative referenda	
All three	1.00
Any two	.75
Any one	.50
Ratio of cube root of population to size of lower house (size of lower house divided by cube root of population): The score for this element is this ratio divided by three, rounded to nearest .05.	
Maximum score	1.00

for establishing popular control as how a constitution is adopted (a possible maximum of 1.00 points).

Imagine a political system that combines the highest scoring variation for each element. It would have a constitution written by a convention elected expressly for that purpose, be approved in a referendum by an absolute majority of the eligible electorate, and be amendable by the same process used in its initial adoption. There would be a specific statement in the constitution certifying that the people as a whole are sovereign and that all government officials, elected or unelected, are the agents of that sovereign. All major national officials – legislative, executive, judicial, and administrative – would be directly elected annually by at least one-half plus one of the total electorate. The people could initiate legislation, pass judgment on proposed legislation, and recall elected officials who displeased them – in each case using a relatively easy-to-initiate referendum. Finally, the lower house would be exactly in accord with the cube root rule. This hypothetical political system would score 13.20 points on the index and reflect a higher level of popular control than any political system now in existence or ever likely to exist. By comparison, the United States would have a score of 7.15.

The index is not intended to indicate precise values but instead to show that in a constitution the attempt to create popular control rests on the cumulative effect of many rules or provisions, and no one rule is decisive. Scholars could argue convincingly and at great length that values for various institutions should be higher or lower, but the essential point of the index would still be intact – popular control is defined by the cumulative effect of many rules. Ideally we could assign empirically determined values for many of the provisions, as will be done in a comprehensive analysis of the amending process later in the book. In the meantime, these relative valuations are offered as points of departure in debate over the relative importance of different aspects of popular control.

The index just devised consists of institutions that together support and tend to produce popular control. These institutions must be distinguished from other, more general conditions that undergird popular control. For example, the high incidence of politically relevant midrange voluntary organizations is an important condition for the creation and preservation of popular control, but one cannot produce these by passing laws, although the laws can encourage and sustain such organizations by preserving a wide latitude for citizenship initiative free from government regulation.[39] Another condition is the widespread and inexpensive availability of reliable information about public matters. A constitutional provision establishing a free press will be helpful, but once again it is not so much a case of passing laws as it is of not passing laws that interfere with spontaneous citizen coordination. An educated citizenry that can act independently, knowledgeably, and effectively is also a condition supporting popular control. However, it may be more accurate to say that popular control tends to produce cheap public education rather than the other way around. For one thing, democracy was born before public education had even been conceived. For another, it can be argued that both Nazi Germany and the Soviet Union had inexpensive public education and rather well-educated, certainly highly literate, populations, and yet this condition did not produce popular control. Many also argue for relative economic equality as a condition or precondition for popular control. Again, it seems just as likely that popular control comes first, and then relative economic equality tends to be produced by popular control. Compare the level of economic inequality today in the most inegalitarian constitutional republic with predemocratic Britain where the monarch and about four hundred families laid claim to about 80 percent of Britain's land area; or with the distribution of wealth in any other predemocratic monarchy, aristocracy, or empire.

This brief discussion is intended to underline the institutional and constitutional basis for the operational definition that is being developed here, as distinguished from a more sociological or "historical forces" perspective. Constitutional design as an enterprise concerns itself with the creation of institutions with reasonably well understood and predictable institutional characteristics, although not predictable institutional outputs. The approach here must therefore also be distinguished from more output-oriented operational approaches. For example, one could use the congruence between public opinion and public policy as an empirical indicator of the relative strength of popular control – especially the speed with which public policy is adjusted in

[39] For a trenchant discussion of this factor, see Robert Putnam, *Making Democracy Work* (Princeton, N.J.: Princeton University Press, 1993).

light of shifting public opinion. Or one might use the relative symmetry between electoral outcomes and the distribution of offices as a measure of popular control. We do not do so here because we are interested not in popular control per se, but in limited popular control, or popular sovereignty. In a situation of popular sovereignty, there might not be a very high congruence between public opinion and public policy in the short run. Nor might there be a very high congruence between electoral outcomes and the distribution of seats.

It is fair to ask why maximum popular control is not found in real-world regimes. It is also fair to ask if we would want such a system. The answer to the first question is heavily predicated on our answer to the second, which is that generally we do not want extreme popular control. Instead, democratic theorists and citizens alike prefer popular sovereignty, which requires that popular control be limited in certain ways. We usually codify the need for such limits with reference to minority or individual rights, but we also prefer popular sovereignty to popular control because extreme popular control tends to produce political instability as the agents of popular control enact rapidly changing laws in response to the ill-considered whims, momentary passions, and undigested hopes of the people. As a result, the benefits of coordination are seriously compromised because long-term, mutually beneficial policies cannot be formulated or pursued. Imagine the space program, national defense, or safety-net welfare in the face of short-term swings in public opinion enforced by extreme popular control. Extreme popular control also destroys the role played by leadership in the formulation and execution of policies that are unpopular in the short term but popular in the long term once the effects are experienced.

For these and other reasons, constitutional republics usually reflect a preference for including many elements of popular control, but then reducing the extent to which extreme popular control is approximated by also instituting constitutional limits that structure the effects of popular control. Put another way, popular sovereignty is characterized by first enabling a relatively high level of popular control and then limiting popular control in ways that are beneficial for the entire project of popular sovereignty. This project has two parts. The first is to establish a supreme power capable of creating and maintaining the order necessary for a people to enjoy the benefits of coordinating the activities of the many – preservation, liberty, sociability, and beneficial innovation. The second part of the project is to control this supreme power so that it will not threaten the benefits for which it was initially created. Thus, as with all sovereignty, popular sovereignty is predicated as a self-limiting supreme power, which implies that the most fundamental requirement for a political system grounded in popular sovereignty is a people among whom constitutional attitudes are widely diffused.

The first part of the constitutional project, the creation of a supreme popular sovereign, has now been explicated and codified. It is now time to do the same for the second part of the constitutional project.

4

The Separation of Powers

Why the Term "Separation of Powers" Is Used

"Separation of powers" is usually associated with so-called presidential systems, but all political systems use separated powers to some extent. We later use the concept of a "pure parliamentary system" to explicate precisely the codification of an Index of Separation of Powers and demonstrate that only two or three political systems reasonably approximate a pure parliamentary system. At this point it is useful to consider how framers of parliamentary systems develop ways to limit majority rule and to indicate in preliminary fashion why such limits are best considered as manifestations of a separation of powers.

In a "pure" parliamentary system, an electoral majority is translated into a parliamentary majority, and that parliamentary majority selects a prime minister who serves as the sole executive. Also, parliament is the final court of appeal for judicial matters. As we will see, this model is almost always rejected in practice for a more complex one. For example, almost all parliamentary systems also have a separately elected or appointed executive outside of parliament, as well as a supreme or high court that serves as the final body for legal appeals. Regardless of the actual powers of these two separate entities, they articulate institutionally a reluctance to place the power for all governmental functions in the same hands. If an executive is elected separately from parliament, or has a veto power or the power to send either pending or approved legislation to the supreme court for review, the separation of powers has been significantly strengthened.

In a pure parliamentary system, the functions of ultimately resolving judicial appeals as well as determining whether a piece of legislation is constitutional remain in parliament's hands. Giving either final judicial appeal or the function of constitutional review to a body outside of parliament strengthens the separation of powers, and invariably both are farmed out to one or more high courts in actual parliamentary systems. A number of parliamentary systems even require that all legislation be sent to the high court for a constitutionality review before the legislation can be adopted. Another common practice in parliamentary systems is to have two high courts, one to consider constitutional issues, and another to serve as the highest court of appeal for civil and criminal cases. Some systems have a high court for criminal cases and one for civil cases, which is still another way to strengthen separation of powers. Typically, members of the high court have life tenure or very long terms of office. In each instance, the separate institution serves to thwart direct majority rule.

Framers of constitutional republics have shown great ingenuity in this regard. Aside from bills of rights that prohibit majorities from reaching certain sets of policy decisions, a wide array of governmental functions is placed in extraparliamentary bodies so as to insulate them from majorities acting though parliament. Examples include the creation of electoral commissions that oversee and regulate all elections, constitutionally creating independent bureaucratic courts and commissions that oversee and regulate various aspects of the bureaucracy, placing certain categories of policy within the competence of elected or appointed bodies other than the national parliament, subjecting certain policy issues to automatic public referenda, providing for the activation of a referendum by an executive or a specified minority within parliament, establishing a constitutional amendment process that includes parliament as only one of the required actors or bypasses parliament altogether, and requiring a supermajority for certain issues or for amending the constitution. Also, some political systems create a national council with extraparliamentary competency, or subject executive vetoes to judicial review, or create ombudsmen with considerable powers. The list could go on at great length, but these examples establish the point.

In every instance, some of the power that a "pure" parliament would have for enacting majority will is separated from parliament and given to some entity that is to a greater or lesser degree separated from parliament. The net result is to produce an average separation of powers for parliamentary systems that is close to the average for "presidential" systems. For this reason, we will subsume all means of slowing down, channeling, or thwarting majority will under "separation of powers."

Four Historical Patterns of Devolution from One-Man Rule

What we now call separation of powers rested historically on a devolution of power away from strong-man rule – whether called a king, emperor, pharaoh, or what have you. This devolution proceeded along one or more of the following paths from one political system to another.

1. Popular consent: Using cultural and/or political institutions to limit the center of power to a range acceptable to "public opinion."
2. Separation of functions: Dividing power among multiple more or less specialized and independent entities or offices.
3. Representation: Creating an elective body to share the exercise of power with the central governing agent, who now becomes an "executive."
4. Federalism: Moving significant power away from the center to other, more local arenas of decision making.

These four historical movements eventually developed into the two great principles of Popular Sovereignty and the Separation of Powers, which together undergird and define modern constitutionalism.

As discussed earlier, popular sovereignty rests on the dual impulse for popular control and for limiting that popular control. What was identified earlier as popular consent is the most "primitive" form of the impulse for popular control. As this impulse matures historically and is institutionally codified, it becomes popular control. When the institutions for popular control are in turn limited by other institutions, it becomes popular sovereignty. Elected bodies of representatives, separation of functions, and federalism are prominent among these limiting institutions, and all are variations on the separation of powers. The second face of sovereignty thus implies separation of powers as part of the definition of popular sovereignty, and separation of powers will not occur without at least the most primitive impulse for popular consent, as characterized by Bodin. The stronger the impulse for popular consent, the more it presses toward popular control, and the stronger and more comprehensive the counteracting impulse toward separation of powers becomes.

What we today call separation of powers is actually a blending of the separation of governmental functions and the sharing of governmental powers by the multiple entities that result from the separation of functions. The strongest and most pure form of popular control, an assembly of all the people in the same space, lacks the limits on power that define separation of powers and that thus define popular sovereignty. From the ancient world on, whether expressed in Plato's and Aristotle's disdain for unmixed democracy, or codified in Rousseau's general will, which attempts to avoid the injustice of merely totaling up private wills, simple popular control has had a bad odor in political philosophy. This reaction does not stem from a dislike of popular consent per se but from a recognition that pure, unlimited democracy is a return to rule by a single agent, only this time an assembly instead of a king. Although an assembly may be inherently superior to a king, it is still not a true sovereign until limited in some way, and therefore it poses significant risks. A central concern in Western political philosophy is the attempt to marry justice with power. The fundamental technology developed for accomplishing this we now term "constitutionalism," and constitutionalism rests on popular sovereignty, which requires some significant manifestation of separation of powers. The advent of a representative assembly to embody popular will is that minimum, significant level of separation of powers, which is why elections are usually the first thing that comes to mind when we think of what makes a government a democracy (more properly, a republic).

What we now term "representation" is an institution, or set of institutions, that separates the power of deciding who will be among the decision makers and places this power in the hands of people other than those who will have the power to actually make the collective decisions. So, for example, the same elite that might dominate the legislature cannot also decide who gets to sit in that legislature. Representation also separates the function of judging the merits of the consequences of collective decisions from the function of making those decisions. This central and often overlooked form of separation of powers embodies the double requirement of the concept – a separation of functions coupled with a sharing of powers. Two distinguishable entities, the people and the elected body of representatives, neither of which can control the entire process of collective decision making on its own, share that power. Sharing power requires that we first divide power between two or more entities.

The British parliamentary system, which developed slowly and incrementally in this direction, sometimes serves as a prominent historical example that blurs the double thrust of separation of powers to the point where it is overlooked. The concept of parliamentary sovereignty, if taken literally, denies the existence of separation of powers. As long as Parliament was composed of a virtually self-selecting elite that was minimally connected to popular control, "parliamentary sovereignty" amounted to control by that elite or oligarchy. At some point, when the people gained the ability through universal suffrage to carry out its distinguishable functions of selecting and removing decision makers, at that point we had separation of powers and minimal de facto popular sovereignty. To the extent Parliament was viewed before 1689 as limiting the monarchy, to that extent Britain had a constitutional monarchy as opposed to the constitutional republic that is today the principle underlying parliamentarianism. The concept of king-in-parliament, by negating the earlier separation of powers between the monarch and aristocracy-dominated Parliament, potentially strengthened elite control. However, the Glorious Revolution also significantly broadened the elite to the point where it was no longer homogeneous but composed of competing elite factions. Also, the theoretical rationale for the Glorious Revolution used rhetoric that implied the potential inclusion of even a broader portion of the population. As a result, at some later point, British parliamentarianism evolved incrementally into modern constitutional democracy (republicanism) with the separation of powers between the people and parliament that we now take for granted as the hallmark of parliamentary government. That the shift was so incremental as to be almost invisible should not blind us to the reality of the distinction between constitutional monarchy, constitutional oligarchy, and constitutional democracy (republicanism) – all of them were at one time or another the reality of what historically appears to be a continuous parliamentary system.

Federalism is a form of separation of powers, and thus constitutionally subsumed under it. At the same time, federalism is an independent theory of government that, when it is present in a political system, leads to significant differences in thinking about constitutionalism in general and separation of powers in particular. Much, if not most of what distinguishes American from British constitutionalism can be traced to the prominence of federal theory in the former. However, a fuller explication of this federal theory must be made elsewhere. For our present purposes, describing the level of separation of powers in a given political system, we treat federalism as part of a separation-of-powers paradigm.

To return to our discussion of separation of powers as a devolution of power away from concentration of political power in a single entity, the type of political system that results from the devolution depends to a certain extent on the agent carrying the impulse for devolution: the agent carrying the demand for devolution will tend to define "the people," and thus citizenship, in terms of itself. Because the historical trend among constitutional polities was initially away from monarchy and toward parliamentary systems, and because historical political systems had different agents carrying the impulse for devolution, parliamentarism is not one thing but several. To clarify this, let us consider the historical tendencies in the devolution from monarchy.

If the agent for devolution is the many "poor," as Aristotle would have it, the system will tend toward the ideal of a pure democracy where government resides in an assembly composed of all the citizens, as in ancient Athens. We can call this the "pure democracy model." Numerical equality in the distribution of citizenship, political influence, goods, services, honors, offices, and duties is the hallmark of this tendency. Theorists also cite honesty, patriotism, and an inclination to the common good as important values, whereas others cite intolerance of minorities, a tendency toward homogeneity, and reduction of political discourse to the lowest common denominator as pathologies. Liberty tends to be defined in this instance in terms of the ability of the people as a whole to get what they want – that is, in communitarian terms. Popular elections and popular approval and amendment of constitutions are some of the consequences of this tendency, as are popular initiative, referendum, and recall.

Originally, the agent for devolution of power was an elite of some sort, and for this reason we may term it the "elite model." Initially there was a tendency toward the separation of executive decision-making functions as the preferred path for limiting power. The decision-making body, usually open to everyone with elite status and thus to a significant degree honorific, tended to be advisory vis-à-vis holders of political power. The precise nature of the regime depended on the criteria for membership in the elite – large landholdings, social status, contributions to the society, military prowess, knowledge and education, religious titles, or simply wealth. If one class of people dominated all or most of these possible criteria, the elite was "coherent," as in late medieval England. If there were a number of avenues to full citizenship rights, and these avenues were used by different sectors of the population, then elite competition resulted, and competition among a fractured elite itself induced limits on the central power, as in the Austro-Hungarian Empire. Honor, proportional equality, territorial expansion, and competition for positions of privilege and honor concerned such agents of devolution from monarchy. Liberty was defined in this instance in terms of maintaining independence of will vis-à-vis the government and in terms of preserving the privileges of members of the elite class. Constitutional expressions of this tendency come down to us in the form of a privy council, cabinet, or other advisory committees to the king (or head of state); ministries or independent commissions that carry out duties or functions usually considered as part of a fully endowed head of state, such as the power to pardon; the requirement that certain major executive actions, such as making treaties, appointing people to major administrative posts such as attorney general, and selecting members of the judiciary be countersigned or approved by some independent body, such as a senate.

Related to the elite model, in which the representative body is essentially advisory or subordinate to the king, is another kind of elite model in which the representative body is actually at the center of power. We can term this the "cohesion model." Post-1689 Britain, early modern Venice, the Iroquois Confederation, and the contemporary Iranian legislature may all be exemplars. In each instance an elite, based on landholding, commerce, virtue, and religious commitment, respectively, is dedicated to preserving the social structure and the culture that underlies it. Politics is seen as the venue of political amateurs using informal as well as formal institutions of decision making. Stability is sought by emphasizing internal peace, often through the distribution of goods and services to alleviate the suffering of the nonelite classes in a way that elicits their continued support but does not threaten existing power relationships. The elected legislature is either the center of elite power, or the primary counterelite institution to induce pursuit of community rather than class goals. None of the four examples cited could be termed a democracy, although all might be called republics.

If the middle (bourgeois) class is the agent for devolution, the emphasis will be on representation per se. Not inclined to spend time away from personal economic pursuits, members of the dominant middle classes will select representatives to serve as agents much the way they will select lawyers and accountants to provide a service. The representatives are agents, not instructed delegates, whose function is to determine how best to achieve the broad needs and goals of the citizens – productivity in the sense of increasing gross national product, efficiency, economic liberty, and infrastructure development. These representatives are also supposed to guard against extremes of numerical equality (economic redistribution) and proportional equality (privilege). Liberty is defined in terms of the rule of law (especially in terms of equal and neutral juridical treatment) and the relative absence of coercion (especially with respect to economic matters). Constitutional expressions of this tendency include bicameralism, an independent judiciary, limited government (denying the competence of the government to interfere in certain areas), and bills of rights. This describes what could be called the "liberal model."

Another type of parliament might be called the "general will model." In this model the representative body is ideally seen as a mirror image of the larger population, including ideological divisions, such that it should act in ways identical to how the people would act if assembled in the same room. Representatives are viewed as delegates sent by the people to carry out their general will. Potential representatives align according to platforms of proposed legislation that they will in fact support unerringly and in detail if elected. Emphasis is on close control by the people through frequent elections by a very broad electorate. Large assemblies, the relative absence of legislative complexities that might hide legislative intent or slow down popular will, open galleries, a free press, and detailed public minutes are hallmarks of this model. The relative absence of requirements that might restrict who can run for office, the provision of public funds for all candidates for office, term limits, automatic voter registration, and mandatory voting are also in line with this model. Originally, multimember districts and proportional representation were seen as key aspects of the delegate model, but empirically the results in this regard have been mixed. Some might prefer to term this the democratic model, but the next model could also be viewed as democratic since it attempts to respond to all of the people using many of the same democratic institutions but is structured differently to reflect and respond to a diverse population with differing characteristics, goals, and needs.

The final type of representative system might be termed the "common good model." It is grounded in a view of representatives as delegates rather than as trustees, and bound more by general goals than by specific instructions. Platforms are considered more advisory and illustrative than binding. A legislator, like a lawyer hired to represent one in court, is supposed to be better at achieving the common good than the people using the agent, or else they would not have bothered to hire or send the agent in the first place. These legislative agents are seen more as policy entrepreneurs and brokers in the bargaining among various societal interests in a complex and ambiguous situation than as carriers of a general will. Unlike the previous model, where the preferred outcomes are assumed to be known at election time, the specific policies that will be in accord with the common good are seen to be largely unknown and subject to emerge through the deliberations of an assembly, where the representatives are not too closely tied to volatile public opinion. The common good model is more liberty-oriented than equality-oriented, a matter more of emphasis than anything else. One consequence is a greater use of legislative complexity in the organization of the institution so as to produce more "choke points" to be used by minorities in protecting their respective interests against majority coercion. This model is concerned more with producing legislation that is balanced, gives everyone something, and privileges solutions that increase the economic pie to everyone's potential benefit rather than redistributing the pie. Ideological outcomes are frowned upon.

Therefore, the history of devolution away from one-man rule had three broad results:

1. Power centralized in a single person was replaced by power focused increasingly in an elected assembly.
2. This led to the creation of multiple types of representative models.
3. These multiple representative models developed varying degrees of separation of powers.

Parliamentarism versus Presidentialism?

If the history of the separation of powers led to several models of representative government, what about the presidential system that is supposed to be coterminous with separation of powers? The fundamental difference between parliamentarism and presidentialism is that the latter has a popularly elected executive who is not part of the legislative branch, whereas the former has an executive, usually termed a prime minister, who is selected by the parliament, sits in it, and leads it directly. Britain is usually cited as the exemplary home of parliamentarism, while the Unites States is usually cited as the exemplary home of presidentialism. The distinction between the two constitutional forms is indeed important, but categorization schemes that rest upon it are failing to account for most of the difference between the two, which is essentially one in the degree of the separation of powers.

Several recurring problems in comparative studies result from this approach. First, a minority of political systems appear to fall into simply one category or the other. This results in the creation of awkward and ambiguous middle categories often labeled "hybrid" or "mixed." These middle categories hide more than they reveal about constitutional design. Second, by singling out the United States as the paradigm case of presidentialism, researchers fail to see that presidentialism is not the major defining characteristic of the American political system. Invariably, on most empirical measures, the United States is a polar opposite to the British system, so it is reasonable to conclude that presidentialism is the cause of the difference. However, students of American politics will readily note that strong bicameralism, federalism, and an independent court together constitute most of what the United States has contributed to constitutional design. A separate executive accounts for, at most, one-third of what distinguishes the American political system from the British parliamentary model, and perhaps as little as one-fourth of the difference. The separate executive is only a minor part of what distinguishes the U.S. from the British model.

Moreover, focusing on the president in the American political system is slightly perverse because the American executive is not only among the weaker presidents compared with those in other presidential systems, but he is even weak when compared with virtually all executives, whether president or prime minister. Because of this relative weakness the American president cannot be considered the true focus of American politics, its defining characteristic, or the explanation for the variance in empirical measures between presidential and parliamentary systems. In sum, for all of these reasons, to term the American political system "presidential" is to essentially miss the phenomenon – and that phenomenon is the separation of powers.

A little American history can shed light on this phenomenon, put supposed American presidentialism in perspective, and help explain why the American presidential exemplar is so different from and, on most empirical measures, more extreme than other "presidential systems." It will also explain why it is useful to consider the British model as the grounding point of any comparative analysis, and other forms as deviations (in a certain sense, also derivations) from this basic parliamentary model.

If we take a look at James Madison's notes to the federal convention that drew up the U.S. Constitution, we find that he and his supporters presented the Virginia Plan during the first week of deliberations. A modified version of this plan was adopted after some debate, and the rest of the convention was spent in further modification of this adopted plan. The Virginia Plan laid out, to the extent possible in America, a copy of the British parliamentary form in existence at that time. The first branch of the national legislature would be directly elected, with representatives apportioned according to the number of free inhabitants in each state. The first branch would then elect the second branch out of "a proper number of persons nominated by the state legislatures." The national executive would also be chosen by the national legislature, as would the national judiciary. There was no aristocracy in America, but the Virginia Plan attempted to use the first branch to identify a natural (nonhereditary) aristocracy and thereby to create the equivalent of a House of Lords through the selection of men of reputation by the first branch in the creation of the second branch. The Revolution had broken ties with monarchy, but the first branch would create a functional equivalent through selection of an executive outside of the legislature. Legislative selection of a high court, with final appeal resting in the legislature, completed the American approximation of the British parliamentary system. The prior existence of the states as polities led to a constitutional innovation that reflected "parliamentary supremacy." The Virginia Plan also proposed that the national legislature could veto state laws that it viewed as contrary to the national constitution. However, national legislation could in turn be vetoed by a national council of revision composed of the national executive and several members of the national judiciary. Because the executive and judicial branches could be altered by it, they were essentially creatures of the legislature. This makes the hereditary British king, and the judiciary under the king, look more independent from the legislature than the American "copy." The one parliamentary power that was removed from the American national legislature in the Virginia Plan was the amendment process. The plan proposed that amendments be "recommended by the several [state] Legislatures to be expressly chosen by the people, to consider & decide thereon."

As the convention debates went on, five major innovations were made in this plan. First, bicameralism was made much stronger than in Britain by having the second branch elected by the state legislatures. Second, the federalism implicit in this move was woven throughout the document to carve out the states as relatively independent polities that, while not sovereign, had more actual power than the national government by retaining competencies in the vast majority of policy areas. One example was the amendment process, which now involved both national and state entities, either conventions or legislatures at both levels. Third, the Supreme Court was removed from legislative control through presidential nomination, senatorial approval only, and the granting of life tenure. Finally, at the very last minute, and almost as an afterthought, the executive was removed from legislative control and given an independent basis in an electoral college that was selected by state electorates.

In every instance the basic British model was altered so as to devolve or separate what were seen in Britain as part of parliamentary powers to other branches and agencies. Thus was the separation-of-powers model derived from the parliamentary model. The various innovations were done piecemeal and for politically pragmatic or utilitarian reasons rather than out of commitment to a principle. Still, the result was the highest level in the separation of powers seen up to that time. That ultimate expression of the separation of powers rested only in part on an independent executive centered around a president.

When we look at the relative weakness of the executive branch in the constitution and the dominance of the legislative branch, we can see both the residual effects of beginning from a British parliamentary model and the final reason why it is a misnomer to characterize the U.S. model as simply "presidential." Nor has the U.S. Constitution strengthened the presidency since 1789. The strength of the presidency continues to rest, as Neustadt famously pointed out in the 1960s, on the prestige and prominence of a single person who is the only American political agent who can lay claim to a national constituency, and who resides in a "bully pulpit" that permits access and recourse to the people as a whole. Constitutionally speaking, the U.S. president, even with the advent of things like executive orders, remains constitutionally a relatively weak institution.

The easiest way to demonstrate this is to run quickly through the checks and balances of the current political system. The principle balances are three: bicameralism, different constituencies for each of the three national branches, and different terms of office for each. Together these "balances" make it extremely unlikely that national power can fall into the hands of any minority – indeed, it is difficult for any identifiable majority to gain such control. The balances thus in part result from and reinforce the separation of powers. However, a number of constitutional checks counteract the centripetal forces created by the separation of powers. Laying out all of these checks at once proves to be an interesting exercise.

The first check most students will mention is presidential veto, but veto override gives Congress the final word. The president nominates men and women to his cabinet and other major executive posts, but the Senate gives Congress the last word. The same is the case for treaties. The president is commander in chief, but only Congress can declare war to make this power meaningful, and only Congress can appropriate funds to give the commander in chief a fighting force. In addition, Congress can impeach the president, investigate executive functions and actions, create and abolish executive agents and agencies, and set or alter executive branch salaries. The president can pardon on his own, but he is left out of the amendment process completely. The president cannot affect the sitting of Congress through prorogue or calling sessions. If the electoral college fails to select a president, Congress shall select one. If the president and vice president die, are removed, or are incapacitated, Congress determines who shall be the executive – currently the Speaker of the House. No other elected president in the world has so many legislative checks and restrictions placed upon him. Even most symbolic presidents can prorogue or call the legislature into session.

The Supreme Court is even more constitutionally dependent on Congress. Although judicial review is now generally considered a constitutional check, this is technically incorrect since judicial review is not found in the text of the constitution. The text does allow Congress to impeach the justices, set their salaries, set and alter the size of the court, and alter the court's appellate jurisdiction. This last point is especially important because less than 1 percent of the court's cases come to it through its original jurisdiction in Article III. The rest come to the court through appellate jurisdiction added by Congress. Put another way, while there is no reason for Congress to want to do so, it could take away much of the court's power by reducing its jurisdiction. Thus, as written, the Constitution leaves the levers produced by the Constitutional Convention largely in the hands of Congress. This is perfectly understandable once it is recognized that the Constitutional Convention began by adopting what was essentially a parliamentary system. As the executive and judicial branches were drawn away from Congress into an independent status, the fear of these branches possibly misusing their power, plus the absence of direct elections to control them, led naturally to a system of checks whereby the elected Congress could keep them in line.

The point of this diversion into American history is to underline how inappropriate it is to characterize the American political system as "presidential." It was not designed to put the president in the center, and the independent executive is only a part of the separation of powers that defines the document's originality that differentiates it from the British model. It seems more than odd to view the U.S. system as an outlier on most empirical measures primarily because it has an independent executive, when its executive was designed to be, and remains, weaker than is found in many "presidential" systems that do not result in outlier status because they lack some combination of bicameralism, federalism, judicial independence, and other separation-of-powers institutions.

Modern constitutional analysis, therefore, requires that we begin with the least separated version of parliamentarism; that we move beyond a simple parliamentary-presidential dichotomy to a separation-of-powers continuum; that we learn to distinguish parliamentary and presidential systems that blend into one another; and that we attempt to develop a Separation of Powers Index that can be more useful in testing empirical propositions about constitutional design. In short, our analysis must be able to deal with political systems that have different degrees of separation of powers that do not permit easy dichotomization, or even categorization.

The Pure Parliamentary Model

We can describe a minimal separation of powers in the following manner.

1. There is an elected unicameral legislative body.
2. The sole executive is selected by this body, resides in it, and presides over it.
3. All other executive personnel (cabinet, etc.) who are to implement and oversee policy are selected by and removable by the legislative body (not the prime minister).
4. This body is the final court of appeal on all judicial matters – there is no separate court of final appeal.
5. There are no limits on the power of this body to deal with any matter.
6. The system is unitary – there is no federalism or local governmental discretion.
7. There is minimal legislative organizational complexity.

This might be termed the Pure Parliamentary Model or a Minimal Separation of Powers Model, which will be used to anchor an index for distinguishing higher levels of separation. However, there is a history to the separation of powers that does not begin with pure parliamentarism. Instead, powers first devolved from a monarch, and then from a parliament that had replaced the king at the center. That is, separation of powers is a political principle that we can identify and discuss theoretically, but the political institutions that embody separation of powers did not generally result from the application of a theoretical principle as much as the principle evolved from the gradual discovery that political power could be institutionally distributed, as well as the gradual discovery of new functions that could be distributed in new ways. For example, during the colonial era in America, legislatures developed the principle of no multiple officeholding as a means of preventing the "buying off" of legislators through the governor giving them paying positions in the executive branch. This was termed a "separation of powers" even though no powers were actually separated. Only later did Americans begin to apply the term separation of powers to the separate election of an executive.

As we follow the history of constitution making down to the present, we find an increasingly complex set of institutions for separating powers as we learn to identify "functions" that were not previously identified as specific powers. Some countries, for example, have established electoral commissions to regulate and oversee elections. Until this century, no one really considered this a separate "function" or power, and it resided undiscovered in the legislative branch as the ability to determine who had been properly elected when he arrived to take his seat. Other constitutional systems have seemingly divided the executive into several persons (or commissions) and subjected these several persons to elections as independent entities. My favorite is the state of Texas, which has a separately elected governor, lieutenant governor, attorney general, treasurer, railroad commission (to regulate intrastate commerce), utility commission, and so on. One of the general post–World War II tendencies noted in Chapter 1 has been the gradual but persistent increase in constitutional separation of powers. This tendency is much older than half a century – it goes back to at least the seventeenth century. However, the long-term trend is not toward the U.S. model. Instead, there is a simultaneous movement away from both the pure parliamentary model and from the extreme U.S. version of separation of powers toward a general middle ground.

The comparative politics literature has attempted to respond to these changes by developing middle categories between the "presidential" and parliamentary forms, such as "presidential-parliamentary" or "parliamentary-presidential," or perhaps something like both of these to indicate which way they lean. The Separation of Powers Index is designed to move beyond simple, rough categorizations that focus narrowly on one office – the president. To illustrate how rough the conventional schema really is, one must realize that the paradigmatic example of the presidential form, the United States, actually has one of the weakest executives in the world – something that students of American politics generally recognize but that seems to be ignored by students of comparative politics. The federal, bicameral, and two-party aspects of the U.S. system, along with an independent judiciary with review powers, are arguably together more important than the fact of a relatively weak, independently elected president for explaining the political process and political outcomes. And yet the U.S. political system is categorized as "presidential." What this term is really meant to say is that the U.S. has a high degree of separation of powers, which is true, but as the index implies, a separately elected president accounts for less than 25 percent of the phenomenon of separation of powers as it exists in the U.S.

The same is true for countries designated "parliamentary." As the analysis using the Separation of Powers Index will show, because an independently elected executive is only a minor aspect of separation of powers, some so-called parliamentary systems lacking a separately elected president still have greater separation of powers than a number of the so-called presidential systems. Terming a system "parliamentary" misses whether or not it is also federal, has an independent and active court, is two-party or eleven-party, is bicameral or unicameral, and so on. For example, let us compare two parliamentary systems on a single point that seems to go generally unremarked in the comparative politics literature. In New Zealand the constitution can be amended by an act of a unicameral parliament and is the easiest in the world to amend. Australia, on the other hand, largely because it is federal, has probably the most difficult constitution in the world to amend because of its much stronger separation of powers as a whole. Yet, these two systems are generally categorized together as "parliamentary."

There is a need to capture the differences among political systems in the distribution of separation of powers. An index that captures these differences would be, at the very least, a useful supplement to the general categorization schemes currently in use. It would also permit the use of statistical techniques that assume a continuous variable. Statistical analyses, however, would now read "Political systems with a higher level of separation of powers tend..." rather than "Presidential systems tend..."

A Separation of Powers Index

The Separation of Powers Index is constructed by assigning weights to the various alterations in the minimal separation-of-powers model developed earlier as the pure parliamentary model (Table 4.1). That is, the various aspects of separation of powers are defined by their contribution to a move away from the pure parliamentary model outlined earlier where all powers are concentrated in a single political entity. As with the Popular Control Index, the final score is additive of a number of institutional elements, and the score assigned each institution is an estimate of each element's relative importance for producing separation of powers. One apparent anomaly is that under element B the apparent creation of two executives produces less separation of power than the independent election of a single executive. However, if the head of government is in parliament, this prime minister prevents the separately elected executive from devolving much power away from parliament. It should be noted that it is also possible for some institutional elements to produce more than one incremental addition to the total index. For example, if an executive veto is subject to legislative override *and* judicial review, .25 would be added twice to the total. Or, if there is a second national court, .25 would be added to whatever other score was generated by that element.

Technically, the zero point on the index is represented by a pure democracy – all citizens assembled in one place, who together have all political power through majority rule. However, to keep matters simple, the zero point on the index is defined by a system with the characteristics of a pure parliamentary model. To this most basic model,

TABLE 4.1. *A Separation of Powers Index*

Institutional Element	Contribution to Index Score
Bicameralism	
Strong bicameralism (separate, popular elections)	+1.50
Weak bicameralism – upper house selected by lower house	+.25
Weak bicameralism – appointed by executive	+.25
Independent executive	
Separately elected single executive who is both chief of state and head of government	+1.5
Separately elected chief of state, but there is also a head of government in parliament	+.50
Outside executive is hereditary but has real power	+.50
Executive outside of parliament elected by parliament	+.25
Outside executive is hereditary and essentially symbolic	+.25
Outside executive appointed by British monarch	+.00
Dual executive (add this score to any from above)	+.15
Executive veto power	
Executive outside legislature has absolute veto power	+.50
Executive veto power subject to legislative override	+.25
Executive veto subject to plebiscite	+.25
Executive veto subject to judicial review	+.25
Selection of cabinet or ministers	
Outside executive selects ministers without legislative approval	+.75
Outside executive selects cabinet with legislative approval	+.50
Prime minister selects with or without parliament's approval	+.25
Prime minister selects through formal intermediary (e.g., governor general)	+.25
Judicial independence	
A separate, elected judiciary	+1.00
Separate judiciary approved by more than one agent (e.g., executive, senate, judicial commission)	+.50
A separate judiciary selected by one agent	+.25
Any of these *plus* a second high or constitutional court	+.25
Any of these *plus* life tenure for judges (or good behavior)	+.25
Level of judicial review	
Supreme court can nullify legislative acts	+.50
Supreme court precertifies constitutionality of legislation	+.50
Supreme court has judicial review only over lower courts	+.25
Degree of federalism	
States or provinces elect national upper house	+.75
States or provinces elect own assemblies	+.50
States or provinces have separate, significant competencies	+.50

(continued)

TABLE 4.1 *(continued)*

Institutional Element	Contribution to Index Score
A completely federal (not merely decentralized) system	+2.00
Degree of difficulty in amending constitution	
Two legislative houses using simple majority rule	+.25
Two legislative houses using two-thirds to three-quarters majority	+.35
Two houses approving twice with intervening election	+.35
Two houses plus approval by external executive	+.50
Two houses plus referendum	+.75
Two houses plus at least a majority of state or provincial legislatures	+.75
One legislative house – half + 1 majority	+.00
One legislative house – two-thirds to three-quarters majority	+.00
One legislative house approves twice with intervening election	+.00
One legislative house plus approval by external executive	+.25
One legislative house plus a national referendum	+.25
One house plus at least a majority of state or provincial legislatures	+.25
Limits on the range or scope of legislative powers	
Legislative and executive powers limited by a bill of rights	+.25
Significant constitutional exclusions of or limits on power	+.50
Legislation can be initiated by referendum	+.25
Other separation of powers provisions (exemplary, not exhaustive)	
Reasonably independent ombudsman with investigative powers	+.15
Council of state drawn from two or more agencies to advise executive	+.10
Multiple agents, any one of whom can force judicial review	+.05
Most laws must also be approved in a referendum	+.25
Elected officials can be recalled by plebiscite	+.10
Independent election commission to oversee election process	+.10
For every major executive official elected beyond president (e.g., attorney general)	+.10
For every such executive official selected by two or more agents	+.05
For every elected executive commission (e.g., mercy commission)	+.10
For every such commission selected by two or more agents	+.05
Some in lower house are selected by provincial governments	+.25

we then add the score for each separation-of-powers institution used by a given country. On the index, Britain has a score of 1.0 (an elected parliament with weak bicameralism, a cabinet appointed by the prime minister, a monarch as a separate but symbolic executive external to parliament, and an amendment process that requires approval by both houses and the external executive). One might argue that a more refined index would allow us to capture the "softness" of factors contributing to the British score, and a better score might be closer to .5 or at least below 1.0. However, the purpose is not to capture some objective phenomenon in all of its nuances, but rather to give us a useful way of comparing political systems. For an initial comparison, the United States has a score of 8.00. The Separation of Powers Index developed here retains the parliamentary and "presidential" forms as virtual opposites. New Zealand's parliamentarism comes in with a score of .50, and the scale ranges up to a probable high score of around 10.00. We can now array political systems between these two "polar" types without having to force any country into a category that destroys the possibility of taking into account degrees of difference in the separation of powers. It also allows us to identify systems that have a rough equivalence in the separation of powers, even though they use a different institutional mix.

Popular Control versus Popular Sovereignty: An Empirical Test

Over the past three chapters, the discussion has driven home the paradoxical nature of the two faces of sovereignty, and thus of popular sovereignty. Sovereignty is a theoretical concept that simultaneously requires the presence of a supreme power and of limits on that supreme power. A Popular Control Index, developed in Chapter 3, permits quantification of the relative extent to which the people have supreme power in a given political system. A Separation of Powers Index, developed in this chapter, measures the extent to which there are limits placed on popular control. These indices are essentially based on the presence of a variety of institutional provisions in national constitutions. Table 4.2 codifies the relevant data for seventy-five nations that appear to have passed the tests required to be termed constitutional republics. These data include their respective scores on the Popular Control Index and the Separation of Powers Index. Using these data

TABLE 4.2. *Data on Constitutional Republics (Democracies)*

Rank Country	Population (in millions)	Freedom House Score	Separation of Power Score	Size of Lower House	No. of Political Parties[a]	Size of Upper House	No. of People per Representative (in thousands)	Percent of Vote by Largest Party	Popular Control Score
1 India	966.8	3.0	5.35	545	17+	250	1,888	36	5.50
2 United States	268.0	1.0	8.00	435	2	100	616	52	7.15
3 Brazil	164.5	3.5	7.00	513	7+	81	320	21	6.35
4 Mexico	97.6	3.5	6.70	500	6+	128	155	44	5.65
5 Japan	125.7	1.5	3.25	500	6+	252	251	48	5.55
6 Germany	84.1	1.5	5.75	656	7	68	128	38	4.75
7 Philippines	76.1	2.5	6.50	204	8	24	373	63	6.35
8 United Kingdom	58.6	1.5	1.00	659	3+	1,200	90	45	4.55
9 France	58.2	1.5	4.75	577	9+	321	101	42	6.85
10 Italy	57.5	1.5	4.90	630	5+	31	91	45	6.60
11 Korea (South)	45.9	2.0	4.00	299	5		154	52	5.80
12 South Africa	42.3	1.5	5.15	400	7+	90	106	63	4.75
13 Spain	39.2	1.5	3.40	350	4+	208	112	39	6.15
14 Colombia	37.4	4.0	6.25	161	6+	102	232	55	7.45
15 Poland	36.7	1.5	4.20	460	6+	100	80	37	6.25
16 Argentina	35.8	2.5	6.00	254	5+	46	141	52	6.10
17 Canada	30.3	1.0	4.25	305	5+	104	103	41	4.45
18 Venezuela	22.4	2.5	6.85	203	5+	50	113	28	6.35
19 Taiwan	21.7	2.0	3.50	164	4		132	46	5.05
20 Romania	21.4	2.0	4.40	343	6+	143	62	30	6.70
21 Australia	18.4	1.0	5.10	146	5	76	126	64	6.10
22 Netherlands	15.7	1.0	3.60	150	4+	75	104	24	4.60
23 Chile	14.5	2.0	6.55	120	7	32	121	31	7.05
24 Greece	10.6	2.0	2.50	300	6		35	42	4.90

25 Czech Republic	10.3	1.5	3.35	200	7	81	5	34	4.65
26 Belgium	10.2	1.5	4.05	150	11	70	68	19	4.60
27 Hungary	9.9	1.5	2.80	386	8		26	54	6.35
28 Portugal	9.9	1.0	2.60	230	7		43	44	6.05
29 Sweden	8.9	1.0	1.40	349	9		26	45	5.45
30 Dominican Republic	8.2	3.0	4.35	120	3+	30	69	48	5.80
31 Austria	8.1	1.0	4.50	183	5+	63	44	38	6.10
32 Bolivia	7.7	2.0	3.60	130	10+	27	59	40	5.30
33 Switzerland	7.2	1.0	5.00	200	11+	46	36	28	6.90
34 Benin	5.9	2.0	3.85	83	9+		71	24	5.00
35 El Salvador	5.7	2.5	2.45	84	9+		67	35	4.60
36 Israel	5.5	2.0	1.85	120	15		46	28	4.55
37 Denmark	5.3	1.0	2.25	179	10		29	35	6.15
38 Finland	5.1	1.0	2.25	200	11		26	28	5.00
39 Papua New Guinea	4.5	3.0	1.75	109	13		41	22	4.40
40 Norway	4.4	1.0	2.75	165	8		27	37	4.85
41 Nicaragua	4.4	3.0	3.75	93	11		47	46	5.30
42 Lithuania	3.6	1.5	3.00	141	6+		26	50	5.95
43 New Zealand	3.6	1.0	1.35	120	6+		30	34	4.75
44 Ireland	3.6	1.0	4.30	166	7+	60	21	39	6.05
45 Costa Rica	3.5	1.5	4.60	57	2+		61	49	5.00
46 Uruguay	3.3	1.5	5.95	99	4+	30	33	36	6.75
47 Panama	2.7	2.5	3.65	72	12		37	44	6.60
48 Latvia	2.4	1.5	2.25	100	9+		24	18	4.85
49 Slovenia	1.9	1.5	2.75	90	7+		22	27	5.90
50 Botswana	1.5	2.0	1.35	44	2+	15	34	61	3.40
51 Estonia	1.5	1.5	2.55	101	7+		14	32	4.90
52 Mauritius	1.2	1.5	2.15	70	4+		16	65	3.95
53 Trinidad and Tobago	1.1	1.5	2.50	36	3+	31	31	47	3.95
54 Fiji	.8	3.5	3.65	70	6+	34	11	44	4.10
55 Guyana	.7	2.0	1.50	65	4+		11	53	3.40

(continued)

TABLE 4.2 *(continued)*

Rank	Country	Population (in millions)	Freedom House Score	Separation of Power Score	Size of Lower House	No. of Political Parties[a]	Size of Upper House	No. of People per Representative (in thousands)	Percent of Vote by Largest Party	Popular Control Score
56	Cyprus (Greek)	.5	1.0	4.00	56	5+		10	35	3.25
57	Solomon Islands	.4	1.5	1.65	47	5+		9	45	3.40
58	Luxembourg	.4	1.0	2.00	60	5		7	35	4.10
59	Bahamas	.3	1.5	2.65	40	2+	16	7	85	4.30
60	Iceland	.3	1.0	4.15	42	6		4	63	5.05
61	Barbados	.3	1.0	2.20	28	3	21	9	64	4.15
62	Belize	.2	1.0	2.10	29	3	8	8	52	4.15
63	Vanuatu	.2	2.0	2.70	50	5		4	34	4.70
64	St. Lucia	.2	1.5	2.30	17	2	11	9	65	5.05
65	Micronesia	.1	1.5	3.50	14	0[b]		9	0	7.10
66	St. Vincent	.1	1.5	1.50	21	2+		6	57	5.25
67	Grenada	.1	1.5	2.35	15	3+		6	53	4.10
68	Kiribati	.1	1.0	4.45	41	3+		2	32	6.45
69	Dominica	.1	1.0	2.15	30	3		2	57	4.75
70	Antigua and Barbuda	.1	3.5	2.30	17	2+	17	4	65	4.45
71	Marshall Islands	.1	1.0	1.90	33	0[b]		2	0	3.60
72	St. Kitts and Nevis	.04	1.5	2.95	14	4		4	64	4.60
73	Liechtenstein	.03	1.0	2.35	25	3	1	52	4.90	
74	San Marino	.03	1.0	1.15	60	6		.4	43	4.65
75	Palau	.02	1.5	4.25	16	0[b]	14	1	0	5.80

Note: This list includes data on new, emerging (unconsolidated) democracies as of January 1, 2000, and includes all countries except Andorra and Monaco that scored at least 2.0 on the Freedom House scale, which includes all liberal democracies. However, the list also includes a number of nonliberal democracies that are often not included in studies of democracies or democratization.

[a] The number of parties that won seats in the two most recent elections – a + indicates there are more parties contesting than won seats.

[b] No parties – everyone runs as an independent.

and indexes, it is possible to empirically test for the existence of popular sovereignty.

If there is such a thing as popular sovereignty in the political world we inhabit, it should be revealed by the tendency for those who write constitutions to include more and more constitutional limits through the introduction of a higher level in the separation of powers as the level of popular control increases. If there is no distinction between a sovereign and a supreme power, and thus between popular control (democracy) and popular sovereignty (a limited popular control), it will be revealed in one of two ways. There will be no significant statistical relationship between the Popular Control Index and the Separation of Powers Index; or else there will be a negative relationship, which implies something radically different from what has been developed theoretically.

The data set includes at least twice as many political systems as is usually the case in cross-national comparative studies of democracies and democratization to this date. In part this is because the small democracies are almost always ignored. It also results from an attempt by other researchers to avoid inclusion of possibly controversial cases that might undermine their respective study's credibility. In this study, however, we are focusing on principles of constitutional design rather than on democracy per se. Countries that might be considered marginally "democratic," or perhaps unconsolidated democracies, can still qualify here as constitutional republics if the minimal test described in Chapter 1 has been met. Indeed, the presence of constitutional republics, whose democratic commitments might be called into question in studies of democratization, or only securely consolidated democracies allows here for the introduction of a wider range of variance. Nation-states with a currently weak commitment to popular control should also demonstrate a weak development in institutions for limiting a majority rule that is not yet consolidated.

All but seven of the countries listed in Table 4.2 scored at least a 2.5 as of June 2000 on the widely used and respected Freedom House scale. Every country that scores 1.0 to 2.5 falls into one of their liberal democracy categories. India, which has a score of 3.0, is usually referred to as the world's largest democracy, and Colombia and Brazil are often included in studies of democracies. Including them does not seem to do violence to normal academic usage. Finally, excluding the half-dozen more controversial nations listed in Table 4.2 does not alter the empirical results, except to marginally improve the correlations in some instances.

When we look at Table 4.2, the Popular Control Index scores are listed in the right-hand column. The first thing to note is that, on an index that ranges from a theoretically possible 1.0 to 13.2, these seventy-five countries range from 3.25 to 7.45, with a mean score of 5.3. Because the use of competitive elections is the minimal definition used historically for republican government, and because on the Popular Control Index competitive parliamentary elections every four years would produce a score of about 3.0, anything below 3.0 would not be a constitutional republic in terms of the index used here. The seventy-five countries, then, tend to be clustered in the low to middle portion of the effective index range of 3.0 to 10.0. Put in standard democratic theory terms, strong democracy characterized by frequent and effective popular participation is almost everywhere avoided. Still, there is more than enough variance in the index scores to test some obvious hypotheses.

One hypothesis might be that the smaller a country's population, the higher its score would be on the Index of Popular Control. Given the honored position of classical Athens as a model of democracy, and the strictures against small republics by theorists ranging from Montesquieu to Madison, it is intuitive to suppose that smaller populations can and will organize with a higher level of popular control. In fact, regressing each country's Popular Control Index score against its population produces a virtually flat curve. Eliminating the sixteen countries with the smallest populations reduces the correlation very slightly (by .029), which indicates that smaller democracies are slightly more inclined toward popular control, but not to a statistically significant degree. The strength of popular control varies independently of population size.

Another hypothesis might be that the number of political parties is for some reason associated with a greater degree of popular control. Again, there is a virtually flat regression curve that indicates no relationship. This finding is important for several reasons. First, empirical studies of political systems tend to focus heavily on electoral and party systems, even though these two important political institutions are usually not mentioned in the formal constitution. Some argue that formal constitutional provisions are not as important as the nonconstitutional institutions that shape political behavior, and usually electoral and party systems are prominently mentioned. However, party and electoral systems turn out not to be important for predicting the level of popular control. All that matters is that there be some form of honest elections and any type of party system as long as it is competitive. Put another way, party and electoral systems are not critical constitutional variables. Second, since multiparty systems are associated with the various parliamentary forms of constitutional republicanism, the flat regression curve indicates that the Popular Control Index favors neither parliamentary nor "presidential" systems. Third, this last conclusion is in line with the argument made earlier that the traditional parliamentary-presidential dichotomy usually used in comparative analysis may not be the most useful approach.

A third hypothesis might be that the higher the level of popular control, the higher the score on the Freedom House index; or, conversely, the higher the level of popular control, the lower the Freedom House score. In the first instance, we might assume that higher levels of popular control make it more difficult for those in government to abuse the rights of the people. In the second instance, we might assume, with theorists like James Madison, that higher levels of popular control tend to produce something usually termed "tyranny of the majority." In fact, regressing the Freedom House scores against the Popular Control Index scores produces, again, a virtually flat curve.

This final conclusion, however, ignores a critical variable emphasized in the present study. Higher levels of popular control may not endanger rights because those who design constitutions with higher levels of popular control also build in a higher level of separation of powers to compensate for the dangers to rights posed by higher levels of popular control. When we control for the effects of separation of powers, the relationship between the Popular Control Index and the Freedom House index is a negative .370. That is, as the Popular Control Index scores increase, the scores on the Freedom House index for protection of rights tend to decrease when controlling for the level of separation of powers. Put another way, as the level of popular control increases, failure to increase the separation of powers results

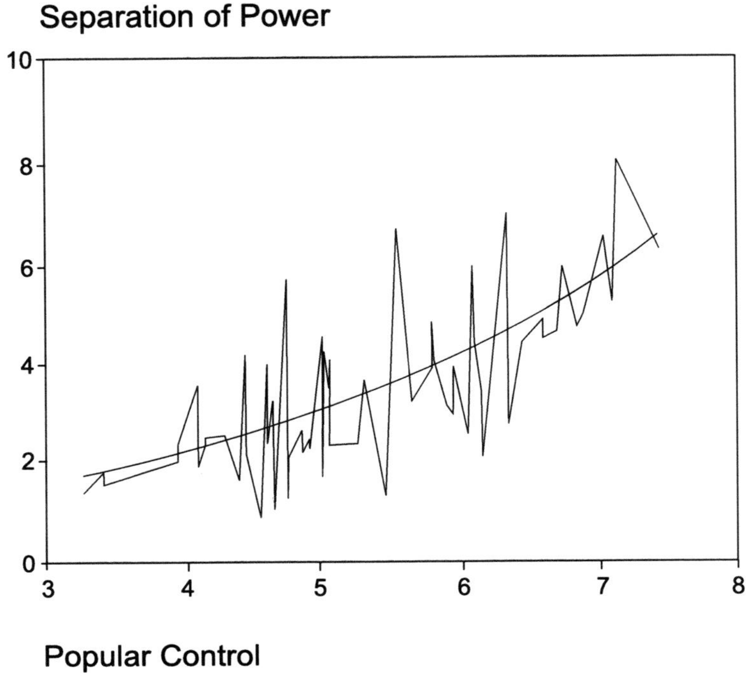

FIGURE 4.1. Popular control and separation of powers using the seventy-five-nation sample. SEPPOW QUA: $r^2 = .497$; d.f. = 72; F. = 35.59; significance = .000; bo = 1.8817; b1 = −.5009; b2 = .1508.

in a greater probability that the country will fail to qualify as a liberal democracy under the Freedom House definition.

James Madison would not be surprised by this finding, nor would he be surprised by the underlying relationship that explains it. The most important empirical relationship uncovered by this study is that the level of separation of powers increases as the level of popular control increases. The r square for the linear curve of best fit for the relationship is .487 (significant at the .001 level), and the quadratic curve of best fit has an r square of .497 (significant at the .001 level – see Figures 4.1 and 4.2.[1] It is of interest that the empirical results here that

[1] The relationship between the Popular Control and Separation of Powers indexes was also tested using multiple regression techniques. The model used a number of variables including the country's population, land area, number of parties, average constituency size, per capita income, size of lower and upper houses, and other standard variables.

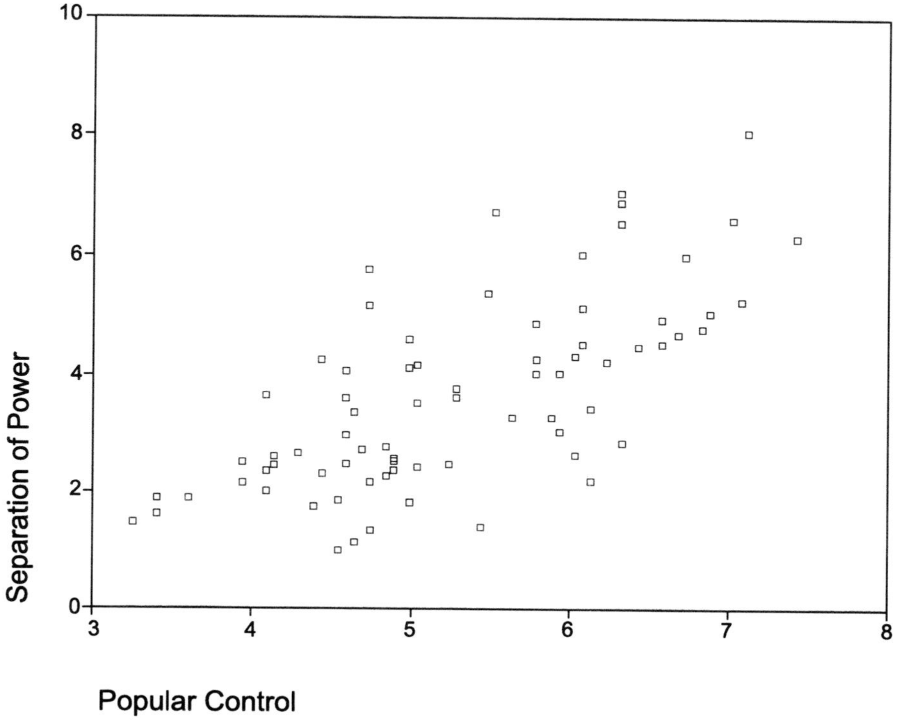

FIGURE 4.2. Bivariate relationship between popular control and the separation of powers using the seventy-five-nation sample. Pearson correlation: .698; significance (two-tailed) = .000 (correlation is significant at the 0.01 level).

use contemporary cross-national data indirectly confirm the insight first codified by Jean Bodin more than four hundred years ago. There is an important difference between power and limited power, and those who frame national constitutions tend to separate or distribute power as it increases in strength.

Although this study includes a larger than normal sample of nations, it is still possible that the combination of countries in some way affects the results. One way to test for this possibility is to use the sample of countries found in Arend Lijphart's widely read 1999 book *Patterns of*

The model explained 81 percent of the total variance, with the Popular Control Index explaining 51 percent of the total variance in the separation of powers – which is virtually identical to the strength of the relationship represented by the quadratic curve of best fit for the simple regression test.

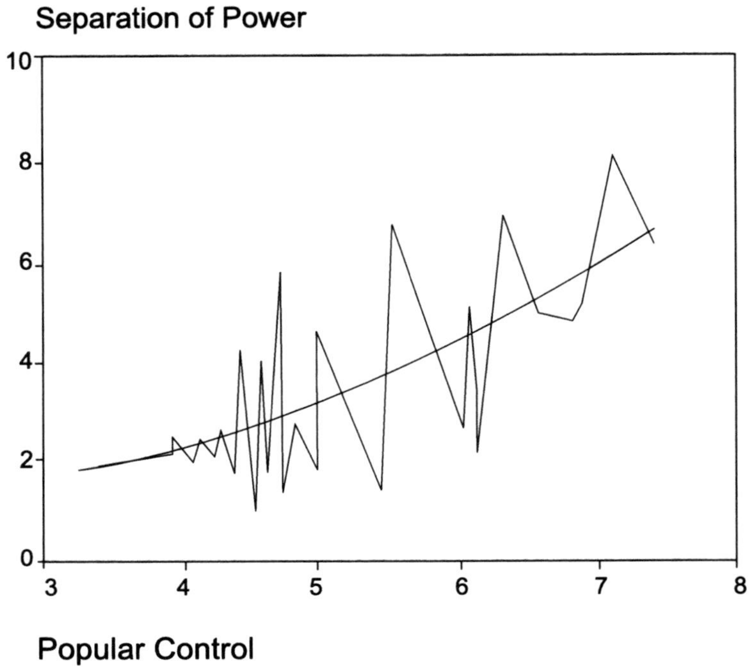

FIGURE 4.3. Quadratic curve of best fit for popular control and separation of powers using Lijphart's thirty-six-nation sample. SEPPOW QUA: $r^2 = .444$; d.f. = 33; F. = 13.16; significance = .000; bo = 1.9637; b1 = −.5343; b2 = .1543.

Democracy.[2] Testing the relationship between the two indexes using his thirty-six countries, which also uses several countries not found in the seventy-five-nation sample used here, produces an r square of .436 for the linear curve of best fit, and an r square of .444 for the cubic curve of best fit with the same level of significance. The regression curve using his sample shows an almost identical set of curves, with the quadratic curve indicating a gradual increase in separation of powers as popular control increases (see Figures 4.3 and 4.4).

If instead of a regression curve we use a simple bivariate Pearson correlation, the seventy-five-country sample used here produces a .668 correlation, and Lijphart's thirty-six-country sample results in a .660

[2] Arend Lijphart, *Patterns of Democracy: Government Forms and Performance in Thirty-Six Countries* (New Haven: Yale University Press, 1999).

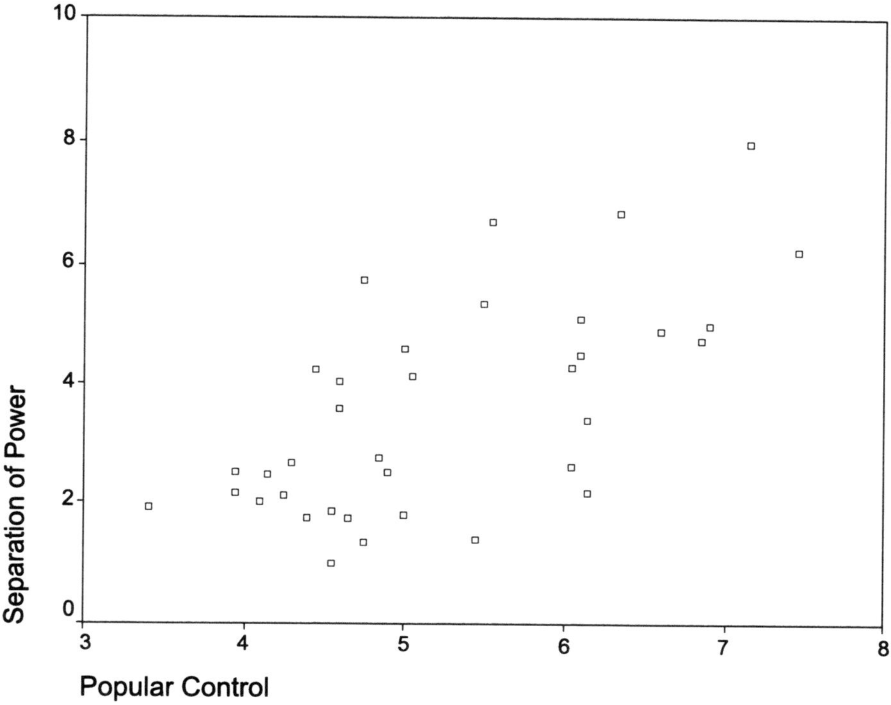

FIGURE 4.4. Bivariate relationship between popular control and separation of powers using Lijphart's thirty-six-nation sample. Pearson correlation: .660; significance (two-tailed) = .000 (correlation is significant at the 0.01 level).

correlation. The effects of sample size and content were tested further by randomly selecting samples of thirty-six, fifty, and sixty countries from the seventy-five-nation data base for analysis. The strong correlation between the Popular Control Index and the Separation of Powers Index holds and is almost identical, regardless of the specific cross-national sample used. Finally, an analysis of the residuals in the seventy-five-nation study confirms that the regression analysis meets the tests for linearity, normality, and constant variance that are required to establish the statistical independence of the two indexes.

What we have uncovered empirically is the advantage of popular sovereignty versus simple popular control apparently perceived by framers of constitutions at different times and in many different countries around the world. It does make a difference that we seek a sovereign rather than simply a supreme power, and this is as true of popular control as other forms of supreme power. The empirical evidence supports the efficacy of the long-standing theoretical usage of sovereignty, as well as the almost universal penchant of those who design constitutions to seek something other than simply more democracy. Thus, if popular sovereignty is the sine qua non of constitutionalism, and separation of powers converts popular control into popular sovereignty, separation of powers is also at the heart of constitutional design.

Some Further Considerations

Although it has been argued here that de facto popular sovereignty underlies all political systems centered around popularly elected representatives, popular sovereignty is often not part of the theory used to explain or justify what are unquestionably constitutional republics. For example, in the United Kingdom a doctrine of popular sovereignty was explicitly rejected during the 1688 convention that produced the Glorious Revolution, and for the past three centuries the concept of "parliamentary sovereignty" has been official constitutional doctrine. Elsewhere, statist assumptions sometimes hold sway. The reification of the state has resulted in the notion of the state as sovereign, and many would argue that this is the proper view of sovereignty. Political theorists holding to a statist perspective would probably argue also that the limits identified here are not designed to limit popular sovereignty but to limit "state sovereignty."

Bodin suggested that a realistic analysis requires us to push our analysis through the chain of power until we come to the entity that first grants power and that has ultimate control over the chain of power holders and power grantors. According to Bodin's method, if the people have the ability to elect and remove those who are at the top of the chain of power, they are in fact sovereign regardless of the legal or constitutional doctrine used to explain and justify the operation of the political system. Suppose, on the other hand, we for some reason prefer another theory that assigns the word "sovereign" to parliament or to the state. The theory under development here does not require agreement on which entity should be termed "sovereign" legally, which is why the phrase de facto popular sovereignty has been used. The fact remains that constitutional republics worthy of the name, regardless of who or what is called sovereign, markedly tend toward de facto popular sovereignty.

The second statist argument is more interesting, in part because it is true. Constitutional republics do develop constitutional limits and the separation of powers to protect the people against governmental tyranny, but this is only part of the picture. James Madison, in an attempt to develop a comprehensive theory of tyranny, distinguished between majority tyranny and governmental tyranny. In this view, the dangers of creating a sovereign became doubled when the sovereign was the people itself. He dealt with majority tyranny in *Federalist Papers* 10, where he famously developed the theory of the extended republic. In this theory, he argued that small republics were prone to majority tyranny because there was a high probability that a majority faction existed from a widely held local interest, and it was easy for this already existing majority to organize itself for action because distance was not a factor. His solution was twofold. Representation, he argued, tended to elevate cooler-headed, wiser, and more statesman-like people to office. Such representatives could resist passionate majorities asking for policies that were inimical to both minority interests and the permanent and aggregate interests of the whole. Aside from noting that "statesmen will not always be at the helm," he also expressed doubts that representatives seeking reelection would be up to the task without ancillary precautions. If a republic were large enough, it would encompass enough diversity of interests such that standing or natural majorities would tend not to exist, and the distances associated with a large republic would make it difficult for a passionate majority both to discover its strength and to organize for action. Representation helps, but the extended republic is the major solution to the problem of majority tyranny. Left unsaid was what we should do when the republic was not extensive in size, as is the case with most constitutional republics today.

In *Federalist Papers* 51, Madison summarized the solution to governmental tyranny as involving the division of governmental power into a number of competing institutions such that ambition would be made to counteract ambition. The total package of separated powers, which then also allowed for the possibility of multiple checks and the three great "balances" of bicameralism, different modes of election, and different terms of office, together prevented governmental tyranny. Often unremarked in analyses of the Madisonian model is that, in the absence of an extended republic, the separation of powers also comprised the primary ancillary means for preventing majority tyranny. That is, a government that could not easily organize to tyrannize over the people was likewise constrained from easily translating popular majorities into tyrannical policies no matter how passionate the majority was. James Madison works out this connection between a separation of powers and both governmental and majority tyranny in *Federalist Papers* 63. Although his discussion is generally about the U.S. Senate, it is here that he points out the combined consequences of bicameralism, different modes of election, and different terms of office – the three great "balances" – that a separation of powers makes possible.

It is helpful to parse out how the theory worked. Assume the existence of a passionate majority bent on gaining policies contrary to the permanent and aggregate interests of the people. Such majorities, in pursuing apparent short-term interests, would in fact be operating against their long-term interests. In order to gain the policies they think they want, but in fact do not, the majority would need to capture more than a single representative body. In order to capture the government for its purposes, the majority would need to first capture a majority in the House of Representatives. Even if it was successful on the first try (an unlikely occurrence), the majority could, at best, capture only one-third of the Senate. This would require that it wait two more years for the Senate, as well as for the president. That still left the Supreme Court with its life tenure, but the impeachment process was available at the cost of more time. Madison did not seem to see the Supreme Court as much of an obstacle to popular will, which our summary of the behavior of supreme courts around the world since World War II tends to confirm. Still, a majority must wait at least four years, and probably longer, to get its way.

During the four years or longer it takes the majority to get its way, the passion in the majority must be maintained, and Madison expected that such enforced waiting would cause the passion in the majority to burn out, so that the people would come to understand its true interests. The system of delay requires several key assumptions. The first is that given enough time the people can distinguish policies that are in the permanent and aggregate interests from those that are not. This requires the deeper assumption that once the distinction is made, the people will tend to choose that which is in their permanent and aggregate interests. This in turn requires the deepest assumption of popular sovereignty, that the people are "virtuous"; that is, that they possess the characteristics necessary for self-government. Any popular political system based on majority rule must make this deep assumption or else it makes no sense to establish popular government in the first place. A prime characteristic for republican government is that the people be able and willing to pursue the common good, which was termed during the seventeenth and eighteenth centuries "republican virtue."

The institutions of delay introduced by the separation of powers in the United States had specific American twists to them. First of all, as originally designed, each separated function had a different constituency, different mode of election, and different term of office (including staggered elections for the Senate as part of these last two characteristics). The resulting institutional structure required that the majority first elect a majority of the House from many small districts, each of which had specific, local interests that required appealing to a wide range of interests overall. The Senate was elected by the state legislatures, which meant the national electoral majority first had to capture a majority in the House and Senate in a majority of the states. Federalism, in this and in other ways, was an integral part of the separation of powers. Finally, capturing the Supreme Court required capturing both the presidency and a majority of the U.S. Senate. At this point the different terms of office came into play.

The separation of powers in the United States was designed to slow down significantly the capture of government by a majority. One does not have to duplicate or even approximate this institutional design to achieve the same effect. A wide array of possible institutional arrangements can and have been developed to introduce the complexity of separation of powers. Even if such institutional complexity is introduced and justified in terms of preventing governmental tyranny, it also tends to control the effects of passionate majorities. Thus has the separation of powers been introduced in a variety of institutional guises around the world. Larger constitutional republics can use the effects of geographical size to help convert popular control into popular sovereignty in addition to a separation of powers and the institutions of delay thereby created. Smaller constitutional republics, on the other hand, are left entirely with the creation of institutional complexity for handling both majority and governmental tyranny. There is no way to introduce any form of institutional complexity without first generating some separation of powers, which is why "separation of powers" is used to identify the entire complex of institutions used to convert popular control into popular sovereignty.

An interesting consideration is that framers of constitutions have not needed to be taught to do so, or convinced to do so. The paradox of sovereignty, and thus of popular sovereignty, seems to be implicitly understood by careful framers of national constitutions. Thus, this is not a normative recommendation to constitution framers. In constitutional republics some institutional form of the separation of powers just tends to happen. Much like the "cube root rule," where constitutional framers tend to reach a size for the lower house or unicameral legislature that approximates the cube root of the population without being taught the principle, so too separation of powers just tends to emerge. Despite a hiatus in understanding sovereignty and the paradox of sovereignty among academics in recent years, the logic of constitutional design under conditions of de facto popular sovereignty seems to result in similar results using a wide variety of institutional designs.

The discussion thus far has illustrated the possibility of studying constitutionalism empirically as well as analytically and normatively. The discussion thus far has also emphasized the cumulative effect of many constitutional provisions. We will now turn to study empirically an important aspect of popular sovereignty in order to emphasize the interlocking effects of institutions in a constitution – the amendment process.

5

Analyzing the Interaction between Popular Control and the Separation of Powers in the Amendment Process

Why the Amendment Process Is Important in Constitutional Design

We have seen that framers of constitutional republics tend to increase the level of separation of powers as they increase the level of popular control. This principle of constitutional design seems to emerge from some logic inherent in the design process rather than from designers following explicit, articulated normative rules. It was suggested in Chapter 2 that the inherent logic of constitutional design results from humans, on the one hand, seeking to create a supreme power that allows an expanded pursuit of self-preservation, liberty, sociability, and beneficial innovation and, on the other hand, seeking to prevent that supreme power from itself threatening these pursued values. As a secondary principle, framers of constitutions tend to balance the consequences of constituency size with the consequences of legislative size to produce a primary legislature whose size approximates the cube root of the population.

Put another way, under conditions of popular control the elective legislatures that are the core of a constitutional republic should have constituencies that as are as small as possible; but also, under

Much of this chapter was earlier published as Donald S. Lutz, "Toward a Theory of Constitutional Amendment," *American Political Science Review* 88 (June 1994): 355–370. Research for this article was supported by a grant from the Earhart Foundation of Ann Arbor, Michigan. Assistance in data analysis was provided by Patricia Gail McVey of the University of Texas School of Public Health.

conditions of popular control, the legislatures should not be so large as to fall under the control of legislative elites. As the population of a constitutional republic grows to a size where the attempt to achieve this balance results in both a constituency size and legislative size too large for preventing government itself from threatening popular control, a second house is usually added to the legislature and gradually strengthened as the population grows larger. This division of power simultaneously helps to control governmental tyranny as it helps to control the effects of public opinion that is increasingly mass-based and subject to temporary passions unchecked by the familiarity and identity with each other that citizens enjoy in small constituencies. The tendency of second branches of the legislature to emerge as population size increases in constitutional republics thus also results from the logic inherent in constitutional design where popular control and the separation of powers interact in pursuit of the benefits of establishing a supreme power.

Another principle tends to emerge with the creation of a constitutional amendment process. There is a straightforward logic that says if a constitution rests on popular consent, and thus on popular control, amending the document should return to the level of popular control that created it. Although constitutions are subject to replacement, replacement is much less frequent than amendment. Analyzing amendment procedures allows us to do several useful things at the same time.

First, it is one of the measures for the relative strength of popular control as the Index of Popular Control indicates. Amending a constitution through a popular referendum on a proposal made through popular initiative, for example, is very direct popular control. An amendment process that combines a popular referendum with a majority in the legislature that proposes the amendment is also quite direct, although somewhat weaker. Amendment by a convention popularly elected only for that purpose would be somewhat weaker still. Other possible amendment procedures can be arrayed along a scale that indicates the strength of popular control relative to these examples.

Second, the amendment process is also a measure of the strength of the separation of powers. Notice how each weakening in popular control of the amendment process involves the separation of functions (usually between the function of proposing and the function of adopting), so that another institution is included in the process. Separating functions with a sharing in the overall power of amendment is the definition of separation of powers. As the amendment process grows more complex and difficult, the separation of powers has invariably been increased. Difficulty of amendment thus becomes a rough surrogate for the level in separation of powers.

Third, analyzing the amendment process allows us to examine a fundamental principle of constitutional design that has been only implicit in the discussion thus far. This principle is that constitutional outcomes result from the interaction of many institutions embedded in a constitution. Analyzing a single institution in isolation does not tell us very much about constitutional design, whereas analyzing institutional interaction is at the very core of constitutional design.

Finally, a careful, comparative look at the amendment process reemphasizes the need to blend the three parts of a comprehensive theoretical analysis – normative, analytic, and empirical. We can assume rational actors in an analysis, but in the end the predictions of such an analysis must be matched with actual empirical outcomes. It does little good if an analysis predicts minimal winning coalitions if minimal winning coalitions almost never occur empirically in functioning legislatures.[1] By the same token, failure to consider the normative goals that are in competition leaves formal and empirical analyses unanchored for purposes of constitutional choice. Constitutionalism rests on goals, hopes, and values that can be thwarted or undermined by institutional design, especially since these goals, hopes, and values often require that we move beyond the mere "efficiency" of an institution to consider how the total constitutional package invariably requires that we balance and trade off between goals and values that inherently conflict. This was one of the points discussed at length in Chapter 1. The cultural, power, and justice elements contained in a constitution struggle with each other, and choosing between their relative strengths requires a set of normative choices that cannot be resolved analytically

[1] That minimal winning coalitions are infrequent occurrences in American legislatures is well known to students of Congress and state legislatures. For explicit tests of the hypothesis, see the articles by Donald Lutz and Richard Murray: "Redistricting in American States: A Test of the Minimal Winning Coalition Hypothesis," *American Journal of Political Science* 18 (May 1974): 233–255, and "Issues and Coalition Size in the Texas Legislature: A Further Test of Riker's Theory," *Western Political Quarterly* 28, no. 2 (June 1975): 269–315.

or empirically. Instead, we must be guided by philosophical analysis of the sort exemplified by our discussions of Montesquieu, Bodin, Hobbes, and Madison. Also, as mentioned earlier and discussed at length in the next chapter, matching the constitution to the people is a paramount consideration.

The cross-national examination engaged in here will use a somewhat different set of constitutional republics than was used in earlier chapters. This results from the availability of reliable data on amendments in some countries but not in others. Another departure from earlier chapters will be to begin with an analysis of the amendment process in American states. This departure permits the empirical derivation of an index to be used in the cross-national analysis.

A constitution may be modified by means of a formal amendment process, periodic replacement of the entire document, judicial interpretation, and legislative revision. What difference does it make whether we use one method rather than another? What is the relationship between these four methods? What do we learn about the constitutional system and its underlying political theory by the pattern of choice among these alternatives? These are some of the questions to be addressed.

Although it is true that a constitution is often used as ideological window dressing and that even in places where constitutions are taken very seriously these documents fail to describe the full reality of an operating political system, few political systems, whether dictatorial or democratic, fail to reflect major political change in their respective constitutions. Constitutions may not describe the full reality of a political system, but when carefully read, they are windows into that underlying reality.

This chapter attempts to use a critical, if often overlooked, constitutional device – the amendment process – as a window into both the reality of political systems and the political theory or theories of constitutionalism underlying them. A good deal has been written about the logic of constitutional choice using rational-actor models, but little has been written about the empirical patterns that result from constitutional choice. The classic example of the first approach is the work of James Buchanan and Gordon Tulloch. The second approach is exemplified by the work of Douglas W. Rae; but see also Bernard Grofman,

Adam Przeworski, and Matthew S. Shugart and John M. Carey.[2] I shall use the latter method and attempt to be systematic, comparative, and, to the extent possible, empirical. I begin with a brief overview of the theoretical assumptions that underlay the formal amendment process when it was invented, identify a number of theoretical propositions concerning the amendment process, and then look for patterns in the use of the amendment process in order to create empirical standards upon which to erect a theory of constitutional amendment for those engaged in constitutional design.

The Original Premises Underlying the Amendment Process

The modern written constitution, first developed in English-speaking North America, was grounded in a doctrine of popular sovereignty.[3] Even though many in Britain were skeptical at best, Americans regarded popular sovereignty not as an experimental idea but rather as one that stood at the very heart of their shared political consensus.[4] American political writing had used the language of popular sovereignty before Locke's *Second Treatise* was published, and the early state constitutions of the 1770s contained clear and firm statements that these documents rested upon popular consent. Although the theory of popular sovereignty was well understood in America by 1776, the institutional implications of this innovative doctrine had to be worked out in constitutions adopted over the next decade. Gradually, it was realized that a doctrine of popular sovereignty required that

[2] James Buchanan and Gordon Tulloch, *The Calculus of Consent* (Ann Arbor: University of Michigan Press, 1965); Douglas W. Rae, *The Political Consequences of Electoral Laws* (New Haven: Yale University Press, 1967); Bernard Grofman, *Electoral Laws and Their Political Consequences* (New York: Agathon, 1986); Adam Przeworski, *Democracy and the Market: Political and Economic Reform in Eastern Europe and Latin America* (Cambridge: Cambridge University Press, 1991); Matthew S. Shugart and John M. Carey, *Presidents and Assemblies: Design and Electoral Dynamics* (Cambridge: Cambridge University Press, 1992).

[3] See Willi Paul Adams, *The First American Constitutions* (Chapel Hill: University of North Carolina Press, 1980); Donald S. Lutz, *Popular Consent and Popular Control: Whig Political Theory in the Early State Constitutions* (Baton Rouge: Louisiana State University Press, 1980); and Edmund S. Morgan, *Inventing the People: The Rise of Popular Sovereignty in England and America* (New York: Norton, 1988).

[4] See Donald S. Lutz, *The Origins of American Constitutionalism* (Baton Rouge: Louisiana State University Press, 1988), especially chap. 7.

constitutions be written by a popularly selected convention, rather than the legislature, and then ratified through a process that elicited popular consent – ideally, in a referendum. This double implication was established in the process used to frame and adopt the 1780 Massachusetts and 1784 New Hampshire constitutions, although the referendum portion of the process did not become standard until the nineteenth century.

Americans moved quickly to the conclusion that if a constitution rested on popular consent, then the people could also replace it with a new one. John Locke had argued that the people could replace government but only when those entrusted with the powers of government had first disqualified themselves by endangering the happiness of the community to such a degree that civil society could be said to have reverted to a state of nature. Americans went well beyond Locke by institutionalizing the power to change the constitution and civil society whenever they wanted. It is of considerable importance that this included not only replacing the constitution but also formally amending it.

The first new state constitution in 1776, that of New Jersey, contained an implicit notion of amendment, but the 1776 Pennsylvania document contained the first explicit amendment process – one that used a convention process and bypassed the legislature.[5] By 1780 almost half the states had an amendment procedure, and the principle that the fundamental law could be altered piecemeal by popular will was firmly in place.

In addition to popular sovereignty, the amendment process was based on three other premises central to the American consensus in the 1770s: an imperfect but educable human nature, the efficacy of a deliberative process, and the distinction between normal legislation and constitutional matters. The first premise, identified and clearly explicated by Vincent Ostrom,[6] held that humans are fallible but capable

[5] While this was the first explicit amendment process in a state constitution, a formal amendment process was first used in William Penn's 1678 *Frame of Government*, which may explain why Pennsylvania was the first state to adopt one. See John R. Vile, *The Constitutional Amending Process in American Political Thought* (New York: Praeger, 1992), pp. 11–12.

[6] Vincent Ostrom, *The Political Theory of the Compound Republic*, 2nd ed. (Lincoln: University of Nebraska Press, 1987).

of learning through experience. Americans had long considered each governmental institution and practice to be in the nature of an experiment. Because fallibility was part of human nature, provision had to be made for altering institutions after experience revealed their flaws and unintended consequences. Originally, therefore, the amendment process was predicated not only on the need to adapt to changing circumstances but also on the need to compensate for the limits of human understanding and virtue. In a sense, the entire idea of a constitution rests on an assumption of human fallibility, since, if humans were angels, there would be no need to erect, direct, and limit government through a constitution.

A belief in the efficacy of a deliberative process was also a part of the general American constitutional perspective. A constitution was viewed as a means not merely to make collective decisions in the most efficient way possible but to make the *best possible* decisions *in pursuit of the common good* under a condition of *popular sovereignty.* The common good is a more difficult standard to approximate than the good of one class or part of the population, and the condition of popular sovereignty, even if operationalized as a system of representation, requires the involvement of many more people than forms of government based on other principles. This in turn requires a slow, deliberative process for any political decision, and the more important the decision, the more deliberative the process should be. Constitutional matters were considered more important in 1787 America than normal legislation, which led to a more highly deliberative process distinguishing constitutional from normal legislative matters. The codification of the distinction in constitutional articles of ratification and amendment resulted in American constitutions being viewed as higher law that should limit and direct the content of normal legislation.

Popular sovereignty implies that all constitutional matters should be based upon some form of popular consent, which in turn implies a formal, public process. Human fallibility implies the need for some method of altering or revising the constitution. A distinction between normal and constitutional matters requires a distinctive, highly deliberative process and thus implies the need for an amendment procedure more difficult than that used for normal legislation.

Together these premises require that the procedure be neither too easy nor too difficult. A process that is too easy, not providing enough distinction between constitutional matters and normal legislation, thereby violates the assumption of the need for a high level of deliberation and debases popular sovereignty, whereas one that is too difficult, interfering with the needed rectification of mistakes, thereby violates the assumption of human fallibility and prevents the effective utilization of popular sovereignty.

The literature on constitutions at one time made a distinction between major and minor constitutional alterations by calling the former "revisions" and the latter "amendments." As Albert L. Sturm points out, the distinction turned out in practice to be conceptually slippery, impossible to operationalize, and therefore generally useless.[7] Because "revision" is used in the literature to mean several different things, I shall use "amendment" as a description of the *formal* process developed by the Americans and "alteration" to describe processes that instead use the legislature or judiciary. Unless we maintain the distinction between formal amendment and other means of constitutional modification, we will lose the ability to distinguish between competing forms of constitutional modification, and we will lose the ability to distinguish competing constitutional theories.

The innovation of an amendment process, like the innovation of a written constitution, has diffused throughout the world to the point where less than 4 percent of all national constitutions lack a provision for a formal amending process.[8] However, the diffusion of written constitutions and the amendment idea do not necessarily indicate widespread acceptance of the principles that underlie the American innovation. In most countries with a written constitution, popular sovereignty and the use of a constitution as a higher law are not operative political principles. Any comparative study of the amendment process must first distinguish true constitutional systems from those that use a constitution as window dressing and then recognize that among the former there are variations in the amendment process that rest on assumptions at odds with those in the American version. Indeed, my chief concern is the efficiency with which study of the amending process reveals such theoretical differences.

[7] Albert L. Sturm, *Thirty Years of State Constitution-Making: 1938–1968* (New York: National Municipal League, 1970).

[8] Henc van Maarseveen and Ger van der Tang, *Written Constitutions: A Computerized Comparative Study* (Dobbs Ferry, N.Y.: Oceana, 1978), p. 80.

At the same time, a comparative study of amendment processes allows us to delve more deeply into the theory of constitutional amendments as a principle of constitutional design. For example, we might ask the question, what difference does it make if constitutions are formally amended through a political process that does not effectively distinguish constitutional matters from normal legislation? Why might we still want to draw a distinction between formal amendment and alteration by normal politics as carefully and strongly as possible? One important answer to the question is that the three prominent methods of constitutional modification other than complete replacement – formal amendment, legislative revision, and judicial interpretation – reflect declining degrees of commitment to popular sovereignty, and the level of commitment to popular sovereignty may be a key attitude for defining the nature of the political system.

Basic Assumptions and Propositions

Every theory has to begin with a number of assumptions. We have seen how the original American version rested on the premises of popular sovereignty, an imperfect but educable human nature, the efficacy of a highly deliberative decision-making process, and the distinction between normal and constitutional law. Although these help define the working assumptions of one theory of amendments (albeit the original one), they do not provide a complete basis for describing either the American theory or a general theory of amendment. I turn now to developing a theory that includes the American version but also provides the basis for analyzing any version of constitutional amendment. The intent of the analysis is to provide guidelines for constitutional design in any context – guidelines that will allow framers to link the design of a formal amendment process securely to desired outcomes.

My first and second working assumptions have to do with the expected change that is faced by every political system and with the nature of a constitution, respectively.

> ASSUMPTION 1. Every political system needs to be modified over time as a result of some combination of (1) changes in the environment within which the political system operates (including economics, technology, foreign relations, demographics, etc.); (2) changes in the value system distributed across the population; (3) unwanted

or unexpected institutional effects; and (4) the cumulative effect of decisions made by the legislature, executive, and judiciary.

ASSUMPTION 2. In political systems that are constitutional, in which constitutions are taken seriously as limiting government and legitimating the decision-making process they describe, important modifications in the operation of the political system need to be reflected in the constitution.

If these two assumptions are used as premises in a deductive process, they imply a conclusion that stands as a further assumption.

ASSUMPTION 3. All constitutions require regular, periodic modification, whether through amendment, judicial or legislative alteration, or replacement.

"Alteration" (as noted earlier) refers to changes in a constitution through judicial interpretation or legislative action. However, I am initially more concerned with the use of a formal amendment process. Amendment rate, a key concept, refers to the average number of formal amendments passed per year since the constitution came into effect. Many scholars criticize constitutions that are much amended. However, constitutionalism and the logic of popular sovereignty are based on more than simplicity and tidiness. Any people who believe in constitutionalism will amend their constitution when needed, as opposed to using extraconstitutional means. Thus, a moderate amendment rate will indicate that the people living under it take their constitution seriously. The older a constitution is, under conditions of popular sovereignty, the more successful it has been, but also the larger the number of amendments it will have. However, it is the *rate* of amendment that is important in this regard, not the total number of amendments.

A successful constitutional system would seem to be defined by a constitution of considerable age that has a total number of amendments that, when divided by the constitution's age in years, represents a moderate amendment rate – one that is to be expected in the face of inevitable change. A less-than-successful constitutional system will have a high rate of constitutional *replacement*.

This raises the question of what constitutes a "moderate" rate of amendment. Because I hope to illuminate the question empirically, rather than in an a priori manner, I must initially use a symbolic stand-in for "moderate rate of amendment." Since a moderate rate is likely to be a range of rates, rather than a single one, the symbol will define boundaries such that any document with an amendment rate above or below its limits will have an increasing probability of being replaced or an increasing probability that some extraconstitutional means of constitutional evolution is being used. I shall use <#> to represent this moderate range of amendment rates symbolically.

The first proposition is frequently found in the literature, but it has never been systematically verified, or its effects measured.

> PROPOSITION 1. The longer a constitution is (the more words it has), the higher its amendment rate, and the shorter the constitution, the lower its amendment rate.

Commentators frequently note that the more provisions a constitution has, the more targets there are for amendment and the more likely that it will be targeted because it deals with too many details that are subject to change. While this seems intuitively correct, the data that are used usually raise the question, Which comes first, the high amendment rate or the long constitution? This is because a constitution's length is usually given as of a particular year, rather than in terms of its original length. Is a constitution long because it had a high amendment rate, or did it have a high amendment rate because it was long to begin with?

My second proposition is also a common one in the literature, although it too has never been systematically tested before.

> PROPOSITION 2. The more difficult the amendment process, the lower the amendment rate, and the easier the amendment process, the higher the amendment rate.

As obvious as this proposition is, it cannot be tested until one shifts from the number of amendments in a constitution to its amendment rate and until one develops an index for measuring the degree of difficulty associated with an amendment process. I shall present such an index as part of what is needed to develop a way of predicting the likely consequences of using one amendment process versus another.

The literature on American state constitutions generally argues that these documents are much longer than the national constitution because they must deal with more governmental functions. For example, if a constitution deals with matters like education, criminal law, local government, and finances, it is bound to be more detailed and longer and thus have a higher amendment rate than one that does not address these matters. From this, I generalize to the following proposition.

> PROPOSITION 3. The more governmental functions dealt with in a constitution, the longer it will be and the higher its rate of amendment will be.

Constitutions are usually replaced for one of three reasons: a regime change may leave the values, institutions, or implications of the old constitution seriously at odds with those preferred by the people now in charge; the constitution may fail to keep up with the times; the old constitution may have changed so many times that it is no longer clear what lies under the encrustations, so that clarity demands a new beginning. A moderate amendment rate is an antidote to all three.

> PROPOSITION 4. The further the amendment rate is from the mean of <#>, either higher or lower, the greater the probability that the entire constitution will be replaced and thus the shorter its duration. Conversely, the closer an amendment rate is to the mean of <#>, the lower the probability that the entire constitution will be replaced and thus the longer its duration.

A low rate of amendment in the face of needed change may lead to the development of some extraconstitutional means of revision – most likely, judicial interpretation – to supplement the formal amendment process. I can now, on the basis of earlier discussion, generate several propositions that will prove useful toward the end of my discussion on the implications of the major competing forms of formal constitutional amendment.

> PROPOSITION 5. A low amendment rate associated with a long average constitutional duration strongly implies the use of some alternative means of revision to supplement the formal amendment process.

> PROPOSITION 6. In the absence of a high rate of constitutional replacement, the lower the rate of formal amendment, the more likely the process of revision is dominated by a judicial body.

> PROPOSITION 7. The higher the formal amendment rate, the less likely that the constitution is being viewed as a higher law, the less likely that a distinction is being drawn between constitutional

matters and normal legislation, the more likely that the document is being viewed as a code, and the more likely that the formal amendment process is dominated by the legislature.

PROPOSITION 8. The more important the role of the judiciary in constitutional revision, the less likely the judiciary is to use theories of strict construction.

I shall test propositions 1–4 using data from the American state constitutions and then seek further verification by examining the amendment process in nations where constitutionalism is taken seriously and does not serve merely as window dressing. The American state documents are examined first because data on them are readily available and easily compatible, because the similarities in their amendment process reduce the number of variables that must be taken into account, and because together they constitute a significant percentage of human experience with serious constitutionalism.

Amendment Patterns in American State Constitutions, 1776–1991

Albert L. Sturm summarizes the literature as seeing state constitutions burdened with the effects of continuous expansion in state functions and responsibilities and the consequent growth of governmental machinery; the primary responsibility for responding to the increasing pressure of major problems associated with rapid urbanization, technological development, population growth and mobility, economic change and development, the fair interests for constitutional status; and continuing popular distrust of the state legislature, based on past abuses, which results in detailed restrictions on governmental activity.[9] All of these factors contribute to the length of state constitutions, and it is argued that not only do these pressures lead to many amendments – and thus to greater length – but that greater length itself leads to the accelerated need for amendment simply by providing so many targets for change. Thus, length becomes a surrogate measure for all of these other pressures to amend and is a key variable.

Table 5.1 shows basic data for duration, length, and amendments for the U.S. Constitution and the constitutions of the fifty states. It also

[9] Sturm, *Thirty Years of State Constitution-Making.*

TABLE 5.1. *Basic Data on American Constitutions, 1991*

State	Number of Constitutions	Average Duration	Current Constitution Since	Years in Effect	Original Length in Words	Times Amended	Amendment Rate
Alabama	6	29	1901	90	65,400	726	8.07
Alaska	1	35	1959	32	11,800	22	.69
Arizona	1	80	1912	79	28,900	109	1.38
Arkansas	5	31	1874	117	24,100	76	.65
California	2	72	1879	112	21,400	471	4.21
Colorado	1	115	1876	115	22,000	115	1.00
Connecticut	4	54	1965	26	8,800	25	.96
Delaware	3	72	1897	94	19,000	119	1.27
Florida	6	25	1969	22	18,900	53	2.41
Georgia	10	21	1983	8	26,000	24	3.00
Hawaii	1	41	1959	32	16,800	82	2.56
Idaho	1	102	1890	101	18,800	107	1.06
Illinois	4	43	1971	20	12,900	6	.30
Indiana	2	88	1851	140	9,100	38	.27
Iowa	2	73	1857	134	9,700	48	.36
Kansas	1	132	1861	130	10,200	87	.67
Kentucky	4	50	1891	100	21,800	29	.29
Louisiana	11	16	1975	16	47,300	27	1.69
Maine	1	172	1820	171	10,100	157	.92
Maryland	4	54	1867	124	25,200	200	1.61
Massachusetts	1	211	1780	211	11,600	116	.55
Michigan	4	39	1964	27	18,600	16	.59
Minnesota	1	134	1858	133	8,500	112	.84
Mississippi	4	44	1890	101	20,100	102	1.01
Missouri	4	43	1945	46	39,300	74	1.61
Montana	2	51	1973	18	11,600	15	.83
Nebraska	2	63	1875	116	16,100	189	1.63

Nevada	1	127	1864	127	14,100	108	.85
New Hampshire	2	108	1784	207	8,000	142	.69
New Jersey	3	72	1948	43	16,400	39	.91
New Mexico	1	79	1912	79	22,000	120	1.52
New York	4	54	1895	96	26,800	207	2.16
North Carolina	3	72	1971	20	10,300	27	1.35
North Dakota	1	102	1889	102	18,100	125	1.23
Ohio	2	95	1851	140	14,200	145	1.04
Oklahoma	1	84	1907	84	58,200	133	1.58
Oregon	1	132	1859	132	11,200	188	1.42
Pennsylvania	5	43	1968	23	20,800	19	.83
Rhode Island	2	108	1843	148	7,400	53	.36
South Carolina	7	31	1896	95	21,900	463	4.87
South Dakota	1	102	1889	102	21,300	97	.95
Tennessee	3	65	1870	121	11,100	32	.26
Texas	5	29	1876	115	28,600	326	2.83
Utah	1	95	1896	95	13,900	77	.81
Vermont	3	71	1793	198	5,200	50	.25
Virginia	6	36	1971	20	18,100	20	1.00
Washington	1	102	1889	102	16,300	86	.84
West Virginia	2	64	1872	119	15,900	62	.52
Wisconsin	1	143	1848	143	11,400	124	.87
Wyoming	1	101	1890	101	20,800	57	.56
MEAN	2.9	77	1896	95	19,300	117	1.23
U.S. Constitution		202	1789	202	4,300	26	.13

Sources: The data in this appendix are based on James Q. Dealey, *Growth of American State Constitutions* (New York: Da Capo, 1972); Walter F. Dodd, *The Revision and Amendment of State Constitutions*, 2nd ed. (New York: Da Capo, 1970); Daniel J. Elazar, *American Federalism: A View from the States*, 2nd ed. (New York: Thomas Y. Crowell, 1972); Fletcher M. Green, *Constitutional Development in the South Atlantic States, 1776–1860* (New York: Da Capo, 1971); Ellis Paxson Oberholzer, *The Referendum in America* (New York: Da Capo, 1971); Harold W. Stanley and Richard G. Niemi, *Vital Statistics on American Politics* (Washington, D.C.: Congressional Quarterly, 1992); Albert L. Sturm, *Thirty Years of State Constitution-Making: 1938–1968* (New York: National Municipal League, 1970).

presents an index to measure the degree of difficulty associated with each amendment process. The average amendment rate is much higher for the state constitutions than it is for the U.S. Constitution. Between 1789 and 1991 the U.S. Constitution was amended 26 times for a rate of .13 (26 amendments/202 years = .13 amendments per year).[10] As of 1991 the current state constitutions had been in effect for an average of 95 years and had been amended a total of 5,845 times, or an average of 117 amendments per state. This produces an average amendment rate of 1.23 for the states, about 9.5 times the national rate.

Proposition 1 hypothesizes a positive relationship between the length of a constitution and its amendment rate: the longer a constitution when adopted, the higher its rate of amendment. The data on American state constitutions strongly support proposition 1 with a correlation coefficient of .6249 significant at the .001 level. Furthermore, the relationship holds whether we use the original or the current amended length.

The average length of state constitutions increases from about 19,300 words as originally written to about 24,300 as amended by 1991, which raises the interesting question of what difference it makes whether we use a constitution's original length or its current amended length. The surprising answer is that it makes no real difference. The curve of best fit for amendment rates using the original length of a constitution has a slope of .58, whereas that of amendment rates using the amended length results in a slope of .62. There is thus good reason, when testing the propositions against foreign national constitutions, for using either the original or the amended length.

Also, the correlation coefficient between amended and unamended rates is .9936 (significant at the .001 level), which strongly implies that the rate of increase in amendment rate resulting from increasing a constitution's length is virtually constant across all lengths. Finally, since at any point in time the set of constitutions used to test the propositions will vary considerably in age and thus be a mixture of documents ranging from slightly amended to highly amended, we should probably use a composite curve that reflects this inevitable mix. In the case of American state constitutions, the obvious composite curve would be

[10] The addition of the Twenty-seventh Amendment in 1992 results, as of 2002, in the same .13 amendment rate.

one that combined .58 and .62. The resulting amendment rate curve with a slope of .60 indicates that for every ten-thousand-word increase in a constitution's length, the amendment rate will increase by .60.

The relationship between the length of a constitution and its amendment rate is the strongest and most consistent one found in the analysis of data drawn from the American states. The strength of this relationship can be underscored by a partial listing of the variables examined that did not show any significant independent correlation with amendment rate. These variables include geographical size, population, level of industrialization, per capita personal income, per capita state expenditures, size of legislature, partisan division in legislature, geographical region, geographical proximity, and the historical era in which the constitution was written. Controlling for these other variables, the importance of constitutional length remains, whereas controlling for constitutional length, the few weak correlations with these other variables disappear.

State constitutions, on average, are much longer than the U.S. Constitution. Can we account for this difference? Proposition 3 suggests that the wider range of governmental functions at the state level results in significantly longer documents and thus produces a higher amendment rate that makes them longer still (in line with proposition 1).

Data from a recent decade show that amendments dealing with local government structure (4.7 percent), state and local debt (4.3 percent), state functions (9.0 percent), taxation and finance (14.1 percent), amendment and revision (2.6 percent), and local issues (28 percent) compose about 63 percent of all state amendments and pertain to topics that have not been part of national constitutional concern.[11]

If we exclude these categories of issues from the amendment count, we end up with an adjusted state rate of about .47. This figure is still a bit more than three-and-a-half times the national amendment rate, but by eliminating the amendments peculiar to state constitutions we obtain a figure for comparison with the national rate (.13), using what amounts to the same base. The difference between .13 and .47 represents what we might term the "surplus rate" that still needs to be explained. An interesting question – one that never seems to be

[11] These data can be found in Sturm, "The Development of American State Constitutions," *Publius* 12 (1982): 64–98, on p. 90.

TABLE 5.2. *Amendment Rate of a State Constitution, by Average Duration*

	Average Duration (years)						
	1–25	26–50	51–75	76–100	101–125	126–150	151+
Amendment rate[a]	2.37 (3)	1.95 (13)	1.26 (13)	1.10 (6)	.93 (8)	.84 (5)	.64 (2)

[a] The numbers in parentheses indicate the number of constitutions in that range of average duration.

asked – is whether the state amendment rate is too high or the national amendment rate is too low.

The answer depends in part on one's attitude toward judicial interpretation. Propositions 5 and 6 suggest that for one who prefers judicial interpretation as a means of modifying a constitution over a formal amendment process, the amendment rate for the national document is not too low. However, for one who prefers a formal amendment process, such as an attachment to popular sovereignty, the amendment rate of the U.S. Constitution may well be too low and the amendment rate of the states is to be preferred.

Propositions 5 and 6 assume a low rate of amendment coupled with constitutional longevity. Proposition 4, on the other hand, posits a general relationship between the rate of amendment and constitutional longevity. Dividing the number of constitutions a state has had into the number of years it has been a state produces the average duration of the state's constitutions – a measure of constitutional activity that controls for a state's age. Table 5.2 shows that a high amendment rate is associated with low average duration and thus high replacement rate ($r = -.3561$, significant at the .01 level).

Proposition 4, however, predicts that the rate at which constitutions are replaced will increase as the amendment rate moves up *or* down with respect to <#>. In Table 5.2, the amendment rate is the dependent variable. However, if we make it the independent variable instead, we can test directly for the bidirectional effect. Table 5.3 supports proposition 4.

I turn now to developing an index with which to measure the difficulty of a given amendment procedure. I shall then be ready to look at the constitutions of other nations.

TABLE 5.3. *Average Duration of a State Constitution, by Amendment Rate*

	Amendment Rate							
	0–.5	.51–.75	.76–1.00	1.01–1.25	1.26–1.50	1.51–1.75	1.76–2.00	2.00+
Average duration[a]	71 (7)	90 (8)	100 (13)	86 (4)	79 (4)	57 (6)	40 (1)	38 (7)

Note: The average duration of a state's constitution declines as the amendment rate goes above 1.00 and as it goes below .75. This means that for American state constitutions, an amendment rate between .75 and 1.00 is associated with the longest-lived constitutions and thus with the lowest rate of constitutional replacement. This range, then, will be defined as <#>. The thirteen constitutions with amendment rates within <#> (as just defined) average .89, which we will define as # within <#>.

[a] The numbers in parentheses indicate the number of states that fall into this range of amendment rate.

TABLE 5.4. *Method of Initiation and State Amendment Rate, 1970–1979*

Rate and Frequency of Amendment	Method of Initiation: Proposed by Legislature	Popular Initiative	Special Convention
Amendment rate	1.24	1.38	1.26
Percentage of amendments using this method	91.5	2.2	6.3
Number of constitutions in category[a]	50	17	5

[a] The total exceeds 50, since many states specify the possibility of more than one method for proposing amendments.

Source: Albert L. Sturn, "The Development of American State Constitutions," *Publius* 12 (1982): 78–79.

Amendment Patterns and the Characteristics of the Amendment Process

In the American states the method of ratifying an amendment can essentially be held constant since every state but one now uses a popular referendum for approval. However, amendments may be initiated by the state's legislature, an initiative referendum, a constitutional convention, or a commission. It is also believed that the initiative has made the process of proposing an amendment too easy and opened a floodgate of proposals that are then more readily adopted by the electorate that initiated them. Another widely held belief is that the stricter or more arduous the process a legislature must use to propose an amendment, the fewer the amendments proposed.

First of all, as Table 5.4 shows, during a recent decade, relatively few amendments were proposed by other than a legislature. One-third of the states use the popular initiative as a method of proposing amendments, and yet in these states the nonlegislative methods received a lot of attention, especially in California, but in fact the popular initiative has had a minimal impact so far.

What has been the relative success of these competing modes of proposing constitutions? The relatively few amendments proposed through popular initiative have a success rate roughly half that of the two prominent alternatives (32 percent versus 64 percent for legislature and 71 percent for convention initiated). The popular initiative is in fact

TABLE 5.5. *Comparative Effect of Majority Size on Amendment Rate in American State Constitutions*

	Required Legislative Majority					
	50% + 1	50% + 1 twice	60%	67%	75%	67% twice
Ratio of difficulty to simple majority[a]	1.00 (11)	1.04 (6)	1.26 (9)	1.62 (19)	1.83 (1)	3.56 (4)

Note: In this table, the decline in the amendment rate produced by each type of legislative majority has been normed against that of the least difficult method. This norming is accomplished by taking the simple (bicameral) legislative majority and dividing it by the success rate of proposals initiated by a two-thirds legislative majority, a three-fourths majority, etc. – always keeping the other variables constant. For example, the data indicate that in the American states, when the method of initiation is stiffened to require approval by a simple (bicameral) legislative approval *twice*, the amendment rate is reduced from the baseline of 71% to a little over 68%. Dividing 71% by 68% results in an index score of 1.04. Likewise, a requirement for a three-fifths (bicameral) legislative majority results in a success rate of 56%. Dividing 71% by 56% produces an index score of 1.26. A score of 2.00 therefore indicates a method that is twice as difficult, a 3.00 indicates a method three times as difficult, and so on. Table 5.3 arrays the empirical results from lowest to highest level of difficulty rather than according to any theoretical prediction. The results are mostly in line with commonsense expectations (although why a second majority vote has so little effect while a second two-thirds vote has so much is not clear).

[a] The numbers in parentheses indicate the number of states using this required legislative majority.

more difficult to use than legislative initiative and results in proposals that are less well considered and thus less likely to be accepted.

What about the varying methods for *legislative* initiation? States differ in how large a legislative majority is needed for a proposal to be put on the ballot, and some states require that the majority be sustained in two consecutive sessions. Table 5.5 summarizes what we find in this regard.

We can derive three conclusions from Table 5.5:

1. Generally speaking, the larger the legislative majority required for initiation, the fewer the amendments proposed and the lower the amendment rate.
2. Requiring a legislature to pass a proposal twice does not significantly increase the difficulty of the amendment process if the decision rule is one-half plus one.
3. The most effective way to increase the difficulty of amendment at the initiation stage is to require the approval of two consecutive legislatures using a two-thirds majority each time.

Beyond these three interesting proposals, it is also useful to discover that the variance in the degree of difficulty between alternative legislative majorities is sufficient to establish the core of an *index of difficulty* for any amendment process. An attempt at such an index is presented in Table 5.6, which lists the numbers assigned by the index to every step required by the amendment processes. Table 5.6 identifies sixty-eight possible actions that could in some combination be used to initiate and approve constitutional amendments and that together cover the combinations of virtually every amendment process in the world. The state data on which Table 5.5 is based generate the index scores for actions 14 through 23, rounding off the score to the nearest .05. If we assume that legislative processes for approval are symmetrical with those for initiation, the index scores for actions 50–59 are the same as those for 14–23. If we assume that a unicameral legislative process is one-half as difficult as a bicameral one, the index scores for actions 4–13 and 39–49 are as indicated. As reported earlier, amendments proposed by popular initiative have almost exactly one-half the success rate of those initiated by the legislature. If we weight the difficulty of legislative initiative according to the number of states using each type of majority, we obtain a combined, weighted index score of 1.50 for legislative initiative, and thus an index score of 3.00 for popular initiatives (action 24).

Also, we know from state data going back to 1776 that the success rate of amendment proposals after popular referenda became the standard means of approval is virtually the same as when the agent of approval was the state legislature. We can thus say that a popular referendum used as a means for approving a proposed amendment (as opposed to initiating one) is about as difficult as having the state legislature approve it. We have just seen that the weighted average for bicameral legislative action is 1.50, and so we assign an index score of 1.50 to action 60, adding further increments for larger popular majorities, actions 61–62. If we assume that special bodies act much the same as unicameral legislatures, the assigning of index scores for actions 2–3 and 32–38 is straightforward.

The use of American state data, in combination with straightforward assumptions, allows the generation of index scores for all actions except numbers 27–30 and 63–68. These actions are assigned index scores that seem reasonable in the context of the other index scores.

TABLE 5.6. *An Index for Estimating the Relative Difficulty of an Amendment Process*

Action	Constitutional Requirement	Add
Initiation Requires Action by		
1	An executive	.25
2	A special appointed body	.50
3	A special elected body	.75
	A unicameral legislature	
	Legislative approval	
4	By a majority of 1/2 + 1	.50
5	*Twice* using 1/2 + 1	.50
6	By an absolute majority[a]	.65
7	*Twice* by absolute majority	.65
8	By a 3/5 majority	.65
9	*Twice* by 3/5 majority	.65
10	By a 2/3 majority	.80
11	By a 3/4 majority	.90
12	*Twice* by a 2/3 majority	1.75
13	If an election is required between two votes	.25
	Action by a bicameral legislature	
	Legislative approval	
14	By a majority of 1/2 + 1	1.00
15	*Twice* using 1/2 + 1	1.00
16	By an absolute majority	1.25
17	*Twice* by absolute majority	1.25
18	By a 3/5 majority	1.25
19	*Twice* by 3/5 majority	1.25
20	By a 2/3 majority	1.60
21	By a 3/4 majority	1.80
22	*Twice* by a 2/3 majority	3.55
23	If an election is required between two votes	.50
	A petition	
24	Of 0–250,000 voters	3.00
25	By 250,000–500,000 voters	3.50
26	By more than 500,000 voters	4.00
	Multiple state	
27	Legislatures, 1/2 + 1	2.00
28	Conventions, 1/2 + 1	2.00
29	Legislatures or conventions, 2/3	3.00
30	Legislatures or conventions, 3/4	3.50
Approval Requires		
31	Action by an executive	.50
	Approval by a special body	
32	1/3 or less	.25
33	1/2 + 1	.50
34	Absolute majority	.65

(*continued*)

TABLE 5.6 *(continued)*

Action	Constitutional Requirement	Add
35	3/5 majority	.65
36	2/3 majority	.80
37	3/4 majority	.90
38	3/4 majority	.90
	If any of the above acts a second time	
	Action by a unicameral legislature	
	Legislative approval	
39	1/3 majority or less	.25
40	1/2 + 1	.50
41	*Twice* by 1/2 + 1	.50
42	Absolute majority	.65
43	*Twice* by absolute majority	.65
44	3/5 majority	.65
45	*Twice* by 3/5 majority	.65
46	2/3 majority	.80
47	3/4 majority	.90
48	If an election is required between two votes	.25
49	Legislative approval *twice* by 2/3 majority	1.75
	Action by a bicameral legislature	
	Legislative approval	
50	1/3 majority or less	.50
51	1/2 + 1	1.00
52	Absolute majority	1.25
53	*Twice* by absolute majority	1.25
54	3/5 majority	1.25
55	*Twice* by 3/5 majority	1.25
56	2/3 majority	1.60
57	3/4 majority	1.80
58	*Twice* by 2/3 majority	3.55
59	If an election is required between two votes	.50
	A popular referendum	
60	1/2 + 1	1.50
61	Absolute majority	1.75
62	3/5 or more	2.00
	Multiple state	
63	Legislatures, 1/2 + 1	2.00
64	Conventions, 1/2 + 1	2.00
65	Legislatures or conventions, 2/3	3.00
66	Legislatures or conventions, 3/4	3.50
67	Majority of voters *and* majority of states	3.75
68	Unanimous approval by state governments	4.00

[a] "Absolute majority" is used to indicate a requirement for approval by 1/2 + 1 of the *entire body*, whereas "1/2 + 1" indicates a requirement for approval by 1/2 + 1 of those voting.

The index score assigned to the amendment process found in a national constitution is generated by adding together the numbers assigned by the index in Table 5.6 to every step required by that particular amendment process. Where a constitution provides for more than one path to a formal amendment, the score for each amendment path is weighted according to the percentage of amendments passed by means of it during the relevant time period.

How the index works can be illustrated using it with the amendment process described in Article V of the U.S. Constitution. There is more than one path to amendment, and each must be evaluated. A two-thirds vote by Congress, because it requires two houses to initiate the process, is worth 1.60, whereas initiation by two-thirds of the state legislatures is worth 2.25. The latter path leads to a national convention, which uses majority rule in advancing a proposal, thus adding .75 (under the assumption that this special body is elected). The first path still totals 1.60, and the other now totals 3.00. Ratification by three-fourths of the states through either their legislatures or elected conventions adds 3.50. The path beginning with Congress now totals 5.10, while the path beginning with the state legislatures and using a national convention totals 6.50. Even though the second path has never been successful (and one can see more clearly now why), it is still a valid option. For the total amendment process, we can use the lower figure unless or until the more difficult procedure is ever used. That is, because the 6.50 path has never been used, a weighted composite score would be 5.10, which is what I shall use here. Table 5.7 shows the index of difficulty scores calculated for the national constitutions of thirty-two countries, along with other constitutional characteristics.

Performing the same calculation for the American states, I find that the average index score is 2.92, with very little variance. The highest state score is 3.60 (Delaware), and twenty-six states are tied for the lowest score at 2.75. Another sixteen states have a score of 3.10. Thus, although one can detect variance between select subsets of states, the range of variance in general is very small compared with that found in the constitutions of other nations.

We have reached a point where we can now begin to test our propositions using data from the constitutions of other nations.

TABLE 5.7. *Basic Data on Selected National Constitutions*

Country	Amendment Rate	Index of Difficulty	Amended Length in Words	Years	Time Period
Argentina	1.04	2.10	10,600	87	1853–1940
Australia	.09	4.65	11,500	91	1901–1992
Austria	6.30	.80	36,000	17	1975–1992
Belgium	2.30	2.85	10,700	15	1973–1988
Botswana	2.44	1.30	35,600	18	1966–1984
Brazil	6.28	1.55	58,400	18	1969–1987
Chile	.64	3.05	24,200	45	1925–1970
Colombia	1.73	2.75	25,100	95	1886–1981
Costa Rica	1.26	4.10	15,100	33	1949–1982
Denmark	.17	2.75	6,000	39	1953–1992
Finland	.86	2.30	18,300	73	1919–1992
France	.19	2.50	6,500	24	1968–1992
Germany	2.91	1.60	22,400	43	1949–1992
Greece	1.32	1.80	22,100	17	1975–1992
Iceland	.21	2.75	3,800	48	1944–1992
India	7.29	1.81	95,000	42	1950–1992
Ireland	.55	3.00	16,000	55	1937–1992
Italy	.24	3.40	11,300	46	1946–1992
Kenya	3.28	1.00	31,500	18	1964–1981
Japan	0.00	3.10	5,400	47	1945–1992
Luxembourg	1.80	1.80	4,700	19	1968–1987
Malaysia	5.18	1.60	91,400	35	1957–1992
New Zealand	13.42	.50	180,000	40	1947–1987
Norway	1.14	3.35	6,500	178	1814–1982
Papua New Guinea	6.90	.77	53,700	17	1975–1992
Portugal	6.67	.80	26,700	15	1976–1991
Spain	.18	3.60	8,700	24	1968–1992
Sweden	4.72	1.40	40,800	18	1974–1992
Switzerland	.78	4.75	13,300	119	1873–1992
United States	.13	5.10	7,400	203	1789–1992
Venezuela	.24	4.75	20,500	25	1967–1992
Western Samoa	.95	1.80	22,500	22	1962–1984
AVERAGE	2.54	2.50	29,400	52	

Note: Cross-national constitutional data have been taken from the constitutions themselves and from commentaries on these documents, found primarily in Albert P. Blaustein and Gisbert H. Flanz, *Constitutions of the Countries of the World*, 19 vols. (Dobbs Ferry, N.Y.: Oceana, 1987) and supplements.

Cross-National Amendment Patterns

Comparative cross-national data show that the U.S. Constitution has the second most difficult amendment process. This implies, if propositions 2 and 4 are correct, that the amendment rate for the U.S. Constitution may be too low, because its amendment procedure is too difficult, whereas the average amendment rate for the state constitutions is not too high.

An even stronger relationship exists between the length of a constitution and its amendment rate here than I found with the American state constitutions, with a correlation coefficient of .7970 (versus .6249 for the states) significant at the .0001 level.

The curvilinear relationship found between the amendment rate and average duration of American state constitutions is almost duplicated here in shape, strength, and high point. For the national constitutions <#> is .75–1.24 (# = .95), and the high point is 96 years in average duration. See Table 5.8. In comparison, as Table 5.3 shows, for the states, <#> is .75–1.00 (# = .89), and the high point is 100 years in average duration.[12] Both sets of constitutions studied have a similar moderate range of amendment rate that tends to be associated with constitutional longevity.

The index of difficulty among cross-national constitutions has enough variance for us now to test proposition 2 with some degree of confidence. Figure 5.1 illustrates that there is a very strong relationship (significant at the .001 level) between the index of difficulty and the amendment rate. The more difficult the amendment process, the lower the amendment rate, and vice versa.

That the relationship between amendment rate and difficulty of amendment process is highly curvilinear is more interesting than if it were simply a linear one, because there is a relatively small part of the curve where most of the effect is concentrated. This confirms the existence of a range of amendment rates that is more critical and toward

[12] The test for curvilinearity using cross-national data is neither strictly comparable with that used for the American states nor an adequate test of the relationship using national constitutions. Whereas the entire constitutional history for all fifty American states was used, only the most recent period of constitutional stability that exceeded fifteen years was used for the cross-national data. The arbitrary use of a fifteen-year minimum may well exaggerate the average longevity of national constitutions, and the use of only the most recent minimum period may weaken the results.

TABLE 5.8. *The Amendment Rate and Average Duration of Selected National Constitutions*

	Amendment Rate							
	.00–.24	.25–.74	.75–1.24	1.25–1.74	1.75–2.24	2.25–2.74	2.75–3.24	3.25+
Average duration[a]	43 (6)	50 (2)	96 (5)	47 (3)	19 (1)	17 (2)	26 (10)	39 (3)

Note: Index scores are normed to that of a simple majority approval in a bicameral legislature, by dividing the approval rate for this baseline by the approval rate for each of the other possible actions. The increments are the estimated increase in the difficulty of passing amendments relative to the baseline rules.

[a] The numbers in parentheses indicate the number of countries that fall into this range of amendment rate.

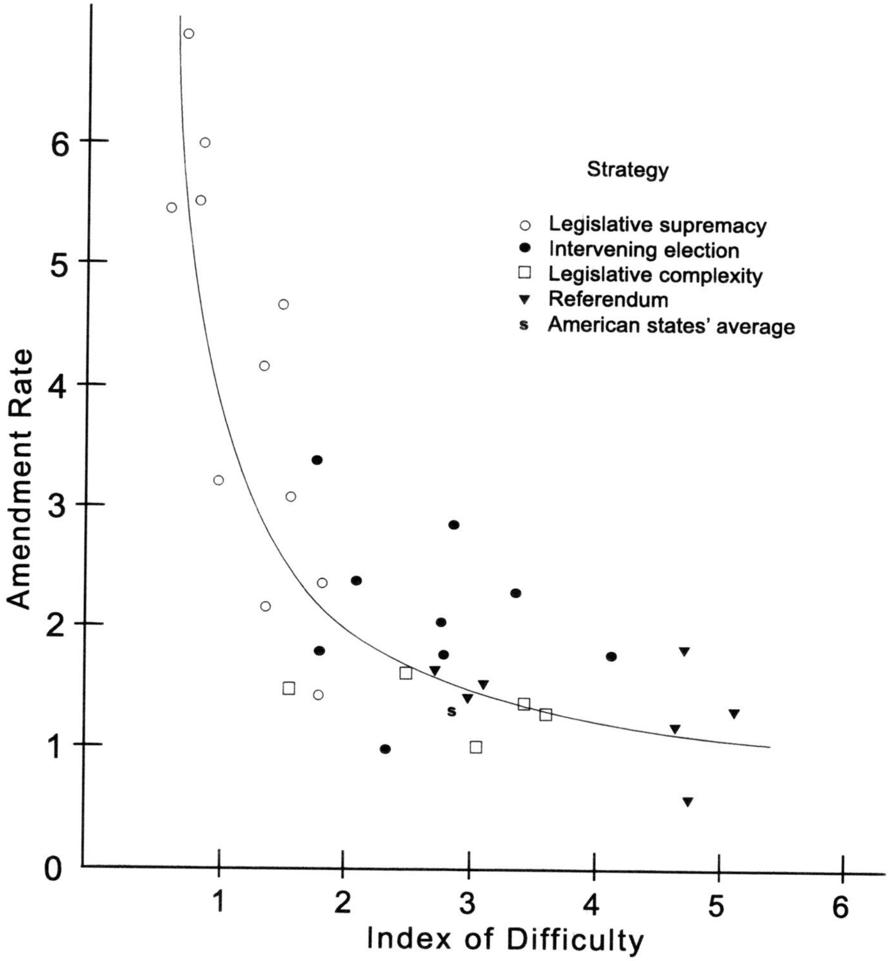

FIGURE 5.1. Cross-national pattern for amendment rate and difficulty, indicating amendment strategy. (The figure was generated using the statistical package STATA and was then reproduced by hand using Geotype overlay techniques to enhance readability.)

which one should aim if constitutional stability is being sought. But it also suggests that one can with some confidence achieve a moderate rate of amendment by selecting an appropriate range of amendment difficulty. This, in turn, suggests that certain amendment strategies are better in this regard than others, the topic to which I now turn.

TABLE 5.9. *Comparison of National Constitutions, Grouped according to Their General Amendment Strategy*

	Amendment Strategies			
	Legislative Supremacy[a]	Intervening Election (Double Vote)[b]	Legislative Complexity (Referendum Threat)[c]	Required Referendum or Equivalent[d]
Average index score	1.23	2.39	2.79	4.01
Length	59,400	13,000	18,300	11,200
Amendment rate	5.60	1.30	1.19	.28

[a] Austria, Botswana, Brazil, Germany, India, Kenya, Malaysia, New Zealand, Papua New Guinea, Portugal, and Samoa.
[b] Argentina, Belgium, Colombia, Costa Rica, Finland, Greece, Iceland, Luxembourg, and Norway.
[c] Chile, France, Italy, Spain, and Sweden.
[d] Australia, Denmark, Ireland, Japan, Switzerland, United States, and Venezuela.

The difficulty of the amendment process chosen by framers of constitutions seems related to the framers' relative commitment to the premises used by the Americans when they invented the formal amendment process: popular sovereignty, a deliberate process, and the distinction between normal legislation and constitutional matters. We can use these assumptions to group our thirty-two national constitutions into one of four general amendment strategies.[13]

Strategy 1 can be labeled *legislative supremacy* (Table 5.9, col. 1). Constitutions in this category reflect the unbridled dominance of the legislature by making one legislative vote sufficient to amend the constitution. The data reveal that the size of the majority required for this vote does not affect the amendment rate. The legislative supremacy strategy

[13] The broad categories were constructed using the theoretical premises developed herein and thus are independent of any categorization schemes developed previously by others. For an instructive comparison, see Arend Lijphart, *Patterns of Democracy, Government Forms and Preference in Thirty-six Countries* (New Haven: Yale University Press, 1999), 189–91. In order for a country to be included, it had to have at least one fifteen-year period free of military rule or serious instability, during which constitutionalism was taken seriously. Reliable data on the number and nature of amendments for that country also had to be available to the researcher. The unavailability of such data explains the absence of the Netherlands, for example, or for Austria before 1975.

reflects a minimal commitment to the three American premises just listed. Strategy 2 is to require that the national legislature approve an amendment by votes in two sessions with an *intervening election* (col. 2 in Table 5.9). The national legislature is still basically in control, but the amendment process is made more deliberative, a clearer distinction drawn between normal legislation and constitutional matters, and the people have an opportunity to influence the process during the election, which implies a stronger commitment to popular sovereignty. Sometimes other requirements diminish legislative dominance; the introduction of a nonlegislative body in the process (e.g., a constitutional commission) is typical. The double vote with an intervening election is the key change, so strategy 2 is termed the Intervening Election Strategy. As we move from strategy 1 to strategy 2, the amendment rate falls by 77 percent. Approximately half (54 percent) of this drop is explained by the 78 percent reduction in the average length of a constitution, and about half is explained by the 94 percent increase in the index of difficulty that results primarily from the double-vote, intervening election strategy.

Strategy 3 relies on *legislative complexity* (col. 3 in Table 5.9), usually characterized by multiple paths for the amendment process, which features the possibility of a referendum as a kind of threat to bypass the legislature. A referendum can usually be called by a small legislative minority, by the executive, or by an initiative from a small percentage of the electorate – and often any of the three. This complexity and easy availability of a referendum emphasize even more strongly the deliberative process, the distinction between constitutional and normal legislative, and popular sovereignty.

The legislative complexity strategy produces only an 8 percent reduction in the amendment rate compared with the intervening election strategy, although this is a 31 percent improvement over what we would expect, given the increased average length of strategy 3 documents. The slight overall improvement is due to the modest (18 percent) increase in the difficulty of the strategy. Strategies 2 and 3 together show most clearly how one can achieve similar amendment rates by trading off between constitutional length and amendment difficulty.

Strategy 4 institutionalizes the most direct form of popular sovereignty and also emphasizes to the greatest extent both the deliberative process and the distinction between constitutional and normal legislative matters. These countries have a *required referendum* as the final part of the process. The United States is placed in this category because the various appeals to the citizenry required by both amendment paths approximate a referendum and because the United States does not approximate any other strategy even remotely.

Compared with that of strategy 3, the referendum strategy's rate of amendment falls off 76 percent. This reduction to what is barely one-twentieth the rate for legislative-supremacy countries is about evenly explained by the 44 percent increase in difficulty vis-à-vis strategy 3 and a 39 percent reduction in average length.

Table 5.9 also shows that countries that use a referendum strategy, as well as those that use the strategy of an intervening election, have, on average, much shorter constitutions than the countries using the other strategies. They tend to have framework constitutions that define the basic institutions and the decision-making process connecting these institutions. The nations using strategy 1 tend to use a code-of-law form of constitution containing many details about preferred policy outcomes. These constitutions tend to be much longer. A code-of-law form, long documents, an easy amendment process, and legislative supremacy are all characteristics of the parliamentary sovereignty model that dominates the list of countries using strategy 1. New Zealand has perhaps the purest parliamentary sovereignty government in the world, and Kenya, India, Malaysia, Papua New Guinea, Botswana, and Western Samoa are not far behind. Although the countries using strategy 2 still have a fairly low index of difficulty, their much shorter constitutions indicate that a much greater divide has been crossed with respect to strategy 1 countries than the addition of a double vote with intervening election might imply.

Table 5.9 implies several interesting things that require emphasis. First, one can trade off between shorter length and greater difficulty to produce a similar amendment rate or use them together to produce a desired amendment rate. One can relax the level of difficulty and greatly reduce the rate of amendment simply by shortening a constitution. Second, it was determined earlier that the amendment rate correlates highly with the degree of difficulty. It is now apparent that different amendment strategies, which reflect different combinations of assumptions and constitutionalism, have certain levels of difficulty associated with them. That is, institutions have definite (and, in this case, predictable) consequences for the political process.

Figure 5.1 demonstrates this rather clearly. The eleven nations that use the legislative supremacy strategy are grouped toward the low difficulty–high amendment rate end of the curve. These are left as an open circle. The seven nations that use referendum strategy, each indicated by an inverted triangle, are clustered toward the other end of the curve. Those that use legislative complexity are indicated by an open square, and those that use an intervening election strategy are represented by a filled-in circle. The clustering of the various countries by amendment strategy shows that the averages reported in Table 5.9 represent real tendencies, not merely statistical artifacts produced by mathematical manipulation. The average for the American states is shown by the letter *s*.

Figure 5.1 shows the relationship between difficulty of amendment and amendment rate while controlling for the effects of length, which has the effect of shifting the curve upward a bit from that created by using raw index scores. The shifted curve is almost hyperbolic, which means that the relationship between difficulty of amendment and amendment rate can be approximated by the equation for a hyperbolic curve, $x = 1/y$.

An analysis of American state constitutions, with the difficulty of amendment held roughly constant by the similarity in their formal processes, reveals a relationship between the length of a constitution and its amendment rate that is described by a linear curve of best fit with a slope of .60 – which is to say that on average, for every additional ten thousand words, the amendment rate goes up by six-tenths of an amendment per year. The curve of best fit for the national constitutions, when controlling for the difficulty of the amendment process and when excluding the extreme cases of New Zealand and Japan, has a slope of .59. Those writing a new constitution can expect with some confidence, therefore, that there will be about a .60 increase in the amendment rate for every ten-thousand-word increase in the length of the document.

Finally, we might conclude from Table 5.9 that both the length of a constitution and the difficulty of amendment may be related to the relative presence of an attitude that views the constitution as a higher law rather than as a receptacle for normal legislation. Certainly it seems to be the case that a low amendment rate can either reflect a reliance on judicial revision or else encourage such reliance in the face of needed change. It is possible that the great difficulty faced in amending the U.S. Constitution has led to heavy judicial interpretation as a virtue in the face of necessity.

The theory of constitutional amendment advanced here has posited a connection between the four methods of constitutional modification. Propositions 1–4 developed the concept of amendment rate in such a way that we were able to show an empirical relationship between the formal amendment of a constitution and its complete replacement. Propositions 5–8 used amendment rate to relate these two methods of modification to judicial and legislative alteration.[14] At this point, I can systematically include these last two methods in the overall theory. Toward that end, it is worth reconsidering briefly propositions 5–8 in light of my findings on the amendment process in national constitutions.

> PROPOSITION 5. A low amendment rate, associated with a long average constitutional duration, strongly implies the use of some alternate means of revision to supplement the formal amendment process.

The countries that have an amendment rate below <#> (defined as .75–1.24 for national constitutions) and also have a constitution older than the international average of fifty-one years include Australia, Finland, Ireland, and the United States. The proposition implies that these four countries either have found an alternate means (judicial review in the United States) or are under strong pressure to find another means. Denmark, Germany, Iceland, Italy, and Japan are all within a few years of falling into the same category, and if the proposition is at all useful, they should experience progressively stronger inclinations toward either a more active judiciary or a new constitution in the coming decades. A trend toward an active judiciary is already well advanced in Germany and is also becoming apparent in Japan.

> PROPOSITION 6. In the absence of a high rate of constitutional replacement, the lower the rate of formal amendment, the more likely the process of revision is dominated by a judicial body.

[14] On this topic, see Chester James Antieu, *Constitutional Construction* (Dobbs Ferry, N.Y.: Oceana, 1982); and Edward McWhinney, *Judicial Review in the English-Speaking World* (Toronto: University of Toronto Press, 1956).

Table 5.9 shows that the lower the rate of formal amendment, the less the legislature dominates. The executive is usually not a major actor in a formal amendment process, so we are left with the judiciary.

Arend Lijphart has found empirical support for proposition 6.[15] A low rate of formal amendment results, as we have shown, from a difficult amendment process. Lijphart and others who work in comparative politics refer to a constitution that is difficult to amend as "rigid." Using his sample of thirty-six countries, Lijphart found a .39 correlation between constitutional rigidity and the use of judicial review (significant at the 1 percent level).

> PROPOSITION 7. The higher the formal amendment rate, the less likely the constitution is being viewed as a higher law, the less likely a distinction is being drawn between constitutional matters and normal legislation, the more likely the constitution is being viewed as a code, and the more likely the formal amendment process is dominated by the legislature.

Discussion of Table 5.9 has supported all parts of this proposition.

> PROPOSITION 8. The more important the role of the judiciary in constitutional modification, the less likely the judiciary is to use a theory of strict construction. In the absence of further research, proposition 8 is a prediction to be tested.

Conclusion

I have examined two sets of constitutions. Each set is composed of documents that are taken seriously as constitutions. Every document in these two sets has a formal amendment process that is self-sufficient – that is, it depends on no other constitution to carry out a formal amendment of itself. The two sets of constitutions examined together comprise at least three-fourths of the existing documents defined by these two characteristics.[16]

[15] Lijphart, *Patterns of Democracy*, chap. 12, especially pp. 225–230.

[16] Canadian provincial and Australian state constitutions are prominent among those remaining to be examined. Also, Israel, Canada, and the United Kingdom, although lacking a simple written constitution, remain to be included. The problem in each of these three cases lies in determining what has constitutional status. An initial attempt to do so, using the content of the New Zealand Constitution as a template, yielded the following very preliminary estimates for two of these legislative supremacy

A comparative, empirical study of the amendment process in these eighty-two documents leads to four specific conclusions about the amendment process, as well as four more general conclusions about constitutions. The first specific conclusion is that the variance in amendment rate is largely explained by the interaction of two variables: the length of the constitution and the difficulty of the amendment process.

Second, it is possible to manipulate these two variables to produce more or less predictable rates of amendment. The strong linear effects of length and the hyperbolic curve that describes the effects of difficulty together allow us to formulate an equation that generates a pattern of amendment rates close to what we found empirically. If we let A represent the amendment rate, D the score on the index of difficulty, and L the length of a constitution in words, the equation representing their interrelationship is

$$A = [1/D + ((L/10{,}000) \times .6)] - .3$$

One part of the equation factors the effects of length in by dividing the number of words in the constitution by 10,000 and multiplying by .60. The second part of the equation approximates the effects of amendment difficulty by using the formula for a hyperbolic curve: A = 1/D. However, this is only approximate, and subtracting .30 from the effects of amendment difficulty results in the curve of best fit for the raw data scores.

Third, there is evidence that the amendment rate affects the probability that a constitution will be replaced and that a moderate amendment rate (between .75 and 1.25 amendments per year) is conducive to constitutional longevity.

Fourth, beyond a certain point, making the amendment process more difficult is an "inefficient" way to keep the amendment rate in the moderate range. Rather, it is easiest to do so by avoiding the extremes of either the legislative dominance or the referendum strategies and

countries. For Israel between 1949 and 1991 with a constitution of 10,000+ words, the amendment rate is 2.5+ and the index of difficulty is .50. For the United Kingdom between 1900 and 1991 with a constitution of 250,000+ words, the amendment rate is 7.5 + and the index of difficulty is .60.

combining either the legislative complexity or the intervening election strategy with a relatively short document (10,000 to 20,000 words).

Among more general conclusions, the first is that institutions have consequences and that the effects of institutional definitions in constitutions can be studied empirically.

Second, the similarity in amendment patterns between the American state constitutions and the national constitutions raises the possibility that for other aspects of constitutional design, one set of documents may be useful in developing propositions for studying the other set and therefore that there are basic principles of constitutional design operating independently of cultural, historical, geographic, and short-term political considerations.

Third, the first two general conclusions together suggest the possibility of discovering a set of principles that can be used to design constitutions with predictable results.

Fourth, the study of the amendment process strongly suggests that constitutional institutions cannot be studied in isolation from each other. Just as the operation of the legislature may strongly affect the patterns we find in the amendment process, the design of the amendment process may affect the operation of the court; and seemingly unrelated aspects of constitution (e.g., its length and formal amendment process) may be linked in their consequences.

Finally, it is interesting that Buchanan and Tulloch's rational cost analysis receives some empirical support, although with a twist. Their general principle holds that constitutional choice rests on a trade-off between decision costs and external costs.[17] Because constitutions contain important political settlements, any amendment carries with it the danger of serious externalities. Although an apparently rational actor might seek a very difficult amendment process in order to minimize externalities, such a one might also attempt to minimize externalities by constitutionalizing its interests, since the more specific the policy content of the constitution on a topic, the less danger there is that unwanted externalities will be imposed. This latter analysis would imply a fairly easy amendment process. However, a process that allows one actor to safeguard its interests allows all actors to do so. The data in this study indicate that the more policy content a constitution has, the longer

[17] Buchanan and Tulloch, *The Calculus of Consent.*

it becomes. Both an easy amendment process (which leads to greater length and thus a higher amendment rate) and a very difficult amendment process (which leads to a very low amendment rate) produce a higher probability that a constitution will be replaced entirely. Thus, the two short-range types of behavior likely to be engaged in by a rational actor are irrational in the long run, because when a constitution is replaced, everything is once again up for grabs – a situation in which constitutional safeguards against external costs are no longer in effect at the very time externalities are threatened on all serious political matters. Therefore, a truly rational actor would seem to be one who attempts to avoid constitutional replacement and instead avoids an amendment rate that is too high or too low. This would seem to argue for constitutional brevity and a moderately difficult amendment process on grounds of rationality.

Still, while an empirical study of the amendment process can suggest some general solutions to a common problem faced by constitutional republics, as Table 5.9 indicates, a number of broad strategies are available to framers of constitutions just as any number of specific possible solutions exist within one of the broad strategies. In the end, those designing a constitution face a more important and difficult problem than simply designing an amendment process. They must find a way to make this institution, and the other institutions in the constitution, "match the people" if the political system generated by the constitution is to endure and prosper. What might be meant by "matching a constitution to the people" is thus a topic worthy of extended, careful discussion. It is to that topic we now turn.

6

Matching a Government to a People

Some Initial Considerations

Constitutionalism and constitutional design are not defined by some set of principles that can be listed, memorized, and then mechanically applied. Nor are they to be discovered through some straightforward logical technique such as that based on rational-actor analysis. Constitutionalism and its attendant design principles have resulted from a centuries-old discussion aimed at understanding how to marry justice with power; how to blend hopes for a better future with the realities of the present; how to construct an order that takes into account human irrationality as well as rational actors; and how to recognize principles that are useful everywhere despite the inevitable diversity among successful political systems. If we are to understand constitutional design, then, it is essential that we reprise some of that conversation for the simple reason that the project does not rest as much on a set of principles as it rests on the reasoning implicitly contained in those principles. That is, constitutionalism and constitutional design rest on a way of looking at the world and on a method of thinking that proceeds from that perspective. The principles are thus important to us primarily to the extent they help us produce a constitutional perspective, and to achieve this perspective it is extremely useful to consider what has been rejected as well as accepted by earlier thinkers who together discovered and developed constitutional thinking. Any list of such thinkers would have to include, at a minimum, Plato, Aristotle, Cicero, Machiavelli, Althusius,

Bodin, Spinoza, Locke, Hobbes, Rousseau, Montesquieu, Blackstone, Hume, Madison and Hamilton, Tocqueville, and Benjamin Constant. At times these thinkers are analyzed explicitly in this book, such as Montesquieu in Chapter 1 and Bodin in Chapter 2. Often their thinking is only implicit in our analysis. A systematic march through the history of political philosophy would be both tedious and too lengthy for one volume. Also, such an approach is often associated with what amounts to an appeal to authority – because a great thinker said something, it must be true. The strategy in this book is to utilize from past thinkers whatever has proved to be useful and defensible given what history and empirical analysis tend to support. Thus, for example, Bodin's thinking is developed at length because of its importance for understanding a central concept, sovereignty, and because a fundamental principle implicit in his analysis turns out to be empirically supportable.

The move from a very contemporary empirical analysis in the previous two chapters to an examination of long-dead political philosophers in this chapter may still strike some as peculiar. A more complete explanation for this move will be laid out in the next chapter. For now, suffice it to say that part of what we need to do in order to understand the principle of matching a government and a people is to reprise what some of the greatest thinkers of the past have to suggest on the topic. As it turns out, part of what they can contribute is the manner and extent to which this principle is connected to the seemingly unrelated question of what a people must share, and what they need not share, if they are to be considered "a people" suitable for matching with a constitution. Addressing this question, however, requires that we raise again the matter of popular sovereignty, in part to illustrate how the various principles of constitutional design analyzed in this book are interlocking and mutually supporting.

One aspect of popular sovereignty that recommends itself to us is its efficiency at matching a government with the characteristics and circumstances of humans in general, and for the specific people in question. One critical aspect of popular sovereignty, the amendment process, allows constitutional republics to preserve this match as the people and its circumstances change. Resting the creation and continued operation of the constitution and the institutions it defines on the consent of the people is a safe way to avoid constitutional and institutional design that will not work because it violates in some important way the history, culture, expectations, or abilities of the people who will live under it. The early lawgivers Draco and Solon gave classical Athens two historically important constitutions, and there are those who still think that wise men are the proper source of good constitutional design. However, it should be remembered that no constitutional system from classical antiquity lasted as long as has that of Britain, the United States, Switzerland, or any other modern constitutional system older than about a hundred years; and modern constitutions are invariably designed by committees, commissions, parliaments, or conventions.

Experience in the modern era has also shown us the high failure rate of constitutions handed down by individuals such as Lenin, Hitler, Mao, Pol Pot, and a whole host of lesser "philosopher-kings." Popular sovereignty is our best way of preventing the imposition of ideologically driven ideas that attempt to change the people rather than accommodate them as humans with differing histories, cultures, demographics, geographical settings, and values. A genie has been let out of his lantern and cannot be pushed back in – the expectation that government should rest on popular consent, at least to the extent that there are free and fair elections. This common expectation, when it is present among a people, must be accommodated, and the result looks invariably like de facto popular sovereignty even when it is not de jure popular sovereignty.

Popular sovereignty, however, implies that the people are limited in some way as the ultimate force, which in turn almost always implies a constitution to encode such limits. Popular ratification of the constitution then amounts to the initial self-limiting that defines a sovereign. These limits can be viewed as resulting from a prudential calculation that a given individual will not always be in the majority, and thus must protect his or her interests as a possible member of a future minority whenever they are part of a majority. This is a reasonable argument, but another argument offers an important supplement. The average human being is a realist and not an idealist. She or he wants to lead a better life but does not expect to achieve perfection on Earth. The essential honesty and realism that result from large numbers of people engaging in political discourse tend strongly to undercut utopian ideas or proposals. Hence, a tiny minority, the revolutionary vanguard of right or left, secular or religious, has always imposed overly idealistic constitutions, whereas popularly approved constitutions tend strongly toward a less than ideal modus vivendi.

One implied principle of constitutional design emerging from this discussion is that a constitution must be written by those who will live under it and not by some outside team of "experts," and must also be approved by the people who will live under it and not by some philosopher-king or cadre of vanguard thinkers. Another principle is that, when designing institutions to produce popular sovereignty, one can only seek the best that is possible under the circumstances, since the ideal political system will not work on Earth, and seeking it will produce only fanaticism, not justice. Because these principles are more complex and more thoroughly grounded than the discussion to this point might indicate, a consideration of Plato and then of Aristotle is helpful.

Plato on Matching a Government and a People

The question of how to match a government and a people recurs throughout the history of Western political thought. Indeed, it is present at the birth of political philosophy. However, even though matching a government to its people is a fundamental principle of constitutional design, constitutionalism may or may not have been present at the birth of political philosophy depending on how one reads Plato. A brief explication of Plato in this regard is instructive for understanding both what constitutionalism is and what it is not.

The matching exercise may proceed within one of several possible frames. Note how it is framed in the first sentence of the preceding paragraph – how to match a government and a people. This way of framing is neutral with respect to the relative status of the two entities – "a government" and "a people." In the second sentence of the preceding paragraph constitutionalism is identified with matching a government *to* its people. In this framing the people have priority over government, and government is considered malleable and subservient to the people. A third way of framing the issue is to think about matching a people to a government. Government now has priority, and the people are viewed as malleable and subservient to the requirements of some ideal political system. One could read Plato's *Republic* as working within this third frame as Socrates and his fellow inquirers construct an ideal city in speech. This reading of Plato would be profoundly anticonstitutional. On the other hand, one can read Plato ironically, in which case the *Republic* is a philosophical cautionary tale against such an anticonstitutional approach. If one sees Plato as using the first way of framing the question, where one takes a neutral view of the relative status of the two entities and engages in what amounts to only a logical exercise, one is engaging in a profoundly nonconstitutional exercise.

A great deal is at stake in deciding which frame to use. If humans have an essence, something without which they would not be human, then any attempt to alter humans so that they conform to the requirements of some political system is potentially an attack on humanity. Today, any philosophical perspective that views humans as having a nature, or an essence, is termed "essentialist." There has been a sustained attack on essentialist philosophy during the modern era. Racists and ethnocentrists have denied that all humans share a single nature and have either emphasized the effects of culture on human identity or argued for genetic or "blood" differences between groups of humans. Moral relativism under various guises, including its recent manifestation as "postmodernism," has attacked essentialism as a cover for privilege and elitism. Although it is true that some elitists have misappropriated essentialist ideas for their own political ends, it is difficult to see how any position that argues for an inherent psychological and moral similarity among humans can support either elitism or moral relativism. It is also difficult to see how one can establish and maintain any political order approaching constitutional republicanism without resorting to some minimally essentialist position. Indeed, modern constitutionalism began with, and continues to rest upon, a notion of human equality that is grounded in one essentialist position or another. Within this philosophical frame humans exist and are fully human prior to any government, so the government must always be matched to the people.

However, Plato was not a modern. In his view, humans could not be fully human outside of a political system. Humans, *qua* humans, have a potential that, although natural, requires development if it is to flower in its fullest form. He considered government, along with family and other sociocultural institutions, as an essential agent for helping humans to develop fully what is in their nature. This view, one held by Aristotle as well, still takes human nature as a given and government as an instrument in the service of humans. However, Plato recognized immediately that because all political systems rest on power, and because power has its own nature with certain inherent tendencies, it is easy for those in power to slip into another frame where human nature recedes into a malleable substance at the service of those holding the reigns of power. The essentialist perspective makes the matching between a people and their government a deeply problematic enterprise. A nonessentialist perspective, on the other hand, can take a neutral position with respect to matching a people and a government. Both are malleable, and matching them is a straightforward and reasonably simple enterprise. The nonessentialist perspective, by avoiding or ignoring any discussion of what is or is not "natural," is profoundly nonconstitutional at its best. This becomes clearer, and Plato's contributions to the discussion on constitutionalism become more apparent, if we consider for a moment the implications of the term "constitution."

The word "constitution" has an interesting etymology that seems to cut across the essentialist-nonessentialist argument. The term comes from a Latin word with the broad, nonpolitical implication of determining the nature or character of something. At the same time, it implies the action of making or establishing something. "Determining the nature of a thing" implies that a constitution is somehow involved with something that has an essence, an unchanging character. On the other hand, the "action of making or establishing something" implies that what is created is not "natural" in the sense of existing prior to human intervention but is, instead, a conventional artifact. When we get to the term's explicitly political meaning, "the system or body of fundamental principles according to which a political system is governed," it simultaneously implies something that is natural in that it has an essence that makes it what it is, and something that is created and therefore not natural in the sense that it does not exist outside of human action. Cicero explicitly recognized that the failure to include the first part of this seemingly paradoxical concept led to the idea of a constitution losing its normative basis and becoming a simple creation of human will. Such a creation would be merely descriptive of a set of institutions, and the description would become unstable because it could be interpreted in any manner decided upon by those in power at a given moment. His famous solution was to suggest that there is an existing order to which the good political system must conform, a natural law, and the essence of constitutionalism is tied to its conformity with this higher law. The political instrument termed a constitution is thus a human creation that is supposed to reflect an existing order against which it is judged. The very meaning of constitutionalism raises ontological issues about what exists by nature, and what it means to say that something exists or that something is natural.

Plato wrote within a political culture that assumed a natural relationship between three things – a *polis*, a *politeia*, and a *politeuma*. *Polis* may be defined as "a way of life," which also implies a way of life that is shared and has a moral content. Because "a people" is essentially defined as those who share a way of life, to the extent the *polis* is a creation and not natural, to that same extent "the people" are a creation and not natural. *Politeia* may be translated as "a plan for a way of life." It may also be viewed as the fundamental principles guiding a way of life, or a constitution in the modern sense. Plato did not, and could not, title his book the Republic because *res publica* is a Latin term not used in classical Greece. Instead, his book is actually entitled *Politeia*, which suggests his project in this long dialogue is generally constitutional rather than supportive of a particular constitutional form.

Politeuma may be defined as "those who write the plan for a way of life." We now commonly translate *politeuma* as "regime," although twentieth-century implications associated with regime make the term less useful than it once was. In classical Greece, when the regime was usually a small part of the population, the resulting political system was considered an oligarchy if the rules benefited the portion of the population that designed the *politeia*, or an aristocracy if it benefited the common good. When the *politeuma* was the body of the people, it was called a democracy if the *politeia* they created benefited the many poor, or a polity if it served the common good. If the *politeuma* was a single person, the *politeia* defined either a tyrant or a monarch, again depending on whom it benefited. The multiplicity of possible regimes suggested to the Greeks that the form of the political system was not natural, although the existence of a *polis* was considered natural because it flowed out of human nature to the extent that they could not think of humans, *qua* humans, living outside of a sociopolitical community. Only deities or beasts could live outside of some political organization. Beasts lack language and reason, and thus cannot create a political system. The deities are immortal and self-sufficient, thus beyond any need for sustaining life. Humans are by nature equipped for creating a *polis*, and by nature in need of creating one. Humans are also by nature inclined to think about turning mere life into the good life, and a political system is instrumental for both. For these reasons the Greeks viewed the *polis* as natural, because it flowed from and helped to perfect human nature. Hence, humans could not be fully human outside of a *polis*.

Plato began by appealing to all of these Greek beliefs, and he also appealed to the belief that the relationship between *polis*, *politeia*, and *politeuma* is a natural one. That is, just as it is natural for humans to exist as members of a people in a polis, it is natural that the way of life for these people has guiding principles set down by someone.

However, Plato raised the ante by suggesting that, contrary to the standard Greek understanding taught by the sophists, there is some way of life among the possible alternatives that is natural – that is, some way of life in accordance with some standard that transcends political creation. The constitution created by human will, therefore, can be held up to some higher natural standard of justice that exists independent of human will. In this sense Plato's project looks very much in accord with constitutionalism. Using the "*polis* as man writ large" approach, Plato constantly asks what is natural for a ship's captain, or doctor, or trainer to do. That is, what would they do without any help from human-made guidelines?

It is difficult, after a careful reading of the text, not to conclude that Plato's ideal city in speech is deeply ironic. After removing all impediments to perfect justice, Plato concludes in book VIII (546 a–e) that even in the city in speech perfect justice is still unknowable to the best among us. The almost comedic equation for justice he describes in this section expresses the mystery entailed in the incommensurability among the elements of perfect justice. The dialogue ends in book X with the Myth of Er, and in this myth it seems that justice is something to be chosen or rejected by individuals rather than achieved through a properly designed political system. Although Plato seems to be telling us that perfect justice on Earth is not possible, his final words in the Myth of Er seem to ultimately reject the constitutional project altogether. Still, one thing Plato appears to be telling us is that seeking perfect justice on Earth is not a constitutional project, and, combined with what Aristotle will later teach us, this cautionary tale does lay out a fundamental principle of constitutionalism: seek what is possible through our *politeia*, not what is perfect.

Plato takes up the constitutional project again in his longest dialogue, the *Laws*. Many students of political philosophy find this dialogue disappointing, because it lacks the flights of originality and memorable images found in the *Republic*. Still, it is in this work that Plato lays out his sense of how to match a *politeia* to flesh-and-blood people who live in a world that is not simply an exercise in formal logic.

In the *Republic*, Plato uncovered the most general principles underlying society. He saw society as resting naturally on a mutual exchange of services that contributed cumulatively to the creation of personal happiness when the exchange rested on virtue. Virtue, in turn, rests on knowledge of the good, and knowledge is conceived of as analogous to the exact, deductive procedure of mathematics to which factual knowledge contributes nothing beyond illustration. Because rulers in the ideal state are to be the most virtuous, the relationship between the rulers and the ruled amounts to one between the learned and the ignorant. Entirely missing from the political equation of the *Republic* are laws, since there is no room for the gradual growth of wisdom through experience and custom. Instead brilliant and virtuous leaders intuit the proper response to any political matter that arises.

In the appropriately named *Laws*, Plato lays out his view on "the second best" political system, one in which laws substitute for philosopher-rulers. That Plato felt such a dialogue was necessary supports an ironic reading of the *Republic*, and thus supports the notion that human nature must be taken as a given. We are not very far into the *Laws* when it becomes apparent that empirical considerations have reentered his analysis through an examination of history. The Athenian stranger, who serves in the role played by Socrates in the *Republic*, rehearses the history of several existing political systems. Each becomes understandable in terms of its respective history seen as a developing experience embodied in laws, customs, religion, myths, and shared events; and conditioned by underlying physical (geographic location, climate, and soil), economic, and social factors. Implicit in this part of the discussion is the evaluation of a government in terms of its appropriateness for the people living under it – matching the government to the people. Still, Plato strains toward some set of principles that will be appropriate for all peoples regardless of how these principles are expressed institutionally.

A lengthy analysis of why certain political systems fail concludes that invariably it is because of a lack of moderation. More specifically, Persia exemplifies how monarchy invariably decays into tyranny, and Athens exemplifies how democracy invariably decays from an excess of liberty. The solution is to combine the principles of monarchy and democracy in a "mixed" government that replaces the rule by one or the many with rule by laws. To this extent his new project is more explicitly constitutional, but only in a partial sense since popular sovereignty is sidestepped in a peculiar fashion. Most of the inhabitants will not be citizens.

The second best political system, the best that can be achieved in the real world, is still informed by the ideal political system laid out in the *Republic*. In order to minimize the effects of economic class on politics, the land is divided into equal allotments that can be neither divided nor alienated. Slaves will do the actual agricultural work on these allotments, and the produce will be consumed in common at public meals. Private property is permitted, but the extent of private property is limited to four times the amount represented by an allotment. Citizens may not engage in trade, business, crafts, or industry. These activities will be engaged in by nonresidents who are freemen but not citizens. Nor is there to be possession of gold or silver, and interest for loans is prohibited. In a certain sense, Plato here ducks an essential problem faced by any constitutional order, participation, by sharply restricting citizenship. Whereas in the *Republic* all inhabitants were citizens, in the *Laws* Plato creates what is in effect an oligarchy where "the people" are only a portion of the many, and thus where popular sovereignty is proscribed.

The mixed government expresses the democratic principle by having the citizens elect a council of 360. For this election citizens are divided into four classes, each class owning one-fourth of the total wealth, and one-fourth of the council comes from each class. In addition, the chief board of magistrates, termed "the guardians of the law," are elected in a three-step balloting. The first vote elects 300, from which 100 are then elected, and on the third vote 37 are elected from this 100 to become the chief board of magistrates. Finally, there is a Nocturnal Council comprised of the ten oldest magistrates, the director of education, and certain priests chosen for their virtue. Strangely, there is no manifestation of the monarchic principle in the second best political system that is supposed to mix the monarchic and democratic principles.

Other important details reinforce the oligarchic basis of this second best political system, but the outline of his proposal is clear. The laws that rule in place of the philosopher-king do not flow from, support, or reflect anything resembling popular sovereignty. Although we may term this system constitutional, the arrangement of institutions does not create what we today term a constitutional republic despite the use of elections. There is an implicit principle of balance in Plato's constitution in the sense that there is some provision for a mutual adjustment of conflicting claims and interests, but the principle is applied only embryonically. Still, Plato has worked his way, perhaps halfheartedly, to the first clear principles of constitutional design – match a government to the people, establish rule of law, include institutions for expressing and balancing the interests of all citizens, and use elections to select and control those who govern. Still apparent by their absence is a comprehensive theory of citizenship, a developed sense of participation, and institutions for effectively balancing the interests of citizens. It is at this point that Aristotle takes over the historic development of constitutionalism.

Aristotle on Matching a Government and a People

In his *Politics*, Aristotle was the first to study constitutional design systematically. Political philosophers who study him often conclude that what Aristotle had to say is of limited use today because it derives from an examination of the Greek *polis*. There are several arguments generally used to dismiss Aristotle's applicability to current political systems. First, the classical Greek *polis* was very small compared with most of today's constitutional republics. Second, the Greeks at that time did not use or understand representation, and modern constitutional republics are by definition built around systems of representation. Third, the *polis* was by definition a political organization with a very deep moral and cultural content that is impossible to reproduce or use as a model in contemporary political analysis.

These objections can be dealt with relatively easily. First, as was shown in Chapter 4, at least twenty of the current seventy-five political systems that can be categorized among constitutional republics are no larger in population than the Athens in which Plato and Aristotle lived. Many are much smaller. Either one arbitrarily concludes that principles of constitutional design are irrelevant for polities below a certain size, in which case we simply write off the relevance of countries like Iceland, or one concludes that analysis of small political systems has something to tell us about large ones, and vice versa.

Second, we are after general principles of constitutional design that are applicable to any constitutional system, including constitutional republics. We are most interested today in constitutional republics, but analysis of nonrepublican constitutions can throw light on the nature of representation by highlighting what this political form is not. Also, although it is true that a direct democracy is not a republic, Plato and Aristotle did not limit their respective analyses to democratic Athens but also engaged in analyses of other constitutional forms that included some form of election, and thus of some form of representation.

Third, it is traditional to emphasize the coherent moral content implicit in a *polis*, but Aristotle in particular examined the manner and extent to which even a *polis* might not require a unified moral content to survive and thrive. That is, because the *polis* did seem to require a high moral content, Aristotle was led to ask precisely what this meant. By rejecting the position he attributed to Plato that everything must be shared, he opened up a deeper analysis of the required minimal moral content of a *polis*, and thus of any political system. He concluded in part that any political system, including a *polis*, would inevitably (naturally) have distributed across its population different notions of equality and thus of justice. If it is natural and inevitable that a given population not include in its political morality a shared notion of equality and justice, then even the classical Greek *polis* did not have the very high level of shared morality that modern commentators are inclined to attribute to it. Aristotle did not say that there was no true justice or equality, but he did say that citizens invariably disagreed about what was just or equal. Indeed, Aristotle was led to suggest the mixed regime as the best possible constitution in the real world precisely because of the natural limits on any shared political morality.

This leads us to consider more carefully Aristotle's "mixed regime." The first thing to be said about this concept is that one cannot mix what is not at least initially distinguishable or separate. Part of Aristotle's contribution to constitutional analysis is to distinguish conceptually three key principles – the monarchic principle, the aristocratic principle, and the democratic principle – and then to show how they can be utilized together to create what he termed the "mixed regime." As indicated in an earlier discussion, "regime" is a translation of *politeuma*, which refers to those who write the *politeia*, or constitution, that defines the shared way of life. Those in the *politeuma*, or regime, have full political rights in that they can hold office as well as assist in the selection of those who hold office. A mixed regime is thus literally a mixture of several possible regimes.

Aristotle used the conventional Greek notion that the regime could be composed of one, a few, or the many. Ignoring for now his distinction between regimes types that sought the good of the regime as opposed to those that sought the common good, rule by one embodied the monarchic principle, rule by a few embodied the aristocratic principle, and rule by the many embodied the democratic principle. A mixed regime utilized all three principles so that the regime was composed of the one, the few, and the many. Speaking only logically, if one established a democracy, it would appear that the regime would include everyone, including any identifiable "few" or any identifiable "one." There would then seem to be no need for any mixing. However, Aristotle rejected simple democracy for two fundamental reasons. First, he noted that each principle was attached to what is usually translated as a "class." Second, he associated each principle with certain characteristics, and because the characteristics associated with each principle were all useful to a political system, he argued that a stable and successful constitution required the inclusion of them all and not just those associated with democracy.

As to his first reason for rejecting simple democracy, Aristotle began by noting that many constitutions were monarchies, and the royal class supported rule by one, the monarch. Other constitutions created oligarchies – rule by a few. Because a hereditary aristocracy invariably supported this kind of political order, Aristotle termed it an "aristocracy" with one critical caveat. "Aristocracy" is derived from the Greek word *aristoi*, which means "the best" or "the better sort" according to some standard of excellence. Aristotle did not accept that members of a hereditary aristocracy were necessarily better in any moral sense of the term, so he distinguished between a theoretical aristocracy, where members of the regime did match the standard of excellence, and actual aristocracies, in which power was based on wealth rather than on merit: "So in fact the grounds of difference have been given wrongly; what really differentiates oligarchy and democracy is wealth or the lack of it" (1279b26).[1] This distinction led Aristotle to conclude that in real-world aristocracies the regime tended to rule for its own ends rather than for the common good. Democracy rested on rule by the many. Becuase most citizens are not wealthy but "poor" compared with those in the "aristocracy," rule by the many would tend to support the needs and goals of the majority who are not wealthy. In sum, after Aristotle distinguished theoretically between the three principles, he then attached each principle to a naturally occurring class. Under this construction, a democracy did not include "the one" or "the few" but was instead just another regime working for some class good rather than the common good. One major goal of the mixed regime, then, was to prevent class domination through the inclusion of all three classes in the regime.

"Mixed regime," then, does not imply a "melted regime" in which the parts become indistinguishable. Rather, the three principles are to be combined in such a way that all parts of the population will feel their citizenship. Aristotle suggests three possible kinds of mixing. In one, legislation favorable to everyone would be provided. However, because he notes elsewhere that mere laws are to be distinguished from a constitution, this form of mixing is descriptive of the effects of a properly operating mixed regime and not descriptive of a constitution per se (1289a11). The second form of mixing is more properly constitutional. Here he suggests that we consider how a given institution would be organized in an oligarchy, and then how it would be organized in a democracy, and then that we design the institution so as to find a middle ground or mean. In the next paragraph, however, he says that the defining feature of a mixed regime is that it is possible to describe the same constitution as oligarchic or democratic because both groups have the impression that it matches their expectations, and this definition undercuts the constitutional efficacy of the second

[1] Aristotle, *The Politics*, trans. T. A. Sinclair, rev. Trevor J. Saunders (Baltimore: Penguin, 1981).

method of mixing. We need only look at the one example of this form of mixing provided by Aristotle. He says that if in aristocracies there is an expectation that there should be a high property assessment for membership in the assembly, and in democracies there is an expectation that there be no property qualification, fixing an assessment midway between these two is a form of mixing. In fact, it is probable that neither side would be happy with this, especially the many nonwealthy who would still see the constitution as aristocratic. Such "blending" is not a very good way to "mix." The third method of mixing that Aristotle suggests is to provide each class with an institution or set of institutions through which it could independently protect its respective ends. Thus, for example, one branch of government could be elected on the basis of property requirements, and another branch of government could be elected by lot. The key point is that Aristotle recognized that there is at least one irreconcilable division present in all polities that makes a simple democratic form of government both impractical and dangerous. The different principles must be mixed in some form within a constitution if alienation of some critical part of the population is to be avoided. The general implication for constitutional design is that major, irreducible divisions within a given population must be given institutional voice.

The second reason Aristotle rejected simple democracy rested on his sense of the natural empirical characteristics associated with each possible regime. Those among the wealthy had the leisure and means to obtain an education, or a much better education than could be obtained by the nonwealthy, who were too caught up in the need to earn a livelihood. The wealthy thus had more elevated tastes that tended to produce moderation and careful thinking. They also had more knowledge of the world at large, were experienced at dealing with large sums of money and with complicated issues, and tended to take a broad and long-term view of matters compared with those whose noses were kept by necessity close to the grindstone. The wealthy few were thus associated with knowledge, wisdom, and virtue. Virtue in this sense did not necessarily have a moral implication, although the aristocratic penchant for moderation was an essential moral virtue. Instead, Aristotle was thinking here more in terms of *aretē*, which was the notion of possessing practical virtues that made one excellent at some activity. The one activity at which "the few" excel is statecraft. By this is meant not only leadership but also the conduct of foreign affairs and the operation of government in pursuit of complex economic and social goals.

The many "poor" or nonwealthy have their own virtues and characteristics. For one thing, their sheer numbers produce strength. Many political philosophers after Aristotle, including Machiavelli, would note the comparative advantage possessed by a state where the many fought in defense of their own liberty and citizenship. On the other hand, if they are not included in the regime, says Aristotle, "they inevitably constitute a huge hostile element" in the political system (1281b21). Their natural strength becomes a danger rather than an asset. The many are also the political system's reservoir of honesty. He means this in the sense that they are both less easily deceived than a few and less easily corrupted (1281a39 and 1286a36). They are less easily deceived because they possess the lion's share of *phronēsis*, or practical wisdom. Aristotle uses the metaphor of building and living in a house. Who knows better whether a house is good, he asks: the person who designed it or the people who must live in it? The much greater cumulative experience with living and solving practical matters gives the many nonwealthy an advantage when it comes to distinguishing fact from fancy. Although individual members of the nonwealthy class may not be good judges of what works and what doesn't, when taken together the large numbers in this class overwhelm those of poor judgment – something that may not happen as easily among the few wealthy. The many nonwealthy are also less easily corrupted. "As a larger amount of water is less easily polluted," says Aristotle, "so the multitude is less easily corrupted than the few" (1286a21). Thus, whatever may tempt an individual to error is much more difficult to induce in a large number than in a small: "It would take a lot of doing to arrange for all simultaneously to lose their temper and go wrong" (1286a21).

Finally, there are certain characteristics associated with "the one" that benefit any political system. The rule of one person is conducive to unity and coherence. Policy is subject to only one will, and thus can move in one direction without competition or dilution. This results in the second characteristic of one-person rule, speed. With only one person involved, decisions can be made quickly, and new circumstances can be responded to immediately. Finally, with only one person involved, there is no doubt who should be held responsible. There is no way to duck responsibility or to hide behind the ambiguity of a complex process involving many heads. As a result, because he knows he will be held responsible, the "one person" will tend to act responsibly to protect his power and reputation. Again, as with aristocracy and democracy, Aristotle is careful to distinguish the monarchic principle from historical manifestations accidentally associated with the principle. There are several reasons why monarchy arose, he says, but almost always it was because one person was perceived to somehow be "the best" in some critical skill such as war or judgment. When that person was replaced by one of his children, however, monarchy came to be associated with inherited one-person rule. As Aristotle notes (1286b22), experience shows that "hereditary succession is harmful," yet a king's not giving his kingship to his children "expects too much virtue of human nature." What he suggests we have learned from experience is that there are certain advantages to be gained from utilizing the monarchic principle but not from tying the principle to heredity.

The analysis of the three regime principles takes place within a larger discussion about what amounts to "sovereignty." As noted in Chapter 2, Aristotle had a notion of some higher law that should serve as a standard against which to measure earthly political systems, which implies something similar to what Bodin meant by a sovereign. However, it is probably incorrect to translate the Greek word *kurios* as sovereign. Instead, it is best translated as "supreme power," so that the opening passage in section x of book III (1281a11) should be rendered: "Another question is 'Where ought the supreme power of the polis reside?' With the mass of the people? With the rich? With the respectable? With one man, the best of all? Or a tyrant? There are objections to all these." After rehearsing the objections to all of these, Aristotle discusses the benefits, though limited, of collective wisdom. There turn out to be reasons for including all of the natural factions described in the passage just quoted, which leads him to conclude eventually that the mixed regime, one that blends the monarchic, aristocratic, and democratic principles, is the least objectionable solution to the problem of where to place supreme political power. Each principle, in effect, represents the natural inclinations of naturally occurring divisions within any political system. A constitution that utilizes all three principles thus has two beneficial consequences. First, it protects the interests of all naturally occurring factions, and thereby contributes to the stability of the political system. Second, it incorporates the various virtues and strengths possessed by each of these naturally occurring factions, thereby contributing to the effectiveness and future success of the political system. What is held in common is not a definition of equality and justice, but a constitution that effectively organizes the people for action in history, for "noble" actions by the people. This leads us to ask what else is held in common if a common constitution is to be possible?

Aristotle on What Is to Be Held in Common

Let us begin by laying out quickly the things that Aristotle says in discussions scattered throughout the *Politics* concerning what are and are not to be held in common by a people. He begins the book by noting that a people have the *polis* in common. This means that they share a way of life, and that way of life is based on a commonly held political association. He then says that in order to understand that common political association, we must break it down into its component parts. Through this analytic method, it becomes clear that we do not share the same household, the same gender, the same status, the same occupations, the same abilities, the same level of development in whatever abilities we inherit at birth, the same notion of equality, or the same notion of justice. All of these differences he terms "natural." In thinking about these differences, however, we find that we do share the same desire for life that the household is designed to provide, the same need for sex that gender entails, the same need to express ourselves through the activity of occupations, the same need to develop our abilities in order to achieve the highest status we can, the same hope to be treated in accord with who we are, and the same hope for justice and the good life – receiving what is due to us as humans and as contributors to the common life. What we hold in common and what we do not thus flow from human nature and are natural.

But while human nature is common to all humans, humans do not all share the same way of life. Instead, humans are naturally divided into different peoples. By the end of section ix in book III Aristotle has set out a number of necessary and sufficient characteristics for a people. A people who share a way of life are necessarily defined by an interlocking set of relationships. Because these relationships require face-to-face encounters that cannot be extended over great distances, a way of life is limited in space by the common human needs for economic exchange, social intercourse, and friendship (*philia*). This requires that "they occupy the same territory and intermarry."

It is notable that when Aristotle describes what he means by social intercourse, he speaks of various "brotherhoods," various religious beliefs, and various "civilized pursuits of life." A political system in his view does not require a common kinship, religion, social memberships, or occupations. Aside from a common territory, however, he does see the ability to intermarry as crucial. Friendship rests on ties of affection that crosscut and bind the various networks of association. One critical aspect of a people, then, is that they are able to intermarry across all of the natural differences. If there is a line across which marriage cannot take place, then we have at least two peoples, and no *polis*. Thus, when it comes to matching a government to a people for purposes of constitutional design, the relative absence of barriers to intermarriage across a population may be a very important consideration. Prohibitions on intermarriage, or high barriers designed to dissuade intermarriage across ethnic, religious, cultural, or racial lines argue against the creation of a people capable of being brought under a common political system. Either one must attempt to match the span of a political system with a highly homogeneous population, or else one must find or legally induce circumstances where intermarriage across all major lines of difference is possible and reasonably well accepted. It is notable that, even in the supposedly highly homogeneous populations of the ancient Greek city-states, Aristotle emphasized that the marriage pool must be held in common in the face of population differences that he held to be significant.

Another thing that must be held in common is the ability of citizens to hold office and take part in political associations. In Aristotle's day this usually implied that citizenship was restricted to only a portion of the adult population. However, his best possible political system in the real world, the mixed regime, clearly implied a very broad definition of citizenship. In today's constitutional republics, with all that we have learned over the past twenty-five centuries, the recommendation implicit in Aristotle's mixed regime would seem to argue that citizenship should be held in common by all adults.

Finally, for purposes of our discussion here, Aristotle argues that a common citizenship makes education a public concern. His discussion at the beginning of book VIII is so clear and efficient, that it will save time to simply quote him directly.

No one would dispute the fact that it is a lawgiver's prime duty to arrange for the education of the young. In a [*polis*][2] where this is not done the quality of the constitution suffers. Education must be related to the particular constitution in each case, for it is the special character appropriate to each constitution that set it up at the start and commonly maintains it, e.g. the democratic character preserves a democracy, the oligarchic an oligarchy. And in all circumstances the better character is a cause of a better constitution. And just as there must be preparatory training for all skills and capacities, and a process of preliminary habituation to the work of each profession, it is obvious that there must also be training for the activities of virtue. But since there is but one aim for the entire [*polis*], it follows that education must be one and the same for all, and that the responsibility for it must be a public one, not the private affair which it now is, each man looking after his own children and teaching them privately whatever private curriculum he thinks they ought to study. In matters that belong to the public, training for them must be the public's concern. And it is not right either that any of the citizens should think that he belongs just to himself; he must regard all citizens as belonging to the *polis*, for each is a part of the [*polis*]; and the responsibility for each part naturally has regard to the responsibility for the whole. (1337a11)

If citizenship is to be held in common, so must education be held in common. This education should inculcate common attitudes, primary among which must be the ability and willingness to pursue the common good.

So where has Aristotle taken us? The basic proposition seems to be that in order to match the government to the people we must first distinguish between what a people holds in common and what they do not. Some of what they hold in common results from their being human and is shared with people everywhere. Other commonalities are limited to the given people to which they belong. Some of the things not held in common need to be taken into account constitutionally, whereas other things not held in common do not. The matching exercise requires that we clearly distinguish all four categories and that we take each into account.

[2] T. A. Sinclair translates the word *polis* as "the state." This modern term, with its European statist implications, is not quite correct. "Political system" would probably be better, but in this instance as elsewhere the original term *polis* is retained.

That Which Is Held in Common by All Humans

The distinction between what is held in common by all humans and what is held in common by the people of a given political system reminds us that any constitution must take into account basic human needs. This seemingly obvious observation is too often the rock upon which a constitutional order founders. Humans cannot be molded by a constitution into something contrary to human nature. A constitution may elicit and encourage any number of possible human responses, but it cannot eliminate any of these possibilities. Aristotle is here the complete realist, and as a result demonstrates his understanding of a deep principle of constitutional design. When one attempts to match a constitution to a people, one must remember that one is dealing with humans and not a completely malleable creature whose natural repertoire of behaviors can be shaped to relegate what is undesirable to the dustbin of history.

Scattered throughout Aristotle's analysis are trenchant observations that lay out these common needs. All humans have a need for self-preservation, which includes the need for order and thus for secure expectations, for families, and for comfort. All humans have a need for sociability, including the need for some minimal level of respect when conducting social interactions. This sociability expresses itself in all kinds moral, economic, and kinship exchanges. He codifies this minimal respect as *philia*, or a friendship that leads one to see oneself in the other. Humans have a need for liberty, including the need for self-expression. Finally, humans have a need for beneficial innovation so that they can look forward to a better life for themselves and their descendants. Aristotle demonstrates one form of beneficial innovation in his creation of a mixed regime but codifies the concept with the phrase "the good life," which is an open-ended set of possibilities that extend into all aspects of life. Aristotle provides a clear argument in favor of private property that flows from the need for self-preservation, the need for family, the need for self-expression, and the need for exchanges grounded in *philia*.

That Which Is Held in Common by a Given People

Aristotle expands upon Plato's insights when it comes to what a people share that make them a people. They share a location with its geographical characteristics such as climate, soil, and relative security from neighbors. They share an identity as a people that results from some level of a shared culture, including language, religion, and customs. Left unsaid is the extent to which these must be shared, although there are some hints. Whereas Plato in his *Laws* suggests that private expressions of religion must be prohibited so that only a common, publicly expressed religion is allowed, Aristotle has no such prohibition. Instead, he speaks of religions in the plural. Thus, while there is no argument in favor of freedom of religion, multiplicity of religions is assumed. It also seems to be assumed that religion belongs to the family and is thus outside of politics per se. Later thinkers such as Thomas More, Machiavelli, and Rousseau speak of the need for a civil religion, either a bland and generalized public worship that does no violence to the multiplicity of private expressions or else an explicitly political nonreligious substitute for a common religion sanctioned by the political system. Successful constitutional republics have tended to use the latter formulation whereby certain shared political principles and basic laws serve as a common "religion." Such an approach is implicitly sanctioned by Aristotle's emphasis upon the need for *philia* among the people that leads to a mutual respect for differences.

Whereas Aristotle is less than clear with respect to religion, he is quite clear that a people must share social networks. That is, they must be free to pursue unregulated exchanges of all types, especially the possibility of intermarriage. This shared gene pool is fundamentally related to the common citizenship that defines a people and has implications for the nature of that citizenship. On one hand, a people result from a myriad of face-to-face interactions through which citizens come to know or at least recognize each other. Intermarriage is one result of people interacting freely and often. On the other hand, all humans, regardless of where they come from, are capable of sexual intercourse and thus of intermarriage. In principle, then, members of a people can intermarry with those who are not citizens. Because frequency of interaction is associated with the probability of marriage, citizens are highly likely to marry other citizens. What happens, however, if for some reason a citizen marries a noncitizen? In the United States this is sufficient grounds for making the noncitizen a citizen. The possibility of intermarriage thus makes differences in religion, ethnicity, and customs secondary in importance. It also, by law, makes noncitizenship a secondary consideration unless the laws distinguish between marriage to a citizen and a noncitizen.

Which brings us to another thing that Aristotle argued must be held in common, the laws, including the constitution. Implicit in Aristotle's treatment of religion is that common laws can dictate the place of religion among a people. Likewise, the laws held in common determine the effects of marriage, including inheritance. Many thinkers since Aristotle have held that citizens must have laws in common, and because today we recognize all adults among a people as citizens, then the people must have laws in common. Rule of law is implicit in common laws, which means in part that the rulers are subject to the same laws to the same extent as everyone else. This in turn implies a constitutional order.

For Aristotle, common laws and a common constitution did not describe something external to the people, but a natural extension of that people. He tried to capture the basis for this natural extension in the concept of *philia*, a basis for political relationships that was expressed in the nature of everyday interactions. That is, the laws and constitutional order rested on something that Montesquieu would later term "the spirit of the laws." Bodin speaks similarly of the laws being undergirded by "the natural temperament of a people," and Tocqueville speaks of the "habits of mind" of a people. A constitution, as well as the laws passed under it if that constitution is matched to the people, is a natural expression of how a people tend to think. This in turn is a natural product of their shared history, which includes the institutions already in place, the political culture shared by potential as well as actual political elites, how the critical political problems faced by a particular people have been resolved, the shared memory of past events, as well as what might be termed the dominant "political myth." All peoples have some sense of how they came to be a people, how they got to where they are, and the sense of this coming to be is often encapsulated in a "narrative" that is in the form of a myth. A myth is not something that is literally true, but a story that captures some deeper truth. The story of Romulus and Remus served as a founding myth for the Romans, and the tradition of George Washington and his cherry tree, along with the story of the Pilgrims and their first Thanksgiving, serves something similar for the United States. A good place to look for the basis of such a myth is in early documents that describe or codify early events in the history of a people. The implicit or explicit values, norms, expectations, hopes, and ideas found in these early documents are often later shaped by a people to explain themselves and their place in history and to serve as the basis for their view of themselves as a people.

Things Not Held in Common by a People but of Constitutional Importance

The discussion to this point has emphasized those things held in common by all humans and those things held in common by a given people. Each of these must be taken into account in constitutional design. A third category consequential for constitutional design is the category of things not held in common by a people. These include, but are not limited to, the sources of wealth; the distribution of wealth and the resulting class structure; the relative prevalence of ethnic, racial, and religious divisions; and the content and distribution of ideological divisions, especially with respect to views on equality and justice. In sum, constitutional design requires careful attention to the structure of interests and therefore the nature of factions. Constitutional design should also take into account the probable consequences of the design itself for future factional alignments.

In classical Greece wealth resulted primarily from ownership of land and slaves. James Madison in *Federalist Papers* 10 argues that viewing wealth as simply a division between those who are wealthy and those who are not is inadequate for purposes of analyzing factional alignments. Landed wealth has different interests from that achieved through manufactures. Both have interests different from those held by men and women engaged in trade and commerce. The interests of those who lend money to manufacturers for production differ from those who must borrow. New and relatively undeveloped industries have different interests from developed industries that can compete on world markets without protection. Owners of small businesses differ in their interests from owners of large businesses. Speculators in land and capital have still another set of interests. Steel companies compete with aluminum and concrete companies for construction. Spice farmers differ in their needs from corn or wheat producers. In sum, the class of wealthy people is not homogeneous and monolithic. Diversity in sources of wealth is both an opportunity and a problem for writers of constitutions. Diversity in sources of wealth makes the task easier, because the resulting class structure will be much less polarized. The task is made harder by the various wealthy factions maneuvering to achieve relative advantage through the process of writing a constitution. Sometimes, as happened with a proposed new constitution for Texas in the 1970s, the combined opposition by these various factions who fear to lose some specific relative advantage can result in the document not being adopted. This is one argument for designing a constitution that has as little policy content as possible. The alternative is to constitutionalize enough policy issues that the factions who see their respective interests safeguarded are sufficient in strength to support the proposed document.

A simple, highly polarized class structure presents one kind of problem, whereas a complicated and fluid distribution of wealth presents another. There are no simple rules for responding to different types of class structure, but careful analysis is called for if the future operation of the political system is not to be destabilized.

In recent years there has been an automatic tendency to emphasize the relative prevalence of ethnic, racial, and religious divisions in a political system. To a certain extent, we may now overemphasize these sources of faction. Certainly these divisions are sometimes extremely important, but a well-designed constitution can fairly easily mitigate such divisions. For example, if the divisions tend to align themselves geographically, a federal structure may well be a good solution. Consociational arrangements may otherwise be a prudent solution. In general, however, it is probably best not to encourage the hardening of such divisions by writing them into the constitution. Aristotle's reference to intermarriage points toward another set of solutions.

Ideological divisions are inevitable, and probably healthy, as long as there does not seem to be a more or less permanent majority ideology as well as a permanent minority. If such a pattern manifests itself, it is probably grounded in some other division, such as religion or ethnicity, and should be dealt with in terms of its source. There always seems to be a party in favor of change and another that wishes to minimize change. As long as the decision-making process is reasonably fair, it is best to just let these factions work out their conflicts in the future operation of the institutional structure.

In the end, constitutional design can take into account the structure of interests and the probable structure of factional alignments, but it cannot resolve these differences. That is what politics is all about, and only the people living under the constitution have a right to decide the eventual outcomes. The job of constitutional design amounts to avoiding the unfair advantaging or disadvantaging of any major, identifiable faction.

7

An Overview of the Constitutional Design Project

It is time to step back and consider how the various pieces discussed thus far fit together. We must consider first how they form a coherent project and then how the various principles are related and the ways they contribute. As a coherent project, constitutional design takes its form from political philosophy in general, because the constitutional project is historically the result of, and an offshoot from, Western political philosophy. This is not to say that constitutionalism is the central concern of political philosophy or that all political philosophers have contributed to constitutional thinking. Instead, constitutionalism is so deeply embedded in Western political philosophy that the content of constitutionalism and the method for pursuing it cannot be separated from Western philosophy. In large part, this resulted from the project being defined by early political philosophers as they engaged in defining the broader philosophical tradition. In Chapter 6 we considered some of Plato's contributions to defining and advancing constitutionalism, but it is to Aristotle we must turn for laying out the coherent project in which we are now engaged.

Political Philosophy as an Integrated Project

Aristotle notes in the *Politics* that political theory proceeds simultaneously at three levels: discourse about the ideal, about the best possible in the real world, and about existing political systems (1288b21).[1] Put another way, comprehensive political theory must ask several different kinds of questions that are linked, yet distinguishable. In order to understand the interlocking set of questions that political theory can ask, imagine a continuum stretching from left to right. At the end, to the right, is an ideal form of government, a perfectly wrought construct produced by the imagination. At the other end is the perfect dystopia, the most perfectly wretched system that the human imagination can produce. Stretching between these two extremes is an infinite set of possibilities, merging into one another, that describe the logical possibilities created by the characteristics defining the end points. For example, a political system defined primarily by equality would have a perfectly inegalitarian system described at the other end, and the possible states of being between them would vary primarily in the extent to which they embodied equality. An ideal defined primarily by liberty would create a different set of possibilities between the extremes. Of course, visions of the ideal are invariably more complex than these single-value examples indicate, but it is also true that, in order to imagine an ideal state of affairs, a kind of simplification is almost always required since normal states of affairs invariably present themselves to human consciousness as complicated, opaque, and, to a significant extent, indeterminate.

Some conclude that the creation of these visions of the ideal characterizes political philosophy. This is not the case. Any person can generate a vision of the ideal. One job of political philosophy is to ask the question, Why is this ideal worth pursuing? Before this question can be pursued, however, the ideal state of affairs must be clarified, especially with respect to conceptual precision and the logical relationships between the propositions that describe the ideal – what can be termed "pretheoretical analysis." In effect, we must first answer the question, Is this vision coherent? Pretheoretical analysis raises the vision of the ideal from the mundane to a level where true philosophical analysis, and the careful comparison with existing systems, can proceed fruitfully.

[1] Portions of this section have been revised from an earlier version, "Political Theory and Constitutional Construction," chapter 2 in Edward Bryan Portis, Adolf G. Gunderson, and Ruth Lessl Shively, eds., *Political Theory and Partisan Politics* (Albany: State University of New York Press, 2000), pp. 33–49.

The process of pretheoretical analysis, probably because it works on clarifying ideas that most capture the human imagination, too often looks to some like the entire enterprise of political philosophy. However, the value of Rousseau's concept of the general will, for example, lies not in its formal logical structure, or in its compelling hold on the imagination, but on the power and clarity it lends to an eventual comparison with actual political systems. Among other things, an analysis of the general will as a concept allows Rousseau to show that anyone who wishes to pursue a state of affairs closer to that summed up in the concept of the general will must successfully develop a civil religion.

Once the ideal is clarified, the political philosopher will begin to articulate and assess the reasons why we might want to pursue such an ideal. At this point analysis leaves the realm of pure logic and enters the realm of the logic of human longing, aspiration, and anxiety. The analysis is now limited by the interior parameters of the human heart (more properly the human psyche) to which the theorist must appeal. Unlike the clarification stage where anything that is logical is possible, there are now definite limits on where logic can take us. Appeals to self-destruction, less happiness rather than more, psychic isolation, enslavement, loss of identity, a preference for the lives of mollusks over that of humans, to name just a few possibilities, are doomed to failure. Much of political philosophy involves the careful, competitive analysis of what a given ideal state of affairs entails. This realm of discourse, dominated by the logic of worthwhile goals, requires that the theorist carefully observe the responses of others in order not to be seduced by what is merely logical as opposed to what is humanly rational. Moral discourse conditioned by the ideal, if it is to be successful, requires that political theorists be fearless in pursuing normative logic, but it also requires that theorists have enough humility to remember that if a nontheorist cannot be led toward an ideal, the fault may well lie in the theory, not in the moral vision of the nontheorist. Constitutional design is always conditioned by some vision of the ideal, but institutions rest on real people in an actual world. It is not helpful, and usually dangerous, to attempt to actualize the ideal that informs a constitution. Human institutions are inevitably prone to imperfect results, and when the institutions based on speech and coordination fall short of the expected ideal, there is a great temptation to use force to command perfect compliance.

Asking why an ideal is worth pursuing thus inevitably leads us to ask how closely the ideal can be approximated in the world of ordinary humans. This level of discourse requires what Aristotle terms *phronēsis*, or practical wisdom, and is largely a matter of coming to understand the nature of the limits imposed by the world of politics. In the past, political theorists have relied on a careful study of political history to develop *phronēsis*, and this is not a bad habit to preserve; but, because the limits faced by a particular political system will vary by time and location, experience in that particular setting is an important part of the platform on which political theory is erected and requires careful attention to the deeper structure of what political experience tells us. What a political theorist has to say to us at this level amounts to an analysis of apparently contradictory and opaque experience where the discourse is limited not only by the imperatives of the human psyche but by the logic of limits and conflicting values and goals. The conversation is still informed by the ideal and motivated by a vision of the best, but it is now proceeding under the assumption that the ideal can only be approximated, not achieved, in politics, as well as under the assumption that, at least in principle, an analysis of limits can lead us to the "best possible." These limits result from the construction of the human psyche, from the empirical facts of human existence, and from the value complexity inherent in any worthwhile vision of the ideal.

The human psyche is so constructed that we have hopes as well as needs. Our hopes lead us to seek something better, something other than what we have, while human needs lead us to prefer states of affairs that satisfy those needs. Because the current state of affairs has been successful to some extent at meeting our needs for food, shelter, protection, companionship, self-development, and self-expression, most of us are also led to seek the preservation of the current state of affairs, or at least to place our hopes in the context of our needs. Political philosophy, and thus constitutionalism, always finds itself stretched between the ideal and the actual, which leads us to seek improvement that is in fact an improvement and not some retrograde "progress" that will lead us to be less well off as a result of the changes induced by our hopes.

We are also limited by the facts of human existence. If there really were such a thing as a "free lunch," or if resources spent in an attempt to achieve greater equality, for example, did not use up resources that could be used for achieving some other good, then we could simply advance in every direction at once. The brute facts of human existence imposed by limited resources, time, space, and attention make us pay a price for our decisions. Time spent trying to make more money is time spent away from human relationships of family and friends. Distance limits our ability to develop high-quality relationships with everyone, and the length of a day plus the need to sleep limits our ability to develop all human relationships to the same degree. The need to engage in activities directed at ensuring food and shelter gets in the way of the need for self-expression. All of this seems obvious but needs repeating in the face of attempts to achieve perfection on Earth. *Phronēsis* reminds us that life is lived in a context of limits, and the relative absence of *phronēsis* too often leads to fanaticism in political philosophy as well as in politics.

Finally in this regard, responsible political philosophy as well as responsible constitutional design must face an important implication from the two previous sources of limits – we invariably want many things and not just one. Another way to say this is that the value complexity inherent in human hopes leads us to want a state of affairs characterized by many values, not just one, and these values are often contradictory in theory and in practice. Seeking unbridled liberty at some point gets in the way of equality, and vice versa. We like comfort as well as excitement, safety as well as danger. I can think of no other reason to explain, for example, why sane human beings who are materially comfortable would want to strap long skis of wood to their feet and jump over cliffs. That ideal polities comprise a number of values that conflict in the real world means that, when carefully analyzed, such ideal polities are self-limiting in any political process involving humans. Thus, it is not uncommon for ideologues to fasten upon one or another of these values and press for its perfection alone. It is a tacit admission that to do otherwise would cause us to moderate our move toward the ideal. For these various interconnected reasons, in the end we are left to ponder the best possible polity we can attain with respect to the ideal polity that informs it.

After considering the coherence of an ideal, why we might want to pursue it, and how closely we might possibly approximate it, we are moved to ask, What are the facts of the situation we face? Another way of putting the question is, Given the continuum we have thus far described, where is this actual political system situated with respect to the best possible regime? Contemporary political science has often attacked the perceived lack of a systematic empirical component to classical political philosophy. Sometimes these political scientists speak as if the only theoretical questions worth asking have to do with empirical relationships. It must be remembered, however, that Aristotle collected well over a hundred "constitutions" and used these descriptions of existing regimes as the empirical grounding for his analysis. His example, and that of others after him, serves to remind us that empirical theory is part of the total project. We now understand that empirical description is always the first step in the discovery of empirical regularities. As such regularities are uncovered, they hold out the possibility of answering at a more advanced level the next question posed by political theory: How do we arrange things so that we can move closer to the best possible political system? That is, it makes little sense to seek empirical knowledge if it is not to be used. If it is to be used, how is it to be used – that is, toward what ends? If voting behavior can be reduced to a set of regression equations, and this allows us to manipulate institutional variables so as to enhance certain outcomes, which outcomes do we choose to enhance? The so-called new institutionalism is essentially predicated on the marriage of empirical and theoretical approaches that are nested in the broader philosophical framework just outlined.

Empirical political theory is limited by the logic of empirical evidence, as well as by the logic of effectiveness (an ends-means logic), but it is ultimately justified by the logic of human hopes and aspirations as well as by the logic of the possible. If it were not, then, an empirical political science focused on the preservation of the status quo, the manipulation of the masses for the benefit of the few, or the pursuit of humanly degrading states of affairs might well be our legacy.

In recent years we have witnessed an increasingly loud set of voices that has leveled just this charge against empirical political science. Critical political theory has worked from a variety of perspectives against empirical political science, from the left as well as the right. To the extent this critique has attacked empiricism per se, to that extent it is an attack on all of political philosophy, because the questions asked by empirical political science are an important and necessary part of the entire enterprise. To the extent critical political theory has attacked a free-floating empiricism isolated from the broader enterprise, it has properly sought to reintegrate the enterprise.

Critical political theory works from the logic of deficiency. It attacks the actual state of affairs in the name of human aspiration for that which is in some sense better. To denounce something as deficient is to compare that reality with an ideal, or else there is no grounding to the critique. In this way, critical theory returns us to the total logic of the continuum. A critical stance is natural for political philosophy and expresses the inevitable conflict between political philosophy and politics as practiced. It is a healthy, necessary antidote to politics as usual inside Plato's cave and, when practiced well, serves as a means of motivating us to work on the entire project. Practiced badly, critical theory is only the contemporary manifestation of the age-old pathology of political philosophy to seek the creation of the ideal in an actual world that will not bear the weight of the enterprise without seriously harming the human aspirations that political philosophy exists to serve. Practiced badly, critical theory also needlessly undermines respect for all institutions, including those that are basically healthy and helpful. The hallmark of the latter pathology is the sophistic stance that there are no discoverable truths transcending culture and ideology upon which we can rest institutional design. This stance, ostensibly in the service of the downtrodden and marginalized, leaves us with no arguments with which to contest the assaults of the powerful against the poor and marginalized. In the long run, such sophistry quietly justifies the rule of the stronger and demoralizes those who would oppose and tame raw power with enduring principles of justice, now reduced to mere expressions of competing ideologies. On the other hand, a political philosophy that serves the integrated questions just outlined leaves open the possibility that political theorists may contribute to the marriage of justice with power by providing arguments, grounded in human aspiration as well as in empirically supported analysis and philosophically sound logic, that will be convincing to political actors as well as to academics.

Constitutional Design as an Integrated Project

As an offshoot of political philosophy, constitutionalism rests on a complex set of normative, analytic, and empirical considerations similar to those just outlined. Like philosophy, constitutionalism does not consist of a set of settled answers, but is instead an ongoing process of questioning and learning. The project of constitutional design, an important part of constitutionalism in general, is thus embedded in a complex set of normative, analytic, and empirical considerations that together define an integrated process of continuous thought and action. For a number of reasons, then, it is hazardous to introduce the notion of "principles" of constitutional design. The unwary might be led to conclude that things are settled, when in fact we are, in medias res, in a long-term historical conversation. Some may be induced to expect a singular solution, when in fact there is no one ideal constitutional design appropriate for all peoples, or even for a given people over time. Given the "plug and play" mentality of the modern world, others may expect that a set of principles allows us to custom-design a constitution using prefabricated pieces from some giant political Lego set. Still, if we are to lay out systematically what we think we know now, some provisional ordering is required; and if the previous provisos are kept in mind, as well as the one to follow, laying out some set of "principles" will do no harm and may do some good.

The term "principles of constitutional design" is potentially misleading in the current context of political studies where emphasis is placed on the discovery of a cumulative body of knowledge modeled after that developed by physics or biology. In the physical sciences a "principle" is an empirically supported proposition that has two characteristics: the empirical test supporting the proposition has been repeated so many times by so many people that it is seemingly "proven"; and the proposition is of such a nature that it logically connects a number of propositions that would otherwise seem to be unconnected. Since we do not yet have in the social sciences a set of cumulative, logically interconnected, empirically supported propositions worthy of being called "principles," to speak of "principles of constitutional design" is to imply something that sounds much like a science. This cannot be the case because, whereas normative questions concerning how or whether to use the knowledge of science lie outside of science as such, the study of politics necessarily involves normative considerations within the enterprise itself. Furthermore, whereas in science the empirical can be completely separated from normative considerations at the highest levels of scientific discourse, the study of politics, rooted in philosophy, is such that the empirical and normative become more inextricably linked as the level of discourse becomes more complex.

When we study constitutional design, several levels of principles emerge as well as different types. That is, there are different levels of complexity and generality within empirical, analytic, and normative discourse. If we look at empirical discourse, for example, some statements are simple in a straightforward sense. An example of this level might be, Single-member electoral districts tend to produce a two-party system, whereas multimember districts tend to produce a multiparty system. The statement is empirically testable and might be termed a "simple empirical hypothesis."

A second level of principles combines a number of these simple empirical hypotheses into a more complex hypothesis that, while still subject to empirical support, rests on a much more complex chain of theoretical reasoning. An example might be, A consensual political system is better at dealing with a heterogeneous population than is a majoritarian political system. We can test this more complex proposition empirically, but only after engaging in a number of careful definitional or analytical exercises, and after testing a number of hypotheses embedded in the general hypothesis. So, here, we first need to determine what is meant by a "consensual system," which turns out to be a combination of institutions including the electoral system, party system, type of legislature, type of executive, type of executive-legislative relationship, and a certain set of decision rules. We also need to determine what is meant by "heterogeneous population" as well as what is meant by "better." Are we speaking of religious, ethnic, economic, cultural, racial, or ideological heterogeneity? Is it the case that all types of heterogeneity can be handled the same way? Finally, this matter of "better" moves us toward the peculiarity of social science principles as opposed to principles in the physical sciences. In the social sciences "better" has an initial empirical referent, or set of referents, but ultimately a normative component. In the case of the principle under discussion, the person who penned the statement meant by "better" that the better system is more effective at distributing material benefits, and thus more stable, and thus will last longer. We can create a scale that measures the level of heterogeneity in a country, and then develop scales to rank "consensual" and "majoritarian" political systems to see how long they have lasted, how often there has been domestic violence, and so on. Note that this requires empirical measurement of a number of variables. A number of political scientists would consider this to be an example of a principle of constitutional design, but it is in fact only a "complex empirical hypothesis."

Hidden within this complex empirical hypothesis are a number of normative assumptions, such as, A good constitution is one that creates a government that is efficient at reaching decisions, and effective at distributing material benefits. Others might counter that efficient government is dangerous, because speed in decision making is not as important as achieving justice. Or they might argue that government is not as good at economic distribution as is the economy itself, so government intrusion into economics is not a good per se but is a supplement to economic inefficiencies and inequities. Regardless, the example used here is designed to show the manner and extent to which normative considerations invariably underlie complex empirical hypotheses and not to argue for one normative position over another.

At a level of analysis one step higher in terms of complexity and generality than complex empirical hypotheses, we consider how to think about constitutional design in a way that includes empirical, analytic, and normative considerations. This level of analysis is also neutral with respect to the outcome. That is, principles or statements at this level do not incline us toward any particular constitutional design. These principles rest on prudential calculations reached by careful students of constitutional design who draw on the history of experience with all kinds of constitutional systems, and these are what should most properly be termed "general principles of constitutional design." Some of these principles are outlined here, along with the topics and considerations to which they lead.

General Principles of Constitutional Design

By this point the principles laid out in this section should all be familiar. These general principles are guidelines for thinking about the overall project rather than dicta to which designers of constitutions must adhere.

Match the Government to the People: All Government, Constitutional or Not, Rests on the "Virtues" of the People

- Analyze the characteristics of a people – use history to evaluate common goals, interests, and values as well as the diversity in these – remember the crucial role of political culture in general (including the use of a political myth), and the attitude of "rule of law" in particular.

- Analyze the material and environmental circumstances.
- Identify the "critical political problems," especially the nature and intensity of factions – localism versus cosmopolitanism, for example.

The Ideal Political System Will Not Work on Earth, So Seek the Best Possible under the Circumstances

- Work from a realistic theory of human nature.
- Consider the difference between the common good and permanent and aggregate interests.
- Distinguish rational-actor coalitions (cost-benefit analysis) versus ideological ones (value analysis).

Political Power Is an Unavoidable Danger That Must Be Understood and Faced If the Design Is to Succeed

- The concept of sovereignty and its offspring, popular sovereignty, must be reflected and/or embodied in a constitution.
- In assessing elite versus popular sovereignty, think realistically about equality, the inevitability of elites, and the means for controlling them.
- Evaluate majority rule versus minority and individual rights, permanent versus temporary majorities, and apathetic versus intense majorities and minorities.

The Idea of a Constitution Is to Marry Justice with Power

- What is a constitution and what are its functions and purposes?
- What belongs in a constitution and what does not?
- What are the different meanings of limited government, and which do we use?

A Critical Problem in Constitutional Design Is the Distribution of Power

- Why should we distribute power, and how should we do it?
- Consider separation of powers, federalism, institutional complexity, and accountability.

- Evaluate basic constitutional models: the parliamentary model (constraint by tradition) versus the separation of powers model (constraint by institutional complexity); the mixed regime model (balance) versus the presidential model (legitimate force); the framework model (process over content) versus the code model (content over process); and the covenant model (communitarian civic relationships) versus the manifesto model (communitarian transformational relationships).

The Process of Collective Decision Making Should Be Viewed as a Complete System of Interlocking Institutions

- Consider the nature of institutions.
- Evaluate systems analysis.
- Evaluate the purpose of collective decision making and the stages in the process.

The System of Institutions Should Be Grounded in a Coherent Theory That Should Be Apparent from the Behavioral Implications of the Institutional Design

- Constrain the behavior of relevant political actors into broadly predictable patterns: the organization of the legislative, executive, and judicial functions, and their mutual relationships in a deliberative process.
- Select and monitor political actors through electoral systems, public opinion, theories of representation, theories of participation, and mechanisms of accountability.
- Evaluate the science of politics (knowledge) versus the art of politics (prudence).

A Constitution Rests Not Only on the History and Present Circumstances of a People but Also on Probable Future Developments

- Provide means for amending, altering, and replacing constitutions.
- Consider the "redemptive" view of politics versus the "realistic" view.
- Distinguish between projection (artful empiricism) and wishful thinking.

8

An Underlying Constitutional Logic: Rational Actors?

Four Interesting Curves

Our aim in this book has been to consider principles of constitutional design in order to better understand the project as a whole rather than to develop formulae for designing constitutions. The nature of the project demands such a stance, because, if a constitution must be matched to the people who will live under it, there is no one ideal or model constitution. Instead, the history of constitutionalism shows that there is a large variety of possible successful designs. Still, various empirical regularities have emerged that can be used by framers of constitutions as they consider the preferred institutional pattern that best suits them; as a result, although there is not an overall science of constitutional design, the design project can be informed by political science.

Several empirical findings fairly plead for further explication, because together they suggest a deeply interesting aspect of constitutional design. Under conditions of liberty, those who frame constitutions exhibit a set of patterned choices that suggest constitutionalism has a certain underlying logic, and perhaps an underlying rationality. We will examine these four curves that designers seem to strain toward without conscious intent: the index of amendment difficulty generating a nearly hyperbolic curve with respect to amendment rate; the size of legislatures tracking the curve for the cube root of the population; the separation of powers increasing as popular control increases; and the historical curve for constitutional democracies tracking the curve for the number of written constitutions. Each reveals a different aspect of possible human rationality in constitutional design, and each contributes to broader questions concerning the nature of rationality itself.

The Hyperbolic Curve Describing the Difficulty of Amendment

Chapter 5 analyzed the amendment process in American states as well as cross-nationally. Figure 5.1 presented the hyperbolic curve describing the basic relationship between amendment rate and the difficulty of the amendment process. The general conclusion, that the amendment rate rises as the amendment process becomes less difficult, is hardly surprising. Empirical political science is often accused of proving the obvious, and if Chapter 5 established nothing beyond this general finding, the charge of proving the obvious would apply here. However, empirical political science has disproved a large number of such supposedly obvious hypotheses over the past half century, so establishing empirical support is always a necessary first step. Chapter 5 goes well beyond this first step and suggests that the project of constitutional design replicates the integrated view of political philosophy as laid out in Chapter 7.

In the integrated project of political philosophy, part of what empirical political science is supposed to determine is where we are on a given continuum defined by some ideal and its contrary. It is also supposed to tell us how to move along that continuum – what we can do to alter the current state of affairs. In both instances we must be able to measure, which implies an ability to quantify. Quantification requires some reasonable, systematic basis for assigning numerical value to an observed event; and this, in turn, requires definitions clear and precise enough to distinguish the observed event for one phenomenon from an observed event of another phenomenon.

The key to Chapter 5 is not that it provides empirical support for an intuitively straightforward empirical relationship or that it measures the strength of that relationship, but rather that it describes and measures the relationship in a way that allows a rational actor to choose a strategy for optimizing a preferred constitutional outcome. The equation

$$A = [1/D + ((L/10,000) \times .6)] - .3$$

describes the curve of best fit for the relationship, and allows us to select an amendment rate by manipulating only two variables: the difficulty of the amendment process and the number of words in a constitution.

The length of a constitution is a surrogate measure for the degree to which a constitution is a simple framework document as opposed to one that also constitutionalizes a number of normally nonconstitutional policy areas. Quantifying the length of a constitution is straightforward by counting sections, sentences, or, as is done here, words.

Quantifying amendment difficulty requires that we first create an index to take into account all of the possible components that could be used in varying combinations to create any amendment process, and then to assign numerical values to each possible component. The numerical value for a given component must reflect its relative possible weight vis-à-vis any other possible component using one of two methods. In the first method the relative weights can be estimated, and the estimates can be indirectly tested by observing how the resulting index "behaves" when it is used to code actual constitutions. The second method is to find a way for weights to be assigned empirically. The latter tactic is available here because American state constitutions hold enough variables constant to permit empirical measurement of many key variables. The weights for these key variables can then be utilized when other variables are obvious equivalents or multiples of the variables we have been able to measure empirically.

An important aspect of Chapter 5 is thus the empirically derived Index for Estimating the Relative Difficulty of an Amendment Process that, together with identification of length as the other important variable, allows us to select some reasonably small range of future amendment rate. It is unclear how much of constitutional design is in principle reducible to such empirically supportable relationships that can be used for institutional manipulation. However, even if we could uncover a large number of such empirical relationships involving constitutional variables, the problems of constitutional design would be far from over. Using the evidence from Chapter 5, we can see that a rational actor would still need to be very clear about what kind of outcome is preferred and why. For example, if someone prefers constitutional stability defined in terms of constitutional longevity, some combination of institutions that produces an amendment rate of about one amendment per year would be optimal. On the other hand, if for some reason framers of a constitution prefer a stronger supreme or constitutional court intervening at a higher rate in future constitutional revision than would normally be the case, an optimal institutional solution might be a combination of some more difficult amendment process with a shorter constitution that is limited to laying out the basic framework of a political system. The longevity of the constitution would be compromised unless other parts of the constitution invited or required a significant level of judicial involvement in constitutional revision. However, a high level of judicial involvement carries other risks for both constitutional longevity and legitimacy under conditions of popular sovereignty. In the end, the relationships described by the equation for the curve of best fit for Figure 5.1 make it easier for constitutional designers to act rationally but do not answer the question of how a rational actor should act.

Much of constitutional design from the viewpoint of positive political theory thus requires that the rational actor first identify the preferred outcome, or set of outcomes, and this requires more theoretical argument of an explicitly normative nature. Furthermore, that normative discussion must proceed at several levels. At the lowest level, the constitution must be made appropriate to the "virtues" of the people, as Aristotle puts it. As Montesquieu and others note, appropriateness refers to the geography, demography, history, and shared values of a given people. As James Madison and others note, appropriateness includes also the behavioral tendencies common to all humans. That is, just as the constitutions should be realistic with respect to the actual situation of a given people, it should also be realistic with respect to human nature. Legislatures that are too small or too large produce broadly predictable consequences for all humans regardless of their culture, geography, or population size. Population size also has broadly predictable consequences that should be taken into account. There are also broadly predictable consequences that arise from human nature when one places political power in the hands of a relatively small part of the population whether through popular elections or other means. Finally, as Aristotle and others have indicated, constitutions marry power with justice, and any constitution must respond to the broader imperatives of constitutionalism itself, which includes some notion of justice, or at least of constitutional morality.

Too often, those who design or analyze constitutions ignore the normative component under the quiet assumption that some value is noncontroversially obvious. For example, parliamentary governments are often described as more efficient than "presidential" (higher separation of powers) systems. Efficiency is usually defined as the relatively rapid and accurate transference of public opinion or popular will into public policies. If there is any concern at all for minority and/or individual rights, such "efficiency" must be more explicitly justified, and probably balanced by other concerns that do not permit an automatic preference for "efficiency." More consensual systems imply a willingness to sacrifice a certain amount of efficiency in favor of other normative considerations, but these other values must not be assumed as preferable either, including minority rights. Part of the underlying constitutional logic thus involves values.

- Constitutional systems do not support single values. Instead, any given constitution tends to favor some set of values over another set, and different institutions in a given constitution will embody or support different values.
- The mix of values supported constitutionally is not necessarily a congruent package – that is, they may not be part of a philosophically coherent system of justice.
- This possible incoherence results from inevitable disagreement within a population over what justice, equality, rights, representation, and other important political values mean, as well as how to best produce them.
- Every constitution will initially embrace some working balance among these values, and the mix of balances will tend over time, under conditions of liberty, to develop and change toward a more or less stable equilibrium.
- Designers and analysts of constitutions and their constitutive institutions can design for long-term rationality by designing a mix of institutions with certain tendencies, but only in the context of what is acceptable to the people in the short term so that the proposed constitution will be accepted and adopted.

Constitutional design does not come down to a set of purely technical, logical solutions. Instead, the curve in Figure 5.1, with its attendant theoretical discussion, demonstrates the need for constitutional design to proceed as an integrated project that takes into account the various related questions laid out in Chapter 7. Empirical, analytic, and normative propositions need to be meshed in a comprehensive manner. One irony is that while those engaged in constitutional design must more explicitly engage the normative consequences of the institutions they design, the basic normative decisions now and in the future must ultimately be made by those who will live under the constitution and not be assumed by some external analyst. The nearly hyperbolic curve in Figure 5.1 could be used to design an amendment process that is technically optimal in some sense, but technical optimality is conditioned by normative concerns that can be analyzed but not determined by the analyst.

Rational-actor analysis is also conditioned by the fact that institutions do not operate in isolation but in an environment of many institutions with interaction effects. If we were to use only the curve in Figure 5.1 to design an amendment process, we would miss the effect of constitutional length. If we use these two together, we would still need to know the ratification process for the constitution, because the overwhelming tendency is for a people to prefer an amendment process that returns to a process that is identical or similar to the process used for ratifying the document. This eminently logical linkage between ratification and amendment processes implies that we consider both at the same time. This still leaves the matter of the reciprocal impact between a supreme court and the amendment process. Other institutions come into play depending upon the specifics of the amendment process. Is the national legislature in any way involved, or is it excluded? The curve in Figure 5.1 tells us how to predict a general amendment rate, but it does not tell us anything about the consequences of different amendment rates other than for constitutional longevity.

Who, then, is the potential rational actor here – the political scientist who proposes a rational-actor solution for an institution, which is then rejected by the people who are supposed to use it? I have been this person more than once when consulting for countries writing constitutions. Are a people who accept an institution designed using rational-actor analysis themselves rational when it turns out that the electoral system that was supposed to be optimal for representation turns out to make it easy for radical ideological minorities to warp elections, and this is one thing those people definitely did not want? I have witnessed

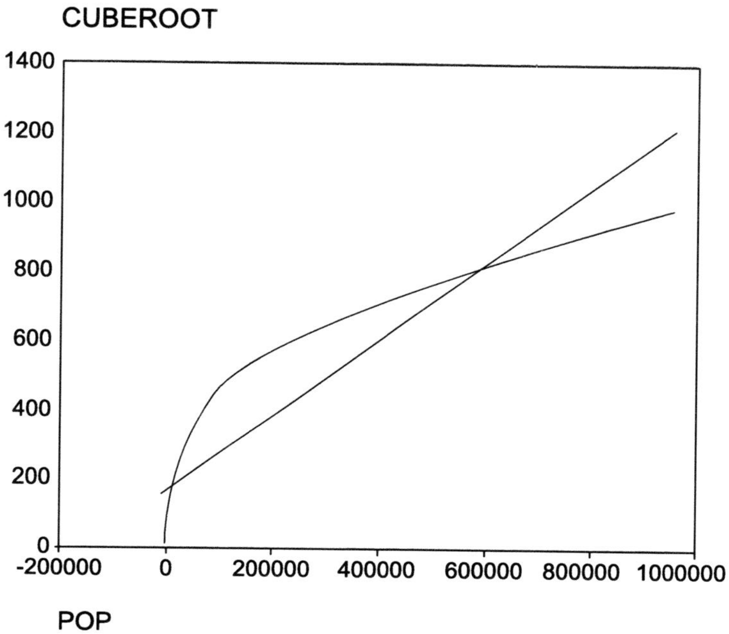

FIGURE 8.1. Cube root curve versus linear curve.

this more than once as well. The rational actor, as it turns out, is a highly useful but mythical creature that tells us about institutional tendencies given the rules that define them, but that cannot tell us which set of institutional rules to choose. The unwillingness to use rational-choice analysis in constitutional design is an error. Failure to use anything but rational-choice analysis in constitutional design is a contrary error. Neither type of disciplinary ideology is a formula for living in a world inhabited by humans.

The Cube Root Curve

The cube root rule – the size of a unicameral legislature, as well as the size of the lower house in a bicameral legislature, tends to approximate the cube root of the country's population – has been known for some time, but little has been made of it. Figure 8.1 shows the shape of the curve generated by taking the cube root of a nation's population compared with a linear curve that represents what we would find if the size of the legislative body increased according to some rule of

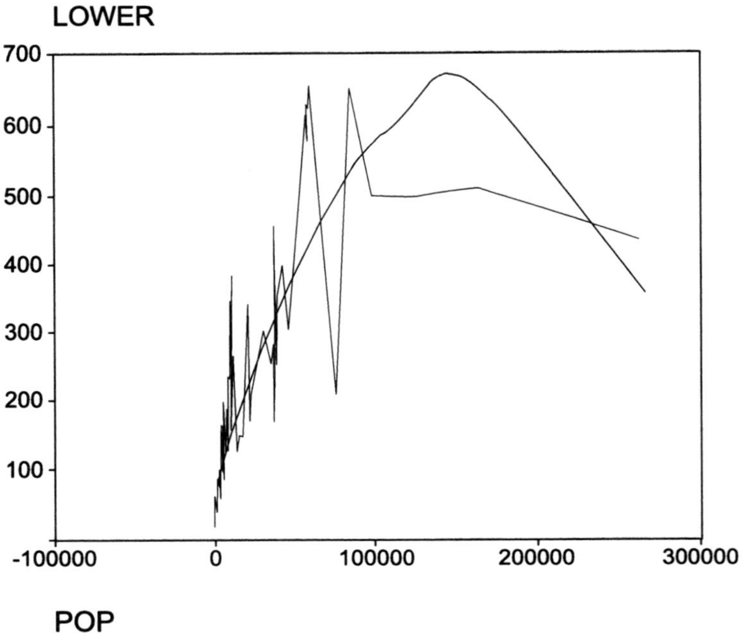

FIGURE 8.2. Size of primary legislative body and population size (excluding India). LOWER QUA: $r^2 = .732$; d.f. = 71; F. = 96.78; significance = .000; b0 = 76.1634; b1 = .0074; b2 = –2.E–08.

proportionality. The cube root curve initially rises more rapidly than does a linear curve but then almost immediately begins to fall off at an increasing rate until it is rising at a much less rapid rate than the linear curve. Consider now Figure 8.2, which shows the curve of best fit when regressing legislative size against the actual population.[1] The curve of best fit between the primary legislative house and population does indeed seem to approximate the cube root curve, with an r square of .732 that is significant at the .001 level. We can directly test for the degree of fit by regressing the size of the primary legislative house directly against the cube root curve as shown in Figure 8.3. If the fit with the cube root curve were perfect, we would find a perfect linear

[1] India is excluded from the calculations for Figure 8.1 because in order to accommodate 1 billion people on the x-axis, the shape of the curve cannot be seen. India's lower house has 545 members, so including it would simply confirm the leveling off in the curve. Including India produces an even higher correlation (.770) because India's lower house fits the overall pattern so well.

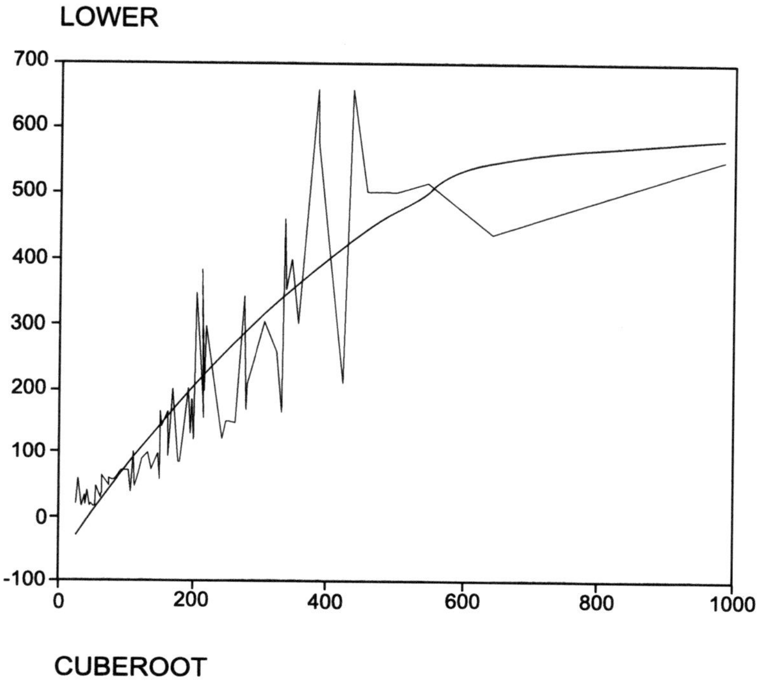

FIGURE 8.3. Size of primary legislative body and the cube root of the population. LOWER QUA: $r^2 = .756$; d.f. = 72; F. = 111.52; significance = .000; $b0 = -64.576$; $b1 = 1.4980$; $b2 = -.0009$.

relationship. Instead, we find a declining curve that resembles the cube root itself until a legislative size around 650 is reached and then the curve flattens out. Although the r square is .756 with a significance at the .001 level, legislative size does not quite track the cube root curve, because designers of constitutions increase legislative size at an increasingly slower rate than the cube root rule would predict and, at a certain point, stop legislative growth altogether. In short, the size of the primary legislative body tracks the cube root curve only within a restricted range of legislative size. The difference between the cube root curve and the actual size of legislatures probably results from a growing reluctance to increase legislative size.

Consider again Figure 8.2. The theoretical reason for this curve is that while framers of constitutions generally wish to keep the size of each representative's constituency as small as possible in order to minimize the "distance" between a representative and those represented, there is also the wish to prevent the legislature from becoming too large to conduct business at all. At the moment, no constitutional republic, regardless of the size of its population, seems willing to utilize a lower house or unicameral legislature larger than about 650 representatives. Although we can account theoretically for the actual curve of legislative size, it is difficult to account for the curve tending to approximate the cube root curve within the restricted range. There is no reason to think that framers know about the cube root curve or, if they do, why they would choose to approximate it per se.

For example, we can just as easily conceive of constitutional framers engaging in a rational-actor analysis of the ideal size for a legislature, given the factors of internal decision making, and settling upon some ideal size for a legislature. In this case the curve would be a horizontal line at the ideal size on the ordinal scale. Or we could conceive of framers using some consistent ratio that added one representative for every set number of citizens, which would produce a rising straight line. Instead, the logic of constitutional design in this instance, as in many others, is based on weighing more than one factor and the effects of more than one institution.

We can pursue legislative size further. In Figure 8.2 we see that at a certain population, around 150 million people, the size of the lower house levels off and declines somewhat. No country with more than 100 million people currently has a unicameral legislature, so we can say for certain that this effect is limited to bicameral legislatures.[2] Thus, at a population of around 150 million people, framers seem to stop worrying entirely about the growing size of the average constituency and focus instead on the size of the lower house. There is no such concern for restricting legislative size in small countries with unicameral legislatures. The curve of best fit for the thirty-five unicameral legislatures in countries with a population less than 10 million is almost linear, with an r square of .832.

Table 8.1 shows that unicameral legislatures are almost entirely associated with smaller constitutional republics. For example, 78 percent of countries with populations less than 100,000 have unicameral

[2] The United Kingdom is technically bicameral, although because the upper house is not elected and has no set size, the United Kingdom is treated here as effectively unicameral. It is thus the only country with more than 50 million people treated here as unicameral.

TABLE 8.1. *Unicameral and Bicameral Legislative Size Compared to Population Size*

Size of Population	Number of Nations	Percentage of Size Category	Average Size of Total Legislature	Average Size of Lower House	Average Size of Upper House
Unicameral legislatures (38)					
0 to .1 million	7	78	31		
.1 to .5 million	6	60	43		
.5 to 5 million	13	72	95		
5 to 10 million	8	67	204		
10 to 50 million	3	18	254		
More than 50 million	1	10	659		
Bicameral legislatures (37)					
0 to .1 million	2	22	33	17	16
.1 to .5 million	4	40	33	29	14
.5 to 5 million	5	28	120	83	37
5 to 10 million	4	33	199	158	41
10 to 50 million	13	82	340	249	91
More than 50 million	9	90	646	507	139

legislatures and 22 percent are bicameral; 72 percent of countries with populations between 500,000 and 5 million are unicameral and 18 percent are bicameral. In countries with a population more than 10 million the two size categories combined show that only 15 percent are unicameral and 85 percent are bicameral. There is a tipping point at about 10 million people where unicameralism is largely replaced by bicameralism, just as there is a tipping point at about 150 million people (as shown in Figure 8.2) where the average lower house stops growing and begins to decline in size. Overall, as populations grow, there is a strong tendency to move toward bicameralism; and as the size of the lower house grows, although at a declining rate, the upper house also grows. Can it be the case that framers of constitutions tend to use increasingly larger upper houses to compensate for the declining rate of growth in the size of lower houses?

The middle column in Table 8.1 under "Bicameral Legislatures" combines the average size of both houses in each size category, but this format does not allow us to test the hypothesis. What happens if we combine the two houses for each of our thirty-seven bicameral legislatures and regress the resulting totals against the size of the population? Figure 8.4 shows that we get the same curve we did in Figure 8.2 where we used the primary legislative body from all seventy-five countries, with the high point at the same approximate population of 150 million people. The curves in Figures 8.2 and 8.4 both have the same shape, the same tipping point, and the same level of significance. Most important for the current analysis, both approximate the cube root rule over the same limited size range. How can we account for these consistent patterns?

Is this the work of a rational actor? Can the approximation with the cube root curve be the work of a rational actor if no one knows about the cube root curve? Is the cube root curve in any technical sense rational? What is the difference, if any, between a consciously rational actor who is attempting to achieve some end, and an actor who turns out to be rational even though she or he is not trying to be rational? Furthermore, what if the "rational actor" is an entire set of constitutional conventions or an entire set of legislatures engaged in writing a constitution? Equally interesting, what if the individuals in that framing body are attempting to act rationally on the basis of different individual goals, and the entire convention ends up acting

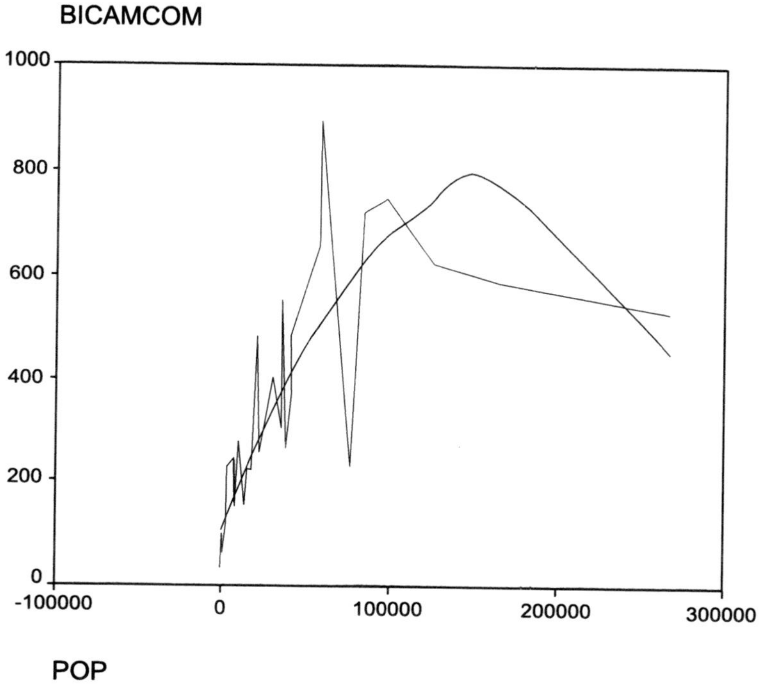

FIGURE 8.4. The combined houses of bicameral legislatures and population size (excluding India). BICAMCOM QUA: $r^2 = .714$; d.f. = 33; F. = 41.29; significance = .000; bo = 108.116; b1 =.0085; b2 = −3.E−08.

in a rational fashion? What do we call this – metarationality? One is reminded of the proposition about individually irrational voters acting together to produce a rational electorate.

There is no inherent rationality to following the cube root rule. However, there is an underlying rationality in balancing the conflicting goals of (A) maintaining reasonable constituency size while at the same time (B) maintaining a reasonable size for the legislature. That the underlying rationality ends up approximating the cube root curve is probably an accident and is therefore only an interesting curiosity. The rational actors here are groups of individual men and women in different cultures who at different times frame constitutions that they hope will be accepted and then be successful. They are balancing the demands of conflicting design goals in the context of their respective individual goals and preferences as well as in the context of their respective country's unique circumstances. Out of the debates among many people in many conventions in different countries with different cultures, we observe a number of predictable results. One of these is that the size of the primary legislative body tracks the cube root curve up to a point. Another is that framers of political systems with fewer than 10 million people basically use a unicameral legislature, and then at around 10 million people framers suddenly start using bicameral legislatures. At around 150 million people the approximation with the cube root rule ends, and legislatures stop growing altogether. It is also at this point that federalism becomes very prominent, perhaps again, in an attempt to minimize the distance between citizen and legislator.

These patterns together reflect an underlying constitutional logic that seems to be shared across cultures and over time. Whether this logic is in accord with rational actor theory will be left for others to determine. What we can say here is that framers of constitutional republics often act in broadly predictable ways when designing basic institutions despite the impressive array of specific institutional combinations they have come up with historically. There seems to be an impressively consistent logic-in-use that may or may not accord with rational-actor analysis, and further study of this underlying logic-in-use may yield important insights into the connection between seemingly unconnected individual political calculations and the creation of commonly accepted solutions that may reflect some widely shared, cross-cultural utility calculus or perhaps some sense of a common good that is shared both within the community and across communities. The general patterns in legislative design uncovered as a result of reflecting on the cube root curve make even more sense if we consider them in the context of the separation of powers.

We saw in Chapter 4 that framers of constitutional republics tend to increase the level of separation of powers as they increase the level of popular control. This principle of constitutional design seems to emerge from some logic inherent in the design process rather than from designers following explicit, articulated normative rules. It was suggested in Chapter 2 that the basic logic of constitutional design results from humans, on the one hand, seeking to create a supreme power that allows an expanded pursuit of self-preservation, liberty, sociability, and beneficial innovation and, on the other hand, seeking to prevent that supreme power from itself threatening these pursued values. Putting it in terms of political economy, humans wish to minimize the opportunity costs and externalities that go with a prepolitical condition, but at the same time humans wish to minimize the external costs and decision costs that result from political organization. It seems to follow as a secondary principle that framers of constitutions, under conditions of popular control, tend to balance the consequences of constituency size with the consequences of legislative size and to minimize external costs.

Let us pursue the logic of this secondary principle. Under conditions of popular control, the elective legislatures that are the core of a constitutional republic should have constituencies that as are as small as possible in order to minimize externalities by keeping those in power close to public opinion; but also, under conditions of popular control, the legislatures should not be so large as to either fall under the control of legislative elites with the resulting externalities or to become ineffective because of the decision costs involved in passing legislation. An increasing population requires an increase in constituency size, in legislative size, or in both. Because continued popular control seems empirically to privilege neither small constituencies nor small legislatures, framers of constitutions allow both to increase in size in an attempt to minimize the overall danger from external costs (although as legislatures become larger, the problem of decision costs is added to external costs in such a fashion as to produce a preference for gradually slowing the growth in legislative size regardless of the consequences for constituency size). At some point, the legislature grows to a size where decision costs simply overwhelm concern for externalities resulting from too-large constituencies, and legislative growth simply halts. This has been termed the "tipping point" and reveals itself empirically as around 650 legislators, a number that in turn occurs empirically at around 150 million people.

Long before the tipping point is reached, however, the population of a constitutional republic reaches a size where there is an attempt to achieve a balance with respect to the possible externalities of both constituency size and legislative size. This point is apparently reached at about 10 million people, for it is here that bicameralism suddenly enters the picture and the rate of growth for the lower house which had hitherto been linear begins to fall off. Minimizing externalities becomes problematic as a population grows for at least one of two reasons, and probably both. First, growing legislative size implies an increasing need for internal legislative organization that favors dominance by an elite, at the same time that growing constituency size implies probable future degradation in the ability of the people to control that emerging elite. Second, any growing population necessarily implies declining homogeneity within that population. Heterogeneity may increase from the more complex economy needed to sustain that population size, the addition of immigrants of a different demographic description of some sort, the addition of new territories that have people with strong local attachments, or some combination of factors. Regardless of why diversity increases, larger populations imply greater diversity such that simple concern for constituency size is supplemented by concern for the nature of the constituencies as well. External costs increasingly include concern for constituency demands that differ in kind. A point is thereby reached where a second house is generally added to the legislature. Empirically the bicameral point occurs at about 10 million people.

Bicameralism is a fundamental step in the separation of powers, and the preceding logic demonstrates one way in which popular control and an increasing separation of powers is linked in an underlying constitutional logic. As constituency size increases with population growth, elections come to be supplemented by any number of a possible array of popular control institutions, such as referenda or popular initiatives. As legislatures also grow in size, separation of powers increases to help prevent government that is increasingly subject to elite control from moving beyond popular control. As separation of powers increases to help control governmental tyranny, it simultaneously helps to control the effects of public opinion that is increasingly mass-based and subject to temporary passions unchecked by the familiarity and identity with each other that citizens have in small constituencies. The tendency for second branches of the legislature to emerge as population size increases in constitutional republics thus also results from the logic inherent in constitutional design where popular control and the separation of powers interact in pursuit of the benefits that are the reason for establishing a supreme power.

The accidental similarity between legislative size and the cube root curve thus has led us to think about an underlying constitutional logic, but that logic has nothing to do with the cube root curve. Instead, the underlying constitutional logic suggested by rational-actor analysis leads us to the curve linking the Separation of Powers Index with the Index of Popular Control. It is to that curve that we now turn.

The Curve Linking the Separation of Powers with the Index of Popular Control

Consider once again the empirical curve uncovered in Chapter 4. The regression curve in Figure 4.1 shows a strong positive relationship between the Index of Popular Control and the Separation of Powers Index. Each index is calculated using a large number of possible institutions that together constitute most of the institutions in any possible constitution, regardless of where it might be placed on the parliamentary-presidential continuum. The Index of Popular Control results from scores assigned to the combination of institutions a people may use to control its government. Presented as Table 3.1, the index reflects eleven constitutional factors: what entity frames the constitution, adopts it, proposes revisions, approves proposed revisions, and has de jure sovereignty; the proportion of directly elected offices, election frequency, electoral decision rule, office holding requirements; whether there is provision for initiative, recall, or referenda; and how closely the legislative size is to what the cube root would predict. We can now see that the last element in the index is a surrogate measure of the attempt to maintain popular control in the face of increasing constituency and legislature size as the population increases.

The Separation of Powers Index, presented in Table 4.1, is similarly based on a large number of institutional factors: constitutional limits on legislative power, the presence and strength of bicameralism, and the complexity of legislative procedures when involved in amending the constitution; the relative independence of the executive in terms of selection and in terms of appointing ministers, plus the nature of the veto power if there is one; the relative independence of the judiciary in terms of selection and tenure, and the level of judicial review; and a host of miscellaneous institutions that illustrate the impressive inventiveness that humans can bring to the separation of powers.

These indexes are far more complex than the three- or four-element indexes usually generated by social scientists, and the relative weights assigned to each element are themselves composites of between three and eleven subelements. Except for the relative weights of subelements in the amendment process, which were empirically developed in Chapter 5, the relative weights for the various elements were estimated. The overall theory developed in this book suggests that the elements should be grouped into the two indexes as has been done, and that the two indexes should be positively correlated. Given the complexity of the construction, the chances of accidentally supporting the basic hypothesis, let alone getting any kind of result, would appear to be quite slim.

The simple bivariate correlation between the two indexes is .698, and the r square for the curve of best fit is .497. The curve goes in the predicted direction. Using Arend Lijphart's smaller sample that includes some countries not considered here produces virtually the same results. Equally important, the two indexes are statistically independent. Others may test for independence using the data in Table 4.2. Furthermore, controlling for other major variables does not significantly alter the statistical relationship found here. The statistical results suggest that each of the two indexes measures some single phenomenon, and the theory suggests that these phenomena are popular control and the separation of powers. The theory and statistical results also imply that the relationship between these two measured phenomena reflects a phenomenon that can be called popular sovereignty, properly conceived. Using the definitions developed in this book, and the theory developed using these definitions, the empirical results allow us to say that de facto popular sovereignty is part of an integral, underlying logic for constitutional republics.

The underlying logic of constitutional design can be viewed as having a structure built around levels of analysis. We can illuminate this structure by summarizing a typical learning process in a class on constitutional design. Let us assume that we have initially assigned a class the problem of designing a legislature and that we have simplified our entry into the problem by focusing initially on the matter of legislative size. This typical entry point allows us to efficiently teach our students about a number of basic concepts, such as decision costs. Concern only for decision costs, ignoring the structure of the internal decision-making process, implies a small body, and logically fearless students will see the optimal solution for minimizing decision cost: a legislature of one. Even when we introduce the effects of internal organization, most students see immediately that decision costs cannot be the basis for sizing a legislature, because the intuitive understanding of representation having something to do with matters outside the legislative body is widely shared. So we introduce the concept of externalities or external costs, operationalized in this instance as a concern for constituency size as a surrogate measure for the sense of connectedness between representative and those represented and thus for popular control. Soon it is apparent that some relative weighting of the two values is required. An equal weighting generates a linear curve with a forty-five degree angle between legislative size and population size, but there is no obvious way to justify equal weighting because a commitment to political equality does not necessarily imply weighting all possible design factors equally. One might recur to game-theoretic results in order to find some empirical basis for weighting the values, but in this instance cross-national data provide a better and more realistic answer. The earlier discussion of the cube root curve is now relevant, and it is possible to show that preferences for weighting the values do not remain constant over the possible range of legislative size but instead vary for reasons that are not immediately obvious.

Further analysis and reflection may lead some to conclude that underlying these two factors relevant for legislative size there may be a deeper single value at work such as maximizing popular control, or democracy, which encompasses and includes the two factors that rational actors are attempting to "balance" – constituency size and the size of the legislature. What does this broadened focus do to our institutional design for the legislature? It does three things. First, it raises questions about legislative selection variables in the pursuit of maximizing popular control. The design of the legislature must accommodate the electoral system used to select its members, and the party system associated with the electoral system. Second, it raises concerns about maximizing popular control through the internal organization of the legislature. Third, it raises questions about the manner and extent to which other political institutions contribute to or undermine the quest for maximizing popular control through the legislature.

The relationship between legislative size and the electoral system is complex and, in the end, indeterminate. After a series of complicated calculations and after reading summaries of electoral system effects, such as that in Lijphart's *Patterns of Democracy*, students generally conclude that the various types of electoral systems that can be used seem to have little or no effect on a designer's preferences for legislative size. The type of party system utilized has a slight effect on legislative size, but does not alter the overall tendency to approximate the cube root curve. That is, multiparty systems tend to utilize a somewhat larger body than the curve predicts, and two-party systems tend to utilize a somewhat smaller body than the curve predicts. The former probably results from multimember districts having more representatives than the overall body needs in order to allow as many parties as possible a chance to win seats in each district. The more parties in the system, the greater this effect. Single-member districts associated with the few reasonable approximations to a two-party system do not need to accommodate as many parties and thus result in, on average, somewhat smaller legislatures. The overall effect of party system variables, however, is to increase slightly the average distance of a given legislature from the predicted cube root size given the country's population. But aside from lowering the formal statistical correlation with the cube root curve, the compensating effects of different party and electoral systems still track the cube root curve generated from the original two-factor analysis where legislative size and constituency size are "balanced."

As to the second concern, the party system does have consequences for internal organization, but these internal arrangements do not affect the size of the legislature since legislative size is a "given" when the popular control effects of internal organization are analyzed.

The third consideration, the effects of other institutions on popular control through the legislature, is a major turning point in class thinking. It is easy to demonstrate that maximizing popular control through the legislature implies either minimizing the power of other branches of government, or eliminating these other branches altogether by folding their functions into the legislature. In short, maximizing popular control through the legislature implies a parliamentary form of government. For this reason supporters of parliamentary government invariably chastise nonparliamentary government as "less democratic." Leaving aside the matter of the extent to which bargaining by the leaders of multiple parties behind closed doors might also be viewed as less democratic than what supporters of parliamentary government project as its primary virtue, Table 8.1 indicates that at a certain population size constitutional framers abandon single-house legislatures for bicameralism. Bicameralism, as we have seen, is a decisive step away from simple parliamentary government toward a separation of powers that eventually blurs the distinction between parliamentary and presidential systems.

Bicameralism has an immediate effect on legislative size. Because the members of the second house can be added to the first when thinking about overall representation, the size of the lower or primary body of the legislature begins to slow in its growth relative to the cube root curve and then to stop altogether. Apparently the "balancing" between legislative size and constituency size is therefore gradually diminished and finally completely abandoned. The initial logic governing legislative size is thus abandoned in favor of a broader logic that increasingly takes into account the effects of other institutions. More important, the broader logic increasingly abandons pursuit of popular control alone and substitutes popular sovereignty that attempts to "balance" popular control with control of popular control. That popular control would itself be brought under increasing control seems to flow from the increasing population diversity that increasing population size seems to imply.

At some point, the second house stops growing in size as well as the first. At this point we are at a population size that, as Arend Lijphart has established, is associated with federal systems.[3] Federal systems have other legislatures that can be added to the national legislature in our calculations of "balancing" legislative size with constituency size. The broader logic that emerges with larger constitutional republics thus incorporates the initial logic used to generate legislative size but transforms it into an integrated institutional analysis based on popular sovereignty properly understood.

By pushing our analysis, we are led to conclude that popular control is itself balanced with another empirically determinable value, the separation of powers, which makes operational a set of values, including but not limited to individual liberty and minority rights, that to some extent complements and to some extent opposes the values associated

[3] See Arend Lijphart, *Patterns of Democracy: Government Forms and Performance in Thirty Six Countries* (New Haven: Yale University Press, 1999), chap. 10, especially p. 195.

with popular control, including but not limited to political equality and majority rule. The analysis that began by considering the optimal size of a legislature has led us to popular sovereignty as the deep value to be maximized, a value that encompasses and includes all of the other values encountered along the way; and by pushing our analysis to this level we end up accounting for virtually everything found in a constitution. The principle of popular sovereignty in this way can be seen as accounting for the artifact of a constitution to the extent that they are virtually coterminous.

Consider now how the design of an institution, in this case the legislature, encompasses various levels of analysis.

1. The optimal size of a legislature as determined by a rational actor taking into account the maximization of any single given value (x) – for example, constituency size
2. The optimal size of a legislature taking into account simultaneously two values (x and y) that lead in different directions – for example, constituency size and decision costs
3. The optimal size of a legislature taking into account a higher value that includes x and y, which we shall call A – for example, popular control
4. The optimal size of a legislature taking into account two higher values (A and B) that lead in different directions – for example, popular control and the separation of powers
5. The optimal size of a legislature taking into account an even higher value that includes A and B – for example, popular sovereignty
6. The optimal size of a legislature taking into account values that encompass and include popular sovereignty in even higher value conflicts and syntheses

At which level should we expect a political scientist to conclude his or her analysis? Level 5 analysis has taken us to popular sovereignty and constitutionalism, but there is no reason to think that analysis should stop here. The theory developed has posited that constitutionalism was developed as a political technology in order to pursue liberty, self-preservation, sociability, and beneficial innovation. These values were taken as a given, although there is no reason to do so. The manner and extent to which these values individually or together animate constitutionalism must be subjected to searching inquiry. It is interesting to note that if one were to begin with level 1 analysis and proceed all the way to level 6, one would recapitulate political philosophy as originally defined by Aristotle and summarized in Chapter 7.

This book is a work in political philosophy because it attempts to address the questions, What is the best political system? and What is a good government? The questions are not addressed head on, since the book does not explicitly argue for one type of government over another. Instead, this analysis suggests recasting somewhat how we think about the available alternatives. Classical political philosophy has always included discussion of regime types. Prior to the modern era, the list was often composed of monarchies, aristocracies, and democracies, for example, as well as their degenerate forms. Without reprising the history of regime categorization schemes, let me suggest that the discussion in recent years has become somewhat impoverished because of several trends. One is the retreat into a continuing attack on liberalism without suggesting alternatives. Another is the reduction of empirically studied regime types to "parliamentary" and "presidential."

When we ask, What is the best form of government? or What is a good government? we are actually asking, What is the best regime? The answer suggested here has two parts. The first is that under conditions of liberty, humans will prefer a regime based on popular sovereignty. The second part of the answer is an attempt to refresh our eyes when gazing upon popular sovereignty. Popular sovereignty does not mean "democracy." That would be, in the terms used here, a regime of simple "popular control." Instead, under conditions of liberty, people will select (A) popular control that is (B) self-limited. Put another way, under conditions of liberty, humans will prefer popular sovereignty, a regime that is limited in what it can do and how it can do it.

Many political philosophers have argued for the creation of unity in a political system, a harmony among its parts, in order to eliminate factions or parties and thus eliminate political conflict. Philosophers as disparate as Hobbes, Rousseau, and Plato (read nonironically) come to mind. That is not the philosophical stance adopted here. Instead, assuming that political conflict flows inevitably from human nature, I argue for a constitutional view of politics. Under such a view, humans can create a political order that has sufficient unity to minimize violence while the inevitable political competition and conflict proceed apace, but at the same time limit the reach of that political order in such a way as to not significantly disadvantage any of the factions or conflicting parties. The constitutional political order thus has to begin by asking what must be shared and what need not be shared. What needs to be shared, at a minimum, are citizenship and whatever that implies – hence the first face of popular sovereignty, popular control. In order not to disadvantage any faction, popular control must then be limited in ways that have together been identified in this book as the separation of powers. The first face of popular sovereignty enlists everyone in the common project, which provides unity and strength; while the second face prevents any faction(s) that might gain control of the governmental apparatus from threatening the basic agreement upon which the system is based, thus providing fairness and stability.

In a sense, modern constitutionalism is an attempt to accomplish what Plato generally suggested in the *Laws*: in the absence of a philosopher-ruler, substitute a regime of laws. The substitution of laws for the philosopher-king does not negate the need for philosophic "gadflies" to inform public discourse by holding up the possibility of improvement and teaching those who will someday be part of the politically active class, but it does remove the need to establish a regime of philosophers. The regime is instead composed of the many, organized under a constitution, acting as citizens within the limits imposed by the constitution, limits to which they have all agreed in order to become citizens. To say, therefore, that at the least citizenship must be shared is also to say that the constitution must be shared – a constitution that simultaneously undergirds order and liberty. Justice, on the other hand, is not embodied in the constitution per se. Instead, because a definition of justice is not shared by the citizens, the production of justice remains the responsibility of the popularly sovereign regime. This failure to share a definition of justice does not mean that justice is dominated by relativism but instead that achieving justice requires free inquiry, searching debate, and individual responsibility. It also means that we have not yet, if we ever will, achieved a universal, cross-generational idea of justice that can simply be taught by rote or written into perpetual laws. Constitutionalism says that we must do the best we can in an imperfect world that we hope we can improve. The well-structured constitutional polity thus does not eliminate political conflict but enables it to occur reasonably free of mob rule and elite control.

Is it rational to pursue in the most effective, efficient manner ends or goals that have not been examined, based only on the assumption that a rational actor wants more of whatever the end or goal represents? Recent developments in positive theory have attempted to include or account for what might be termed nonrational aspects of behavior, and while this is significant progress, it is not enough. Not only is it apparent that humans act in apparently nonrational ways, but it is also true that humans often act to maximize more than one value at a time, which is one way of explaining why apparently rational human beings risk their lives (the self-preservation of the classic rational actor) in the pursuit of other ends. What initially appears to be "irrational," or perhaps inconsistent, behavior may instead be a simple refusal to maximize a single valued outcome while ignoring everything else. Rational action often takes the form of balancing, or at least taking into account, two or more values.

The Rising Curve of Constitutional Republics (Democracies)

As noted in the first chapter, Figure 1.1 shows that the number of constitutional republics tracks the number of countries with a written constitution with a lag of fifty to one hundred years. Both variables are smoothed to the curve of best fit, but the actual historical process has been anything but smooth. There has been much discussion in the comparative literature about three "waves" of democracies emerging, and while the concept of three waves is reasonable, it is as much of a simplification as the smooth curve presented here. During at least four periods between 1800 and 1945, the number of democracies using any definition of democracy fell by as much as 30 percent, with long periods of no real net increase. Although the absolute numbers were not large during this century and a half, the ebb-and-flow pattern more properly represents several waves rather than one. There have been three waves since 1945 – the reestablishment of democracy in countries freed from Nazism, the rapid move of many countries from colonies to independent nations beginning in the 1960s, and the new democracies during the 1990s that arose from the demise of the Soviet Union. Some have asked portentously if the third wave of democratization is over, but this ignores constitutional history. The number of constitutional republics has always ebbed and flowed, and we are probably entering a period of ebbing that is quite natural. The overall trend has been steadily, if not inevitably, upward. A more interesting question is why the trend has continued upward even during periods much less auspicious for democracy than is the case today. Certainly the growth and spread of economic wealth has been an important factor, as has the continuous pressure from existing democracies to spread and protect the idea of democracy. Nor can we discount the impact on the spread of democratic ideas of growing international trade, the proliferation of international organizations, and other forms of cross-national exchange strongly aided by the spread of inexpensive mass communication technology. Still, as was suggested in Chapter 1, the diffusion of written constitutions may serve as both a surrogate for all of these factors as well as an independent variable.

Concluding Remarks

From the very beginning, the existence of a written constitution did not coincide with the presence of democracy. In 1789 the United States was still a developing nation both economically and politically. Some have suggested that in the absence of full adult suffrage the United States did not become a democracy until well into the nineteenth century. Robert Dahl has plumped for the 1960s as the beginning of true democracy in the United States. Certainly this has to be wrong. Constitutional democracy does not rest on a single variable, or on the perfect achievement of an ideal. Furthermore, as has been amply demonstrated, as democracies develop more fully, they actually move away from pure democracy institutionally by increasing the separation of powers as the level of popular control increases. Indeed, many today are loath to term countries with full suffrage but insecure rights as anything but "hollow democracies" or "pseudo-democracies." For this reason, the preference in this analysis has been to refer to constitutional republics rather than democracies as the long-term goal. "Democracy" as an ideal implies the absence of individual and minority rights to thwart majority rule, and the use of constitutions implies a democracy, and a majority, that is not free to do anything it wants whenever it wants. The actual choices made by citizens of "democracies," such as increasing the separation of powers to slow down majority rule and the use of rights to thwart majorities in certain policy areas, prove that "democracy" per se is not what people outside of the academy really want. What democratically inclined people want is popular sovereignty rather than simple popular control.

Using the definition of a constitutional republic from Chapter 1, the United States became one in 1800 with the peaceful transfer of power from one party to another. Curve B in Figure 1.1 represents the curve of best fit using this definition. Other definitions are available. For example, if we use Dahl's definition, curve B would begin someplace well into the twentieth century and rise even more rapidly to a current count of more than one hundred constitutional republics. This curve would track curve A even more closely with a diminishing average time between the use of a written constitution and the emergence of a constitutional republic. Among other things, this would imply a stronger future for democracy than is probably the case. In fact, democracy is a difficult system to implement and maintain, and democratization is not something limited to new nations from the Third World. In a sense, curve B can be viewed as a learning curve that represents the struggle for more peoples to understand what democracy implies and requires, and to implement effective institutions to achieve what has been learned. The people of the United States are still in the process of learning, and to require that they understood in 1820 what they know now is essentially anachronistic. Any reasonably stable democracy will tend toward more effective democracy, and it is argued here that democracy will thus tend toward what is more properly termed a constitutional republic with at least de facto popular sovereignty if not de jure.

Curve A is misleading in one respect. It seems to imply a continuing rapid increase in the number of countries with a written constitution. In fact, there are fewer than half a dozen countries left without a written constitution. As of about 1998 the number has abruptly stopped growing and should be represented by a horizontal line. Curve B should continue to rise gradually, but the prospects for the curve to continue rising at the rate exhibited since 1945 are dim. Perhaps more important, the percentage of the world's population living in a constitutional republic may not increase at all until countries like Russia, China, or Indonesia make the definitive move to such a political form. Most constitutional republics are very small, and some of the medium-sized countries like Venezuela, Mexico, Nigeria, and Turkey tend to slip in and out of the category.

Existing constitutional republics will continue to use economic trade and capital investment as tools for helping in the spread of democracy. There is a very strong correlation between average per capita income and the presence of stable democracy, so this is not an unimportant consideration when predicting future diffusion. Still, it is not entirely clear whether democracy follows wealth or wealth follows democracy. Saudi Arabia and Iraq should be democracies using the per capita income predictor, and many or most of the small democracies should not. Rather than representing the diffusion of wealth, the curves in Figure 1.1 may represent the diffusion of an idea. The United States was well down the road to democratization at a time when most European nations were much wealthier but governed by monarchies and autocracies. Twice during the twentieth century the United States has had to assist European democracies against nondemocratic invaders who were anything but poor, and then engage in a fifty-year Cold War to preserve the fruits of the second intervention. The statistical correlation between average per capita wealth and democracy is so recent as to approximate a historical accident when one takes the long view.

Figure 1.1 implies another hypothesis that probably cannot be tested empirically in any satisfactory way with the statistical techniques and small number of examples currently available to us. This hypothesis is that an idea, or set of ideas, has taken hold and represents a general evolutionary trend. Chapter 2 laid out an evolutionary framework for viewing human history. It was suggested that at some point humans began to evolve culturally at a much more rapid rate than nature does genetically. The eventual result was species dominance over the rest of nature, and the eventual ability to organize larger and larger numbers of people under government. Certain ideas took hold that resulted eventually in the spread of political organization to most members of the species, much as did the control of fire, agriculture, and the mining and working of metals. At different times in human history, similar clan organizations spread over much of the Earth, as then did military kingships, empires, and eventually the nation-state. If one takes the long evolutionary perspective, we find that technical innovations in social, economic, and political organization spread and competed with each other. Over time, politically organized peoples overcame and largely extinguished less competitive forms of organization. There were a few democracies thousands of years ago, as well as peoples with what amounted to constitutionalism. Four hundred years ago, the Iroquois, for example, certainly had a constitutional system, if not a democracy, in the midst of less fully articulated political systems, and the advantage this gave them has been clearly demonstrated. Although it was not a historical necessity that democratic ideas should be linked to the idea of a constitution, even random processes may have inevitably produced the combination.

We may be living in an era when the combination of the two political technologies of democracy and constitutionalism is leading to another evolution in human organization that has a competitive advantage. This is not to suggest the superiority of some peoples over others, but instead to suggest that all humans tend to prefer political organization that better secures for them the liberty, self-preservation, sociability, and beneficial innovation that led them to invent government to begin with. In this view, the political forms we now have are not the end of history. Instead, we as a species are still in the midst of learning, improving, and preserving that which serves us better. Other, better forms of organization lie in the future, and other curves of diffusion as well. At least we can hope. The hope rests on a view of humans as fundamentally "rational" in the sense of wanting more of what we value as humans, as well as seeking appropriate and effective means for achieving this goal.

Index